"With *VisuaLeadership*, Todd has hit the trifecta of what makes a truly great business book: a big idea, supported by real-world experiences and stories, with provocative and fun techniques to help the reader bring these ideas into action. Wow! I challenge any reader to not get at least two dozen new and original leadership ideas they can start implementing immediately!"

—BRYAN MATTIMORE, Chief Idea Guy, Growth Engine Innovation Agency, and author of *21 Days to a Big Idea*

"Todd Cherches is a legitimate Doodle Revolutionary. In this engaging and illuminating book, he skillfully explores how anyone can 'draw on' the power of pictures to more effectively solve problems, amplify insights, innovate, communicate, and lead. *VisuaLeadership* conclusively shows that visually-literate leaders will have a competitive advantage in the future of work."

—SUNNI BROWN, Founder of Sunni Brown Ink, and The Center for Deep Self Design, and best-selling author of *The Doodle Revolution*

"This book is a great example of Plato's dictum that 'learning is remembering what you already know.' So yes, we already know that a picture is worth a thousand words—but Todd gives us a way to really learn what that means and, more importantly, to put it into practice. Anyone who communicates for a living—and that's pretty much everyone—will find useful nuggets in *VisuaLeadership*—and some of us will probably find entire gold mines. What a great book!"

—RON ASHKENAS is an executive leadership consultant and coach whose books include *The Harvard Business Review Leader's Handbook*, and *Simply Effective*

"*VisuaLeadership* does what few leadership books can do: it helps us see our way to a better way to lead. Compelling, engaging, and thoughtful, Cherches's book will help leaders where they often need it most: communicating a compelling and fun vision for their organizations."

—JERRY COLONNA, CEO, Reboot, and author of *Reboot: Leadership and the Art of Growing Up*

"Todd Cherches's book puts into context the meaning behind the idea that a picture paints a thousand words. *VisuaLeadership* is a meaningful departure from the business world of briefs, PowerPoint presentations, and reports. All who implement the principles from this terrific book will benefit from stronger communication and presentation skills that will lead to a greater ability to innovate, influence, motivate, and sell their ideas."

—SETH MERRIN, CEO, Liquidnet, and author of *The Power of Positive Destruction*

"With inflation, a visual image is now worth 10,000 words and climbing. Whatever the number, this book vividly demonstrates visual literacy is the glue that holds all literacy together and produces a literate leader."

—STEVEN HELLER, Co-Chair School of Visual Arts (SVA) MFA Designer as Entrepreneur program

"As a Broadway stage manager my entire professional career, I know firsthand the value and the power of imagery, metaphor, character, and story. In his entertaining and engaging new book, *VisuaLeadership*, Todd Cherches shows us how leadership is continuously hiding in plain sight, and demonstrates how anyone, at any level, can apply his innovative visual thinking-based approach to be a more effective leader at, or on, any stage."

—MICHAEL PASSARO, Production Stage Manager, and Associate Professor,
Columbia University Theatre Arts Program

"Though I've been leading and coaching others, including hundreds of CEOs, for almost forty years, it was not until Todd Cherches became one of our Vistage speakers last year that I truly began to recognize and appreciate the power of visual thinking as an approach to leadership. In his 'eye-opening' and entertaining new book, Todd shares with us one engaging model, metaphor, and story after another to illustrate and demonstrate how any leader, at any level, can use visual thinking to bring their leadership vision to life."

—MARK TAYLOR, NYC Master Chair and CEO Coach, Vistage Worldwide

"In *VisuaLeadership*, Todd Cherches introduces us to an innovative, visual thinking-based approach that is not only practical and easy to implement, but creative and fun as well. Through his collection of tools and engaging storytelling, Todd provides the reader with a wide variety of 'eye-opening' new ways to not only become a better leader, but a better person as well. Todd's visually-based approach to leadership has helped me to see my own business challenges in a new light and to envision a world of possibilities that I had not considered before. I would encourage every leader to read *VisuaLeadership*...and then encourage those leaders to have their people read it as well."

—JEFF SCHWARTZMAN, Head of Learning, Liquidnet, and Adjunct Professor,
NYU School of Professional Studies

"Todd Cherches's new book, *VisuaLeadership*, is a rapid-fire masterclass in leadership development. Reading this book is like being invited into Todd's home where he has cooked up a smorgasbord of delicious entrees for you to dine to your heart's content on a visual array of leadership content. This is not the type of book you will want to read and put on the shelf, but one you will want on your desk much the same way you keep your best kitchen recipe book close at hand. And, in the world of work, we are always in need of a good recipe to help guide us to create a dish that is not just palatable but meets the palette of the pickiest eaters. *Bon appétit!*"

—ROB SALAFIA, CEO of Protagonist Consulting Group and author of
Leading from Your Best Self

"How can black socks, pink spoons, and a yellow ball propel your leadership skills? How about elephants, remote controls, and showers? In *VisuaLeadership*, Todd Cherches demonstrates the unexpected gifts in everyday objects and the transformative power of unleashing your imagination through daydreaming, doodling, and visual metaphors. Through entertaining stories, he offers a bounty of tools to help you master leadership in your professional and personal lives. Cherches is a playful punster—you may never see a drawbridge in quite the same way again."
　　　　—NANCY ANCOWITZ, Career Coach, and author of *Self-Promotion for Introverts*®

"Todd Cherches masterfully uses metaphors, stories, and visual models to share a raft of outstanding insights and tips on both professional and personal leadership. Like a letter from an old friend, this is a book to keep nearby for frequent reference as—in addition to its many practical suggestions—its folksy words of empathy, encouragement, and wisdom will be an invaluable guide as we travel along on our own journey of career, leadership, and self-growth. A truly fun read, *VisuaLeadership* makes for both a highly inspirational and delightful learning experience."
　　　　—DAVID KRUCZLNICKI, President, High Peaks Strategic Business Advisors

"*VisuaLeadership* is a brilliant compilation of Todd's personal and professional experiences defining and refining visual thinking and visual communication through the use of simple, practical visually-based models. Todd's big personality, quick wit, and humor reverberate throughout the book, engaging the reader on a journey of self-exploration and insight while demonstrating the power of visual thinking and its critical place in the future of work."
　　　　—MARYANNE SPATOLA, Founder & CEO, C3 Talent Strategies and author of *Careers in the New World of Work*

"Imagine in your mind's eye a 'key' that unlocks your full leadership potential. Got it? Packed from cover to cover with actionable ideas and superb, real-world examples, *VisuaLeadership* is that key. The very witty Todd Cherches has written a clear, compelling, and comprehensive guide to using visual models, metaphors, and stories to increase your leadership influence and create a profound impact with your communication. Read it—and apply it!"
　　　　—RICHARD KUEPPER, Founder and Chief Experience Architect, L.E.A.D. USA, LLC

"If you've ever struggled to 'picture success' or articulate what great leadership 'looks like,' then this book is for you! *VisuaLeadership*'s smart, practical approach is a gift to anyone who leads people and teams and needs a simple and effective way to communicate more clearly. If a picture is worth a thousand words, *VisuaLeadership* is worth a thousand leadership books."
　　　　—DEBORAH GRAYSON RIEGEL, CEO and Chief Communication Coach, Talk Support

"*VisuaLeadership* is one of the most generous—and entertaining—business books I have ever read! In showing us how he uses visual thinking to lead his clients, his students, and himself to success, Todd freely gives away many of his most valuable models and methods so that we can apply them to our own personal and professional lives. Filled from start to finish with engaging stories and proven, practical tools, this captivating book will expand your horizons, and become a go-to resource for improving yourself at work, and beyond."

> —BRIAN TALLY, Talent Development Consultant and faculty of Liquidnet University

"*VisuaLeadership* is filled with Todd Cherches's world-class expertise in visual elements and leadership ideas. Combine this with his endearing and funny personal stories and this book is a home run! Todd distills his concepts and lessons down to their most important and relevant elements, making them easy to grasp—and to put into practice—both personally and professionally. This book will tickle both your mind and your heart, provide numerous *aha!* moments, and leave you with an undeniable truth: your leadership style is a direct reflection of your view of the world."

> —HELENA ESCALANTE, Founder, Speaker, Bibliophile, and Writer, Entregurus.com

"Filled with actionable insights and superbly-written stories based on many years of experience, Todd Cherches has created a compelling, fun, engaging book that's different from all the other books on leadership. You'll not only learn how to lead in a whole new way, you'll be entertained and coached by a good friend as you do."

> —JENNIFER GOLDMAN-WETZLER, Ph.D., CEO of Alignment Strategies Group, and author of *Optimal Outcomes*

"*VisuaLeadership* will fundamentally change what you think and how you feel. As a strategist, the lessons learned within it will help my clients to picture a better future, execute their strategy, and turn their vision into reality."

> —MARC EMMER, President, Optimize Inc., and author of *Momentum: How Companies Decide What to Do Next*

"I am a huge Todd Cherches fan. He is a powerful storyteller who always finds the right story for the right leadership lesson. It's not just about *being* visual. It's about *having* vision, integrity, and a way forward. This brings together many challenges with examples and perspectives that will help you lead more effectively."

> —FAWN GERMER, global leadership speaker and Oprah-featured, best-selling author of nine books

"In the future of work, one of the most important capabilities of successful leaders will be the ability to tolerate, embrace, make sense of, and utilize chaos and volatility to their advantage. To help navigate this increasingly complex and fast-paced world, Todd Cherches provides an incredible and innovative framework to help leaders visualize and apply mental models in order to make sense of the chaos and transform it into a competitive advantage. VisuaLeadership is a powerful concept and capability that leaders need to embrace if they want their organizations to thrive and succeed in the future."

—ENRIQUE RUBIO, Founder, Hacking HR

"*VisuaLeadership* combines and utilizes our mind's natural inclination to make stories, associations, and mental discoveries with visuals. However, what Todd Cherches does extraordinarily well is make *VisuaLeadership* both practical and inspiring. I can't recommend this book enough!"

—DONNA SCAROLA, Head of Performance Management & Leadership Model,
Johnson & Johnson

"*VisuaLeadership* brings new meaning to the phrase 'what you see is what you get' (or 'WYSIWYG'), as Todd Cherches shows us how the power of visual thinking can greatly enhance our leadership, communication, and understanding."

—BILL MAW, CFO, and author of *The Work-Life Equation*

"If you have ever wondered how to quickly improve your impact, *VisuaLeadership* is an excellent resource! In it, Todd Cherches provides a wide range of practical visual models, metaphors, and self-assessments, accompanied by a wealth of personal stories, quotes—and of course, great visuals—to bring his concepts to life. It's obvious that Todd put his heart and soul into writing this 'masterpiece'… so as to help us all to become more visual thinkers."

—MARY ABBAZIA, Managing Director of Impact Planning Group,
and co-author of *The Accidental Marketer*

"Todd is a master at showing anyone how to leverage visual models to be a more effective leader and communicator at work and in life. *VisuaLeadership* is chock full of simple, powerful frameworks you can put to immediate use to cut through the clutter of today's digital landscape, connect viscerally with distracted audiences, and positively influence behaviors and outcomes."

—JP LAQUEUR, Chief Connector, BrandFoundations

"*VisuaLeadership*, by Todd Cherches, provides a cutting-edge approach to creativity, problem solving, and action-taking. As an author and mental training coach for athletes, I understand the importance of being able to adapt and adjust to situations in seconds. *VisuaLeadership* provides a framework, structure, and plan in which businesspeople, presenters, and athletes can creatively, effectively, and efficiently approach and solve problems, as well as continuously raise the bar on their expertise to enhance their performance."

—ROB POLISHOOK, Mental Training Coach, Inside the Zone Sports Performance Group,
LLC, and author of *Baseball Inside the Zone*, and *Tennis Inside the Zone*

"As a leadership development professional, I've always helped leaders get their message across in a clear and compelling way. Their biggest challenge has always been simplifying the complex and conveying thoughts in an easy-to-understand way. Todd Cherches's *VisuaLeadership* provides a practical and immediately applicable set of tools and approaches for doing exactly that—enabling leaders to convey their vision in images, frameworks, stories, and a variety of other great communication vehicles. This book is a must-read if you want your leadership communications to be more effective."

—MIKE FIGLIUOLO, Managing Director, thoughtLEADERS, LLC, and author of *One Piece of Paper*, *Lead Inside the Box*, and *The Elegant Pitch*

"Todd Cherches's new book, *VisuaLeadership*, is a treasure trove of stories, models, and metaphors illustrating the power of visual thinking and visual communication. Todd, who is an excellent live stand-up facilitator and coach, brings his unique, engaging presentation style to his writing, and his numerous tips and techniques will immediately enable you to be a visual leader. Enjoy it!"

—STEVE GARDINER, President, Gardiner Associates

"Todd Cherches hits a grand slam with this innovative leadership book! Through a mix of engaging stories, thought-provoking metaphors, and illustrative examples that bring his concepts to life, he creatively and playfully reminds us of the value of visuals to both educate and inspire."

—MARC LEVINE, Founder, Improve My Sales Consulting

VisuaLeadership

LEVERAGING THE POWER OF VISUAL THINKING IN LEADERSHIP AND IN LIFE

TODD CHERCHES

Post Hill PRESS

A POST HILL PRESS BOOK

VisuaLeadership:
Leveraging the Power of Visual Thinking in Leadership and in Life
© 2020 by Todd Cherches
All Rights Reserved

ISBN: 978-1-64293-337-6
ISBN (eBook): 978-1-64293-338-3

Interior design and composition by Greg Johnson, Textbook Perfect

Post Hill Press
New York • Nashville
posthillpress.com

Published in the United States of America

*To my wife, Karin, my muse…as well as my greatest source
of amusement. You believed in me even more than I believed in myself.
I couldn't do it without you…and wouldn't want to.*

To my parents, Dee and Harvey, who made me the person I am today.

*And, lastly, to all of the many, many (way-too-many!) horrible bosses
I've had over the course of my career, you taught me more about
management and leadership than I ever wanted to know.*

When I Heard the Learn'd Astronomer

When I heard the learn'd astronomer,
When the proofs, the figures, were ranged in
columns before me,
When I was shown the charts and diagrams,
to add, divide, and measure them,
When I sitting heard the astronomer where
he lectured with much applause in the lecture-room,
How soon unaccountable I became tired and sick,
Till rising and gliding out I wander'd off by myself,
In the mystical moist night-air, and from time to time,
Look'd up in perfect silence at the stars.

—WALT WHITMAN

CONTENTS

INTRODUCTION

The Power of Visual Thinking

When I was a little kid growing up in Queens, I absolutely loved television. I was completely obsessed with it. If I didn't have to go to school—or go to sleep—I really think I could've watched TV twenty-four hours a day. I'm not kidding. So when people would ask me, "What do you want be when you grow up?" I always said that I someday wanted to work in television.

But, actually, that answer wasn't entirely true.

If I'm being completely honest, what I *really* wanted to be…was Superman. Or, if that didn't work out—and it's good to have a fallback option when thinking about your career—then my backup plan was to be Batman. But if I couldn't be either Superman *or* Batman…then my *backup* backup plan was to get some kind of a job in the television industry.

Many years later, after graduating from college and working for a year as an assistant media buyer for a New York City ad agency, it sank in that most of the jobs in the TV industry at that time were based out on the West Coast. So I did the most impulsive thing I had ever done in my entire life: I packed my bags—and my cape—and headed out to Hollywood.

But, as you can imagine, getting a job in the entertainment industry—when you have no experience and no connections—is not all that easy.

So, after a series of unpaid internships, part-time gigs, and dead-end jobs, my friend, Seth, helped me to get hired as a project coordinator for a small theme park design and production company in the San Fernando Valley. It wasn't television, but at least it was kind of in the entertainment industry.

In this job, I was responsible for overseeing the production of seven life-sized audio-animatronic (robotic) animals—two elephants, three sheep, and two cows—for a cultural theme park in Shenzhen, China. Needless to say—having never done anything like this before—I had absolutely no idea what I was doing.

But somehow I figured it out. In fact, I figured it out so well that that they came to me one day and said, "We're putting you in charge of this entire project. Oh, and by the way, you're going to have to go over to China for a few weeks to oversee the installation."

In just a few short months, I had gone from taking a job where I had no idea what I was doing, to now being shipped halfway around the world to do it. I couldn't locate Shenzhen on a map, I had never been out of the country before, I didn't even have a passport…and I was terrified. But I had no choice. So, a few months later, off I went.

Having arrived in Shenzhen with my two technicians, I woke up that first morning all excited and anxious and ready to get to work. It was 110 degrees with 95 percent humidity. And, for some ridiculous and completely unnecessary reason, I had decided to wear a suit and tie that first day in order to make a good first impression on our client's senior executives, who didn't even show up.

Drenched in sweat within minutes of leaving the hotel, I somehow found my way to the theme park job site. The good news was that it turned out that all the robotic animals had arrived safely after their four-week voyage in a shipping container across the Pacific Ocean. The bad news was that we immediately discovered that none of the Chinese workers spoke any English at all—including the translators.

There was no Google Translate back then. And, needless to say, none of us spoke any Chinese. The only Chinese phrase I knew was *"Ni hao ma"*—which means, "How are you doing?" And how were we doing? Not too well at this point, as we had a serious problem on our hands. Just like that famous line from the classic 1967 movie *Cool Hand Luke*, what we had here was a "failure to communicate."

So, how were we supposed to get this installation done when we, literally, couldn't understand one another? We were all just kind of standing there that first morning, staring at each other, trying to figure out what to do first, when it hit me:

If we can't communicate in *words*…maybe we can communicate in *pictures*!

When the Chinese laborers finally showed up with the big Knack toolbox (towed in by a bicycle, did I mention this was an extremely low-tech operation?), I didn't know the Chinese word for hammer, or screwdriver, or tape measure, or nail…but if that's what we needed, we were going to have to get the message across by pointing, and by drawing pictures back and forth. It ended up turning into a nonstop game of Pictionary and Charades! "Two words, three syllables, sounds like… um…'screwdriver'!"

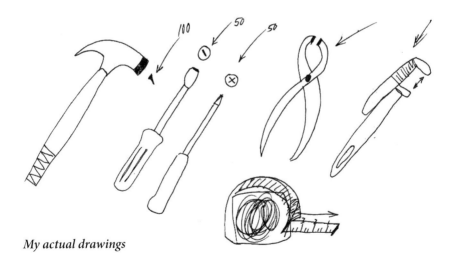

My actual drawings

Long story short…it all ended up working out, and I'm glad to be able to report that the grand opening of the park was a huge success, and one of the highlights of my young career.

When I got back home to Los Angeles and reflected on my experience, one of the biggest things that struck me was how we leveraged *the power of visuals* to communicate, to innovate, to manage, and to lead. And that, in a single phrase, has become the foundation of my thinking—and of all of my work—ever since: the power of visual thinking and visual communication.

So, what, exactly, do we mean by "visual thinking"? In a nutshell, it's about **thinking *in* pictures**. And "visual communication"? That's about **communicating *with* pictures**. They both involve using visually related techniques such as visual imagery; mental models and frameworks; metaphors and analogies; and visual storytelling to (a) formulate an idea, and (b) get that idea out of your head and into someone else's.

And the goal of visual thinking and visual communication? Ultimately, in a simple phrase, it's about getting other people to "*see* what you're *saying*."

If you think about it, that is the objective of *any* communication—whether a one-on-one conversation, a text, an email, a blog post, a presentation, a TED Talk, an advertisement, a novel, a play, poem, song, or TV show…like *Superman* or *Batman*: taking an idea and expressing it in a way that others will be able to see what is being said.

So, why visuals? When we communicate a message visually—as opposed to, say, just verbally—it dramatically increases our impact in three key areas: **Attention, Comprehension, and Retention**. (And these words even rhyme, making them easier to remember!) Without getting into all the science behind it, the use of visuals gets people to *focus*, thereby capturing their attention. The use of visuals increases understanding, helping people to better comprehend. And it enables them to remember, thereby enhancing their retention. And that's why, as the saying goes, "a picture is worth a thousand words."

For example, one of my primary areas of focus is leadership. I design and deliver management and leadership training programs for organizations and teach leadership graduate classes at NYU and Columbia. When I ask participants in my programs to shout out the first word that comes to mind when they hear the word "leadership," what would you guess the most popular response is? How would *you* answer?

Well, by far, the most common response tends to be the word "vision."

But what does it mean to have a "leadership vision"? And what does it mean to say that someone is a "visionary leader"? In a word, it's about "seeing." It's about having a picture in one's "mind's eye" and *envisioning* an idealized (eye-dealized?) future state that is different from, and better than, the current reality. And it is about communicating to others this imaginary picture of the future in a clear, compelling, and inspiring way so that *your* vision becomes *their* vision…and so that others will be able to say, "Yes, I *see* what you're saying."

And if you can find a way to do that, you will inspire others to want to accompany you on a "leadership journey" of exploration and discovery. For, as the saying goes, if you can get people to "see the invisible," you can inspire them to "do the impossible."

In regard to that **"Leadership Journey"** metaphor I just mentioned…

In the picture above, the **Rearview Mirror** represents the past—where we came from…and how we got here. And, as a mirror, it literally reminds us to take the time along our journey to stop…and to "reflect."

The **Dashboard**, with its dials and gauges, represents the present and tells us how we're doing. As the management guru Peter Drucker famously put it, "If you can't measure it, you can't manage it."

And, lastly, the **Windshield** represents the future...and directs our attention to the road ahead. While it appears to be blue skies and clear sailing for as far as the eye can see, what's beyond the horizon is unknown, as our future is unwritten.

So, as *you* travel forth on *your* "leadership journey," I encourage you to think about how you might leverage the power of visual thinking to help you to achieve *your* vision.

For, in the words of the French novelist Marcel Proust, "The real voyage of discovery consists not in seeking new lands...but in seeing with new eyes."

Over-View

"You can observe a lot by watching."

—YOGI BERRA

We've all heard the saying, "A picture is worth a thousand words." In VisuaLeadership, you'll learn how to turn those proverbial "thousand words" into thousands of innovative ideas and leadership solutions. How? Simply by learning how to think, communicate, manage, and lead more visually.

For, if it is indeed true that a picture really is worth a thousand or more words, and finding the right words takes time, and time is money, shouldn't it follow that you should be able to do more in less time by leveraging the power of visual thinking…in leadership and in life?

OK, it may not be that simple, but my hope is that VisuaLeadership will forever change the way you see the world, and the way you lead your teams, and yourself, by approaching your work and life challenges through the lens of:

- visual imagery
- mental models and frameworks
- metaphor and analogy
- visual storytelling.

For those who like things quantified, my formula for success can be summed up in the following equation (and please bear in mind that I was most definitely *not* a math major):

$$VL = (VT + VC) \times (L + M).$$

In essence, this simply means that VisuaLeadership (VL) is the practice of applying Visual Thinking (VT) and Visual Communication (VC) techniques to the art and science of Leadership (L) and Management (M) in order to help you turn your ideas into actions, and actions into results.

There are thousands of leadership books out there. And one of the hottest trends in the business world these days—across all industries—is the emergence of design thinking, visual thinking, and visual communication. You see it everywhere, from classrooms and conferences to C-suites and boardrooms. Yet very few business books out there have explored this powerful new dynamic. VisuaLeadership is here to help close that gap, and to demonstrate how anyone and everyone can use visual thinking and visual communication techniques to give you a competitive edge.

Through this collection of tools, tips, techniques, and stories, this book is intended to equip, enable, and empower you to become more efficient and more effective, in both formulating and communicating your ideas, so as to maximize the performance, the productivity, and the potential of yourself and your people. VisuaLeadership will help open your eyes to a world of new possibilities and new approaches and lead you on a journey of exploration and discovery so that you can become the visionary leader that you want to be, that you need to be, that you can be, and that you are meant to be.

Welcome to the world of VisuaLeadership.

The Big Picture

While this is a leadership book, it is written with the foundational assumption that *everyone* is a leader in one way or another. This book concerns "small l" leadership—as in, leading from any and every level—as opposed to "big L" leadership, which is about having a leadership title. We all know that having a lofty title doesn't make you an effective leader any more than not having one does not. So, even if you don't manage other people or teams, you still need to manage and lead yourself. And you have the power within you to step up to leadership anywhere and anytime…both at work *and* in life. Whether you are a student or an entry-level employee or a senior executive or an executive coach, you can take the VisuaLeadership ball and run with it.

While there is no "one-size-fits-all" solution to, well, anything, this collection of visually-oriented images, models, metaphors, and stories is intended to help you to discover how you can use visual thinking and visual communication to be an even more efficient, effective, and successful idea generator, solution finder, problem solver, decision-maker, communicator, team member, manager, coach, consultant, educator, and/or leader.

A common phrase in the professional development business has to do with helping people to develop their "mind-set, tool set, and skill set." In that regard, this book will help you to develop a more visually-oriented mind-set through seeing the world and thinking about things in eye-opening new ways; it will provide you with a collection of visual tools, tips, and techniques to add to your leadership tool kit; and it will enable you to develop your skill-set to immediately put these newfound approaches into action to achieve extraordinary results.

With that being said, here's a big picture overview of what you'll find in this book, section by section:

In *Part One: Leading with…Visuals*, we will kick things off by taking a look at what VisuaLeadership is all about, answer the big question you may be wondering, "Why Visuals?" and I'll share with you three personal stories that most influenced my thinking and led me down the path to discovering and formulating my visual thinking-based approach to leadership.

In *Part Two: Leading with…Visual Models*, we will take a look at what we mean by "visual models," followed by an exploration of eighteen of my top visual models, or frameworks, that you can immediately incorporate into your leadership tool kit.

In *Part Three: Leading with…Visual Metaphors*, we will discuss the power of metaphors and analogies, along with demonstrating—through fourteen of my favorite examples—how you can use metaphorical thinking and visual language to help you to become a more effective leader.

In *Part Four: Leading with…Visual Stories*, we will discuss the importance of leadership storytelling. I'll also share nineteen of my own personal leadership-related stories, which will enable us to explore how, by making your stories more visual, you can leverage the power of storytelling to inspire others to gain new insights and reach new heights.

And, lastly, in *Part Five, VisuaLeadership…What Now, What Next?* we will wrap things up with an exploration of how visual thinking and visual communication can help us to be more successful in "The Future of Work." I'll introduce you to my "Ten Tough Questions that Every Self-Aware Leader Needs to Be Able to Answer," we'll give some thought to a few things you may want to be thinking about as you continue down "The Road Ahead," and I'll leave you with some final thoughts related to what I call "Reflection, Introspection, and Connection."

Do *Not* Read This Book

Unlike most authors who would probably prefer that you lock yourself away to focus solely on reading their book without interruption or distraction, I am going to encourage you to do the opposite:

I encourage you to read this book with pen in hand and your digital device nearby, so that you can engage with the content the way I often do when reading the works of others: underlining, circling, highlighting, color-coding, making margin notes, doodling, stopping to look things up online, writing in a learning journal, or taking digital photos of content you want to remember afterwards. One of my best practice suggestions to you when reading anything you'd like to get the most out of: "Look things up…and write things down."

So, in regard to the above heading, what I *actually* meant to suggest is: do not *just* read this book…but engage with it—both visually and kinesthetically—interact with it, consume it, play around with the ideas, agree with them or disagree with them, challenge them or put your own spin on them, come up with your own stories and metaphors, sketch out your own models, think of your own examples and real-life applications, and have some fun with the ideas in this book as you take the next leap forward in becoming a more visual thinker.

To that end, I encourage you, as you are reading, to think in terms of this phrase: "Insights, Actions, and Outcomes."

Insights: What can I take from this visual image, model, metaphor, or story?

Actions: How can I apply this insight at work and/or in life?

Outcomes: And if I do, what change will occur and/or what results will I achieve?

To help you do this, at the end of each chapter I will provide a *big lesson* and a *big question* as food for thought, along with a place for you to jot down—while fresh in your mind—one *big insight* that you gained from reading the chapter, along with one *big action* that you can take, or change you can make, to put that insight into action to produce results.

The Tip of the Iceberg

"All I know is that I know nothing."
—SOCRATES

The most difficult part of writing this book was not deciding what to include…but deciding what to leave out. If I had packed everything I wanted to into this single volume, it would have totaled around five thousand pages as I had, literally, hundreds and hundreds of pages of typewritten and handwritten notes and sketches piled up from over the past twenty years since I first dove headfirst into the leadership development field.

For every image, model, metaphor, and story included in this book, there were probably twenty or more left on the cutting room floor. So, using one of my favorite metaphors, I had an "iceberg's worth" of possible content from which to choose, and what you are holding in your hands is just the proverbial "tip." And even though I am fully immersed in this field of study, there is still a veritable "ocean's worth" of information out there related to the topics of leadership, management, visual thinking, and visual communication that I have yet to discover!

So, while I've done *my* best to provide you with some of *the* best of what I know, love, and teach, I hope that this book will pique your interest in this area, and encourage and inspire you to venture out there and to dive beneath the surface to explore what other treasures await. To do otherwise would be a missed opportunity of, yes, "Titanic" proportions.

Regarding that aforementioned tip of the iceberg contained within this book, the concepts herein have been selected from among the most useful, valuable, and popular content that I tend to draw on in my NYU and Columbia leadership graduate classes, my corporate workshops, and my executive coaching sessions, as well as from my own personal and professional experiences in the workplace over the past thirty years. As such, I hope that you will benefit both from my success stories as well as my failure stories.

In terms of the criteria for inclusion regarding the models, metaphors, and stories that made the final cut, they are:

- **Among the Best of the Best:** I included what I think are some of the most useful and popular visual models, metaphors, and stories in my repertoire. The ones I go to most often in my workshops, classes, and coaching sessions, and that (based on feedback from my clients and students) are considered among the most valuable. One of my sayings is, "The true value of knowledge is not in its accumulation, but in its application"—and these are the ones that people seem to get the most value out of applying at work and in life.

- **Original Content**: Sir Isaac Newton once wrote, "If I have seen further it is by standing on the shoulders of giants." No ideas exist in a vacuum. And many are simply floating out there in the ether. So while the majority of the concepts in this book are my own, based on my many years of personal and professional experience, I have no doubt that some of them might have seeped into my brain from all that I have read, heard, watched, and experienced over the course of my lifetime. While I will, of course, give credit where credit is due, and attribution wherever possible, the insights, ideas, and opinions expressed in this book are mine. Although it must be said that, when it comes to the field of management, almost all roads, ultimately, lead back to Peter Drucker. Or Confucius. Or Socrates.

- **Actionable, Rather than Theoretical:** While I love theory, there are other thoughtleaders out there who are far more capable than me when it comes to the science of how the brain works and why visuals rule (for example, John Medina's *Brain Rules* and *How We Learn* by Benedict Carey). Similarly, "neuroleadership," the study of the relationship between neuroscience and leadership, is a new and growing field (spearheaded by David Rock and featured in his book *Your Brain at Work*). So I have chosen to leave the science to the scientists, the research to the researchers, and the academics to the academicians, and focus on what I know and do best based on my thirty-plus years of practitioner-based experience, which is: exploring and helping others to master the real-world practical application of visual thinking and visual communication tools, tips, and techniques to be more effective performers, managers, and leaders.

When asked how long it took him to write the Gettysburg Address, Abraham Lincoln's well-known response was, "My entire life." Whether he actually said that (he probably didn't; I'll discuss the controversy around famous quotes later), and while I am not in any way comparing my writing to one of the most famous speeches by one of the greatest leaders of all time, I can say that the content of this book is, indeed, the accumulation of a lifetime of living and working, and succeeding…and, yes, failing. After all, Eleanor Roosevelt wrote that we should "learn from the mistakes of others. You can't live long enough to make them all yourself."

One of my sayings, and one of the foundational visual models of this book, is, "Wisdom is where Knowledge and Experience Meet." Think about all that *you* know…and think about how you know it. And then think about all the work and life experiences you've had. At the intersection of these two realms is where *your* wisdom comes from.

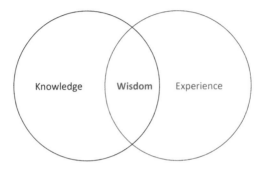

As Bill Nye the Science Guy once said, "Everyone you will ever meet knows something that you don't." Similarly, what I write about in this book, and what I am excited to share with you, is some of the best of what I, personally, have to bring to the table in the form of my favorite and most useful visual images, mental models and frameworks, metaphors and analogies, and visual stories. But my hope in writing this book is that it will not be a monologue, but a dialogue, and that as you read it, you will bring your own knowledge, experiences, and stories to the party. And I look forward to this being—to quote one of the most famous last lines in movie history—"the beginning of a beautiful friendship" as you join me on this journey of exploration and discovery.

A Confession: My Business Book Addiction

After having had so many bad bosses earlier in my career, I started think-ing, there has to be a better way to manage and lead people. So, when I was hired many years ago as a program director for one of the nation's leading training companies with the responsibility of revamping their flagship mini-MBA program, I started reading business books, one after another after another. And I was hooked. Some weeks I'd read one, other weeks I'd read five or even ten. That habit continued for twenty years, from 1998 to 2018, at which point I calculated that I had read over 1,000 business books during that period. And that was in addition to reading the *New York Times* every single day, along with numerous periodicals, like *Harvard Business Review*, as well as hundreds of blogs, including the *Harvard Management Tip of the Day*, and the brilliant and incomparable daily posts by Seth Godin (how on earth does he do it seven days a week?).

One of my favorite books on innovation and creativity is Austin Kleon's *Steal Like an Artist*. And one of the key points he makes is that there are very few original ideas out there. "Nothing," he says, "comes from nowhere. All creative work builds on what came before." And what came before VisuaLeadership is everything I've ever read, heard, and experienced in my life.

With that being said, my objective in this book is to provide you with some of the best of the best of the content I've created over the years, along with references to some of the best of the best of what's out there. As such, my hope is that you will gain some new knowledge from this book, and that you will be able to apply it to your life and work so that you can become the wisest and best version of yourself as a VisuaLeader.

With that…on with the show!

"It sort of makes you stop and think, doesn't it."

PART ONE

Leading with...Visuals

In this section, we'll take a look at what "VisuaLeadership" is all about. We'll then answer the big question you may be wondering, "Why Visuals?" And I'll share with you three personal stories that most influenced my thinking and led me down the path to discovering and formulating my visual thinking-based approach to leadership.

But first...

For many business professionals, when you hear the words "visual thinking" and "visual communication," the initial thought often is "this isn't for me, because I can't draw." Let me put your mind at ease right up front by saying that your drawing ability doesn't matter—at all!

As you'll soon discover, leading with visuals involves so much more than drawing. It's about formulating and communicating a leadership vision; using internal visualization processes; and leveraging visual images, models, charts, diagrams, PowerPoint slides, and visual language—including the use of stories, metaphors, and analogies—all of which I will explore and provide examples of within this book. In fact, you have one of the most powerful visual thinking and visual communication tools in the world right in your pocket: your smartphone! With its picture-taking and video capabilities and other features, when combined with social media... you can, instantly and visually change the world.

That being said, since it came up, here's that I want to say about the subject of drawing, just to get it out of the way. Let's call this, "How to Overcome 'ICD' (I Can't Draw) Syndrome":

1

When we facilitate workshops on visual thinking and visual communication, we often start out by asking the group, "How many of you can draw?" Typically, we get only about 10 percent of businesspeople raising their hands. But if you were to ask a group of kindergarteners that very same question, almost every single kid would have their hand raised. So, over the decades, have we lost our *ability* to draw—or just our confidence?

To answer that question, I encourage you to just pick up a pen and see what you can do. I think you'll be pleasantly surprised. Like anything else, drawing is a skill that you can quickly get better at with just a little bit of practice. If you are capable of playing Pictionary or Charades at a party, then you are fully capable of using a whiteboard to explain a concept by sketching it out—even if only in stick figures and doodles. Moreover, visual communication isn't just about graphics. If you can use body language, hand gestures, and facial expressions to communicate (which I am sure you do naturally, without even thinking about it), then you are capable of doing so more purposefully and skillfully in the future.

Do you remember that classic GEICO campaign, "It's so easy a caveman can do it"? Well, when it comes to drawing, cavemen *did* do it—forty thousand years ago—without any lessons. So, don't ever let "I Can't Draw" syndrome stop you from picking up a pen, pencil, or marker to help you get your point across. To paraphrase Babe Ruth, when it comes to communicating more visually, don't let the fear of striking out keep you from swinging for the fences!

Speaking of cave drawings by the way, that's visual communication before the written word was even invented. And the earliest written languages, including Egyptian hieroglyphics, consisted of pictograms: a form of visual communication that used symbols and images to represent things and ideas. Bear in mind also that in order to communicate visually, one must first *think* visually to figure out what you want to say—and how best to say it. So, now that we have thousands of emojis and emoticons ("emotional icons") at our disposal, it appears that we have come full circle, and that visual thinking and visual communication are back and here to stay.

If you're the type of person who happens to be not too happy about this movement towards using visual symbols in the place of words, your reaction might be expressed something like this: @#$%&! But, did you know that this use of symbols to represent cursing or swear words actually has a name and an origin story; and do you know what it's called? Yes, a "grawlix"! (And if you're thinking, "What the @#$%&! is a 'grawlix'?" I invite you to take a moment to look it up!)

Now, to get us in a "visual thinking" mind-set and mood, and so that you can "see what *I'm* saying," let's start out with a few related quotes and thoughts as a mental warm-up. Just read through the quotes below, "see" what "comes to mind," and let them sink in. Many are familiar, while others may not be. Here goes:

A picture is worth a thousand words.

A good sketch is better than a long speech. (Napoleon; although he probably said it in French.)

Seeing something once is better than hearing it a thousand times. (Chinese proverb)

Changing the way you see the world changes the world itself.

Changing what people see can change what they think, feel, know, and do.

Every picture tells a story.

I'll believe it when I see it.

Seeing is believing.

Picture this…

If you can dream it, you can do it. (Disney; though written by Imagineer Tom Fitzgerald and not a quote by Walt, himself.)

If you can see it, you can be it.

You can't be what you can't see. (Marian Wright Edelman)

If you can see the invisible, you can do the impossible.

If you see far, you can go far. (Slogan from the ASYV in Rwanda)

If you want to go fast, go alone. If you want to go far, go together.

If you see something, say something. (Ads in the NYC subway system)

3

I'm just not seeing it.
Can you imagine...?
Show me what you mean.
Pictures don't lie.[1]

So, to sum up, as Arthur Brisbane, the editor of the *New York Evening Journal* wrote way back in 1916: "In this day of hurry, we learn through the eye, and one picture may be worth a million words."

And I would have to say that in today's increasingly fast-paced digital world, this statement is truer than ever before.

---

[1] Or, do they? Of course they do, now!

CHAPTER 1

What is VisuaLeadership?

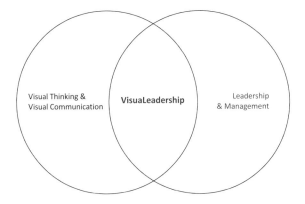

"Leadership is the capacity to translate vision into reality."
—WARREN BENNIS

When you think about the best and worst companies you've ever worked at, and the best and worst managers you've ever worked for, what thoughts comes to mind? As Shakespeare said (in Hamlet), "Nothing is either good or bad but thinking makes it so." So, when thinking about your best and worst jobs…what made them so good—or so bad?

When I pose this question to others, for example, my coaching clients and grad students, the most common response is that what made the good ones good and the bad ones bad could be summed up in two words: passion and purpose. The "bottom line" is that people are engaged, inspired, and motivated not by quarterly reports, balance sheets, and

5

cash-flow statements, but by big picture aspirations, hopes, and dreams. And, so, as leadership guru Warren Bennis succinctly stated, getting an opportunity to work for a leader who can inspire us to translate a compelling vision into a new and exciting reality makes all the difference in the world.

But what does it actually mean to have a "leadership vision," or to be labeled a "visionary leader" or a "leadership visionary"? This question tends to evoke images of iconic leaders like Abraham Lincoln, Martin Luther King Jr., Walt Disney, and Steve Jobs; but who else comes to mind for you? To me, the phrase, "leadership vision" has to do with "seeing" possibilities. It's about "envisioning" a future state that is different from and, ideally, better than the current reality…along with the ability to effectively communicate that vision in a compelling way that engages, empowers, and inspires others to help turn that vision into a reality.

In Shakespeare's *Hamlet*, the title character says that he sees his deceased father in his "mind's eye." But what does that metaphor actually mean? And how do we get an image, a thought, an idea, a vision, out of *our* mind's eye and into someone else's? One way is through the power of visual thinking and visual communication. Or what I call "VisuaLeadership."

First, what is "visual thinking"? At its most basic level, it's about thinking in pictures, as opposed to in words or numbers. And "visual communication"? That's about expressing your ideas visually—by means of visual images, objects, and movement, as well as through the use of visual language, which includes metaphors and stories.

So, VisuaLeadership? Simply put, **VisuaLeadership is where visuals and leadership meet. It is the art and science of applying visual thinking and visual communication tools, tips, and techniques to manage and lead yourself and others.**

For those who like a "magic formula," it can be summed up in the following equation:

$$VL = (VT + VC) \times (M + L)$$
$$\text{VisuaLeadership} = \text{(Visual Thinking + Visual Communication)}$$
$$\times \text{(Management + Leadership)}$$

And how does one manage and lead visually to more effectively get people to "see" what you're saying? Here are four ways (all of which overlap and/or can be used in combination):

1. **Visual Imagery:** Using **pictures**—or other visual means of expression—for the purpose of conceptualizing and/or communicating. Examples may include: pictures, drawings, infographics, videos, video games, virtual reality, simulators, explainer videos, visionboards, graphic recording, visual note-taking, sketchnoting, napkin sketching, doodling, emoticons, emojis, symbols, icons, logos, cartoons, comic strips, color-coding, shapes, body language, facial expressions, hand gestures, sign language, choreography.

2. **Mental Models:** Using **frameworks** for the purpose of conceptualizing and/or communicating. Examples may include: maps, data visualization, gamification, infographics, graphs, charts, diagrams, matrices, tables, circles, squares, triangles, pyramids, ladders, steps, arrows, cycles, acronyms, etc.

3. **Metaphor:** Using **comparisons** of unlike things for the purpose of conceptualizing and/or communicating. Examples may include: sports, arts, nature, animals, business, and so many more; the list of possibilities is endless.

4. **Visual Storytelling:** Using **narrative** to "paint a picture with words" for the purpose of conceptualizing and/or communicating. Examples may include: anecdotes, cautionary tales, drama, comedy.

Exercise: To bring these concepts to life and to personalize them for you, consider these questions:

- What are some of the ways in which you use visual **images** (that is, pictures, sketches, maps) to process information and/or to communicate with others?

- What are some of the **mental models** or frameworks that you carry around in your mind to help you frame your reality, innovate, make decisions, and solve problems?
- What are some of the **metaphors** and analogies you commonly use to understand and to explain things?
- What are some of the go-to **stories**, anecdotes, lessons, and examples that you carry around with you and pull out to illustrate your points and share with others when needed?

One of the ways to think about becoming a more visual leader is to think about how you can develop your VisuaLeadership "mind-set, tool set, and skill set":

To have a VisuaLeadership **mind-set** is to begin thinking more visually. To view the world through an exciting, colorful, and creative new lens. To be more hyperaware and intentional in noticing how you, as well as others, are—either consciously or unconsciously—using visual techniques to think, innovate, problem solve, communicate, manage, and lead. Hopefully, after reading this book, you will see the world around you in an exciting new light.

Once you are more conscious of visual thinking, the next step is to continue to build your VisuaLeadership **tool set** so that you have it at your disposal to access when needed. By that I mean a (metaphorical) arsenal of visual thinking and visual communication tools, tips, and techniques that you can *draw upon* at any time. This tool set will include visual imagery, mental models and frameworks, metaphors and analogies, and stories to help you to be more effective and more impactful in everything you do. And using all these new tools will not only help you to boost your performance, it will make going about your business in this new way more creative, more colorful, and more fun.

And being *aware* of all these new tools is just the beginning; developing the **skill set** to effectively *use* them to achieve better results is another. While these visual concepts are often simple on the surface to understand, they take time, experience, and practice to master. Just as buying a shiny new tool kit from Home Depot or Lowe's doesn't instantly make you a master carpenter, adding all these exciting new tools to your VisuaLeadership tool kit will enable you to become a more visual thinker and communicator, not overnight…but over time.

To continue with the above analogy, if you were to come home from a hardware store with a big new tool box, you would have two ways to approach things. You can say, "I have this new tool kit…now, what can I build?" Or you can look around your house for things that need fixing and ask, "Which tools can I use to do so?"

Similarly, while reading this book, you can start with one of the models, metaphors, or stories and ask yourself: "How can I apply this?" Or you can start with a life- or business-related problem that you're currently facing and ask, "Which visual thinking concepts from this book (or elsewhere) might I apply to help me solve it?"

As the concept of visual thinking can, at first, be perceived as somewhat abstract and nebulous, here are just a few, concrete, real-world business examples, framed as visual thinking-related challenges, just to illustrate and "plant the seed" for what's to come:

- One of the tasks most closely associated with managing is "supervising." The word, "supervise" is composed of "super," which means over or above, and "vise," which means to "see or observe." So, in essence, to supervise someone is to "over-see" the person and their work. With this definition and word origin in mind, why might an employee possibly resent your referring to yourself as their "supervisor"?

- Are leaders born or made? If I were to ask you to "picture" and then describe "a leader," who are the first five people who immediately pop into your mind? If you were to point to a little kid in a playground, and say, "See that kid? She/He is going to be a real leader one day," what are some of the traits, qualities, or characteristics that that child is exhibiting that make you think and say that? Now answer this question: how might your answers to these two above questions relate to any unconscious biases that you—or anyone—might have when it comes to how we define—and visualize—leadership?

- If I were to ask you to describe the differences between management and leadership, or managing and leading, how might you use visual thinking and visual communication to wrap your head around it and then explain it to someone else? What metaphors, analogies, or stories would you use to illustrate the subtle but important distinctions? And, how would understanding the differences between being "a manager" and being "a leader" help you to be better at both?

- Before giving an employee feedback—whether informally, or for their annual performance review—do you visualize in your mind what you are going to say, how you are going to say it, and how they might respond—as well as how you will respond to their reaction—*before* you launch into the conversation? If so, how will that help you to be more successful? If not, what might the possible repercussions be?

And, lastly, if you were curious about the origin and the intended meaning of the word, "VisuaLeadership" itself, I coined this term to serve as both a conceptual and a visual reminder that *how you lead* is inseparable from *how you see the world.*

Now that we've touched on the concept of VisuaLeadership and provided a few examples of some of the types of challenges visual thinking and visual communication might help us address, it is time to just dive in, as the best way to understand what this is all about is, simply, to experience it.

But first, before we do…let's answer one final question that you may be wondering: "Why visuals?"

CHAPTER 2

Why Visuals?

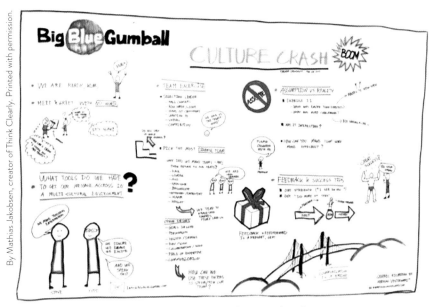

Example of a graphic recording (aka visual note-taking)

When you wake up in the morning and remember a dream that you had while sleeping, or flash back to something you forgot to do yesterday, that's visual thinking.

When you look at your alarm clock, mentally decide on your wardrobe, imagine how you are going to get to work, and look at your calendar to envision how your day might unfold, that's visual thinking.

If, before you leave for work, you decide to meditate, or you jump in the shower only to find your mind wandering off to daydream about your upcoming vacation, that's visual thinking.

If, while listening to a song on Spotify, you visualize the singer or the band or the album cover in your mind, that's visual thinking.

If you are listening to a ballgame on the radio, and picturing in your "mind's eye" what's happening on the field, that's visual thinking.

If you think of your significant other and picture what they might be doing right now, that's visual thinking.

If you text someone an emoji, click a thumbs-up or a heart on their social media post, use Google Maps to navigate your route, or put together a piece of Ikea furniture using one of their diagrams, those are all examples of visual thinking.

You get the point. When you are thinking visually, it's almost as though you're looking at mental "snapshots" or watching a mental "movie" in your mind's eye. In fact, the word, "movie" is short for "moving pictures"... which is, basically, what visual thoughts are. They could involve a vision from the past (as in recalling a memory or a dream), from the present (as when you are focused on the moment), or of the future (as when you envision upcoming possibilities).

Think about it, what percentage of your day—even when you are out there in the world with other people—are you spending alone in your head, starring in your own mental "motion picture"? If you're like most people, the answer is "a lot." And the powerful thing about visual thinking is that it happens anywhere and everywhere. We all have our favorite places to visually think. In fact, the worst place, when trying to innovate, is probably at your desk. The best place—for many people—tends to be anywhere else: walking the treadmill or walking the dog, sitting in a park or at the water's edge. Not to get too personal, but—as many people do—I tend to get most of my best ideas while in the shower. In fact, to be honest, that's where much of this book was written. So, my apologies if some of the pages are still wet.

Translating the concept of visual thinking to the workplace: Before heading to a meeting, you may look at the Outlook invite and picture in your mind: *where am I going, how am I getting there, who else is going to be there, and what's going to happen?* You may project in your mind how you are going to feel while in that meeting: Bored? Excited? Fearful? Anxious, curious, or inspired?

When you know you have an upcoming performance review with your boss, don't you picture what you should wear, what you need to bring, how you should act, what you should and shouldn't say, and how you think it will go in advance? As a manager, when you communicate to your team, do you paint a picture with words and images—that is, communicate your "vision"—of what the future is expected to look like… so that *they* will have that same vision in their heads?

As mentioned, when you use visual methods of thinking and communicating, it dramatically enhances your effectiveness in three key areas: Attention, Comprehension, and Retention. When you see a visual image, such as the VisuaLeadership Venn diagram from Chapter 1, or the graphic recording above, it captures and holds your attention and gets you to focus; it increases your understanding, and it enables you to remember… in a way that is more powerful and effective than words alone.

In fact, the importance of developing one's visual intelligence and visual literacy was considered so important to one of the great visual thinkers of all time, Leonardo da Vinci, that he coined the Latin phrase, *sapere vedere,* which translates to "knowing how to see"—a skill that he deemed essential to understanding the world around us.

Author Scott Berinato, in his *Harvard Business Review* article "Visualizations That Really Work" (June 2016), points out that from a management and leadership perspective "visual communication is a must-have skill for all managers, because more and more often, it's the only way to make sense of the work they do."

For instance, Visual Project Management is a new and growing field that incorporates visual models (including data visualization) and other visually-oriented techniques into traditional project management tools and methodologies to maximize efficiency and effectiveness. Similarly, more and more organizations are embracing digital technologies that harness a visual component (for example, "dashboards") that make them more dynamic, engaging, and user-friendly. (More on this later when we discuss the future of work.)

So, why is this? What is it about using visuals and visual techniques—including visual imagery, mental models, metaphors, and stories—that can make business professionals more productive, more efficient, and more effective?

Without getting into all the brain science behind it, I just want to very briefly and simply introduce two fairly complex, though fundamental, concepts to help answer the question, "Why visuals?" These two foundational concepts are: The Picture Superiority Effect and Dual Coding theory.

In brief, the Picture Superiority Effect (PSE) states that when it comes to the understanding and recall of information, the use of images is superior to the use of text alone. From our own personal experience, this principle is fairly obvious, and the science backs it up. Yet how often do we still sit through tedious and torturous PowerPoint presentations composed of slide after slide of text-based bullet points as the presenter drones on and reads off the screen? As I'll discuss later, visual images, models, metaphors, and stories—especially when used in combination—can dramatically increase our effectiveness in a wide variety of ways.

As for Dual Coding theory (originated by psychology professor Allan Paivio), this concept is in many ways similar to the Picture Superiority Effect. Without getting into the complexities of the brain science behind it, this theory states that when you take factual information and add a visual component to it, the information gets encoded in our brains in *two* ways rather than just one (hence, "dual" coding): verbally (the words) and visually (the pictures). This dual coding, therefore, takes advantage of both the left (language) and right (visual) sides of our brain (metaphorically speaking), thereby dramatically enhancing learning, and increasing recall, by getting your message across more effectively...and helping to make it stick.

For example: Research has shown that blog posts accompanied by a visual image get read—and recalled—twice as much as those that are composed of text alone. People are more likely to accept a stranger's

LinkedIn request if there is a headshot vs. when there is not. Would you buy a product on Amazon or eBay if there wasn't a photo included with the description? Would you rather watch an unboxing video…or listen to an unboxing audio?

The visual factor also explains why the use of video (both prerecorded and live) has taken off on all social media platforms, from Instagram and YouTube to Facebook and LinkedIn. Very simply, visuals capture people's attention, enhance understanding, and increase retention in a way that words, alone, simply cannot and do not. And in this increasingly fast-paced, digital world wherein everyone is battling for limited time and attention spans, the use of visuals in all areas of work and life will, no doubt, continue to rise.

Let's do an experiment: Take a second and thumb through this book, stopping at any random page. Stare at that page for three to five seconds, and then come right back here. Go ahead…I'll wait.

OK…welcome back!

When thumbing, did you happen to stop upon a page containing a visual image (that is, a picture or model)…or one with just plain text? My guess is that there's an 80—100 percent chance that you stopped on a page containing an image. And that your eyes—and your attention—were immediately, intuitively, almost magnetically, drawn to the visual image.

Why was that? Because it's human nature. We are visual creatures, and it is how our brains are wired. We are instinctively and unconsciously attracted to (and, sometimes, distracted by!) visuals like flies to a light bulb. If you had to describe one of your stumbled-upon visuals to someone, could you? Probably. What about the content of the text on the page? Probably not.

Research has shown that not only are we instinctively drawn to visuals, but that our brains process them thousands of times faster than we can process text. That's why billboards on a highway are designed differently than an ad in a magazine: it needs to get its message across to people traveling at 60–80 miles per hour. That's why blog posts containing a visual image get almost twice as many views as those that don't. And why color images get almost twice as many views as those in black-and-white.

And that's why we should, primarily, be using images rather than text when designing our PowerPoint presentations. And why both the Picture Superiority Effect and Dual Coding Theory tell us that when there's a battle between text and visuals, the visual image will win out every time.

You know who recognized these principles long before all this recent scientific research?

Give up?

Well, one of the key proponents was the Confucian philosopher Xunzi, who wrote, in around the third century BC: "Hearing something a hundred times isn't better than seeing it once." Which was, basically, his way of saying, "A picture is worth a hundred words." (If I'm not mistaken, I believe the perceived value of a picture eventually increased from "a hundred words" to "a thousand words" over the past five thousand years due to inflation.)

Similarly, most of us are familiar with the proverb (of which there are many variations, with attributions to everyone from Confucius to Benjamin Franklin): "Tell me and I'll forget. Show me, and I may remember. Involve me, and I'll understand." This saying reinforces the various ways in which we take in information and learn, paralleling the well-known Auditory, Visual, and Kinesthetic sensory learning modalities. Known, collectively, as the "VAK" model, this concept has, more recently, been expanded to add "Reading/Writing," leading to its current iteration as "VARK" (Visual, Auditory, Reading/Writing, Kinesthetic).

While the first three sensory approaches are fairly self-explanatory, for those who may not know, Kinesthetic has to do with movement, and "learning through doing" (that is, experiential learning). And as Sir Ken Robinson cleverly states in his top-ranked TED Talk, the opposite of kinesthetic is…what? Anesthetic. And what does an anesthetic do? It puts us to sleep. Which further supports the contention that using multi-sensory approaches is more powerful than using any one of them alone.

All that to say, while the focus of this book is primarily on the use of visuals, I did not want to ignore or in any way disregard the other sensory modalities, and the various ways in which our brains receive, process, store, and communicate information. When used appropriately, especially in combination, we can dramatically increase people's attention, comprehension, and retention and get them to see what we're saying. The use of images, models, metaphors, and stories helps to make the abstract concrete, the intangible tangible, the unfamiliar familiar, and the invisible visible.

And, speaking of making the invisible visible….

CHAPTER 3

What's Your Sign?

I don't know how many times this happened while I was growing up, but we'd be riding along in our old Chevy Impala—my father driving, my mother in the passenger seat, and my brother and me in the back seat—when my father would suddenly yell out:

"Hurry up! Somebody give me a pencil and a piece of paper! Quick!"

On cue, as if they practiced this routine a thousand times, my mother would roll her eyes and say (with a complete lack of enthusiasm): "Why, Harvey?"

To which my father would inevitably respond: "What do you mean *why*? Don't you see the sign?!"

I know, I know—you're probably groaning right now and rolling your eyes like my mother did. But as corny as that "Dad joke" is—and as many times as we heard it over and over (and over) again, it always made me laugh or at least smile. And to this day, fifty-plus years later, I still smile—and think of my dad (who passed away a few years ago)—every time I come upon a sign that says, "Draw Bridge." I hope that from now on, you will too, as one of my father's favorite things in life was to make people laugh.

And I would venture to bet that from now on—whether you want to or not (sorry about that!)—every time you pass a Draw Bridge sign, you are going to think of this silly story and, perhaps, crack a smile. Why? In short, that's the power of visual thinking in action.

When you use a visual image, and/or a story—and especially if you couple it with humor—it's an extremely powerful and effective way of getting an idea to stick.

And that's the foundation of VisuaLeadership in a nutshell: using visual thinking and visual communication techniques to get an idea out of your head into someone else's so that they will be able to "see"—and to remember—what you're saying.

Think about the two words on the sign, "draw" and "bridge":

At its most basic level, "drawing" tends to be about taking pen or pencil to paper (or, more and more these days, to a digital screen) to create a picture. Whether it's a doodle or a stick figure, a diagram or a sketch, drawing is about creating an image to visually represent a thing or an idea. The word "image" comes from the Latin word for "copy." So, in essence, what we are doing when we draw is visually copying the real world (skillfully, or not…depending on one's level of talent and expertise) in the form of art. And where does all art come from? Our IMAG-ination.

And what about the word "bridge"? Just as a physical bridge connects two pieces of land, "bridging" is, metaphorically, about any connection. In fact, one of my college textbooks was entitled *Bridges Not Walls*, which is a powerful visual metaphor that reminds us that ideas—and the communication of those ideas—can either connect us as a bridge does… or divide us as a wall does.

So, to me, the words "Draw Bridge" serve as a simple representation of what "VisuaLeadership" is all about on multiple levels: the art and science of managing and leading through the use of visual thinking and visual communication techniques including, but not limited to, visual imagery, mental models, metaphors and analogies, and visual storytelling.

Speaking of fathers, by the way, in *Hamlet* the title character exclaims that he saw the ghost of his deceased father in his "mind's eye." Shakespeare was the one who popularized the phrase "mind's eye." But what does it mean? And how do we get a thought from our mind's eye and into someone else's so that they can see what we're thinking…and understand what we're saying?

If you think about it, when you see something in your mind's eye, it's about visualizing something that is not actually, physically, there. It's about "en-visioning" a picture in your head—of either the past (as in a memory), the present (as in a thought), or the future (as in a vision). In all instances it's about "seeing." And, when it comes to being a more visual leader, seeing the invisible will enable you, and others, to do the impossible. In essence, that's what visionary leadership is all about.

A classic example—probably, *the* classic example—of a leadership vision by a visionary leader would be Dr. Martin Luther King Jr.'s "I Have a Dream" speech. If you listen to it or, even better, if you watch it, while focusing on his artful and impactful use of visual imagery, metaphors, visual language, and other rhetorical techniques, you'll find that he used the power of visual thinking and visual communication better than pretty much anyone who has ever lived.

But here's the thing: You don't need to be Dr. Martin Luther King Jr. to be a "VisuaLeader"; you can just be yourself. *And*, by the way, you do not need to be able to draw. All you need to do to be a VisuaLeader is to think and to communicate more visually, so as to get others to "see" what you're saying. If you can do that, you can change not only *their* world, but *the* world.

CHAPTER 4

How My 30-Second Napkin Sketch Solved a Client's Multimillion-Dollar Problem

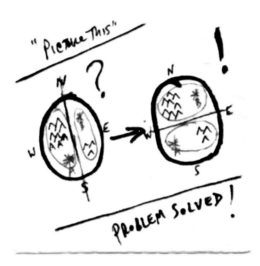

Sitting in a San Antonio bar in 1967 with entrepreneur (and soon-to-be CEO) Herb Kelleher, Texas businessman Rollin King grabbed a now-legendary cocktail napkin and sketched out a simple triangle while posing this question: What if we were to create a local airline that connected these three cities (San Antonio, Dallas, and Houston)? With that simple sketch the idea for Southwest Airlines was born.

(By the way, this classic story is often told by author Dan Roam, who is one of the thoughtleaders most responsible for putting the business application of napkin sketching "on the map," such as in his groundbreaking book *The Back of the Napkin: Solving Problems and Selling Ideas with Pictures*.)

Keeping this classic Southwest Airlines example in mind, the next time you are trying to generate ideas, brainstorm a solution, or convey a complex idea to someone, instead of just trying to explain it verbally, why not use a cocktail napkin—or a piece of paper, or a flipchart, or whiteboard, or tablet—to sketch it out?

Even if you think you can't draw, it's not about your *artistic* ability... it's about your ability to visually represent your idea for the purpose of getting it out of your head and into someone else's.

Early in my executive coaching career, one of my new coaching clients—a regional vice president of sales at a global pharmaceuticals company—was wrestling with a costly, complex, and incredibly challenging business dilemma that had been keeping him up at night for months.

In my first coaching session with him, I helped to solve this problem in less than ten minutes—simply by means of a 30-second napkin sketch.

It's not that I'm so brilliant—in fact, to be completely honest, I didn't really, fully understand all the complexities of his situation (in this instance, that ignorance probably worked to my advantage)—and my drawing skills are elementary at best. And yet my amateurish and rudimentary sketch helped save the day.

Here's how:

In one of the smaller European countries for which he was responsible, this sales VP had two regional sales directors reporting to him: the director of the western region, and the director of the eastern region.

The guy who ran the west was very senior and highly experienced, but near retirement and not all that ambitious. The guy who ran the east was young, hungry, energetic, and looking for a challenge. The problem, though, was that the east was a more mature, settled market with little growth opportunity; so the newer guy felt handcuffed and frustrated. The northwestern part of the country was where all the potential action was. But the guy who ran the west was nearing retirement and not interested, energized, motivated, aggressive, or willing enough to do what it would take to conquer that untapped sales territory.

So, what was my client to do? Neither of these regional directors was interested in relocating. And, for logistical reasons, constant travel was a costly and ineffective option. My client was stuck, with absolutely no idea what to do. He had two unhappy employees on his hands, and he was losing thousands of dollars in potential business with each passing day.

Just to make sure I understood the problem correctly, I sketched out my perception of the situation simply by drawing an oval (representing the country) with a vertical line splitting it down the middle, separating it into east and west.

Instinctively I said, "This may be a stupid idea, and I'm sure you've already thought of it, but what would happen if you did this…?"

At which point (and maybe you've figured it out by now as it's so obvious it's almost embarrassing) I drew a line *across* the country and said, "What if, instead of east and west, you were to redivide the two regional markets into north and south?"

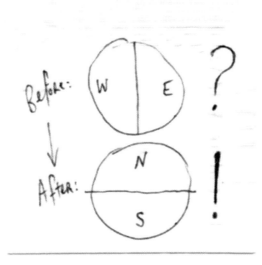

Problem solved. A solution that was so simple and obvious after the fact was imperceptible to my client…until he saw it drawn out on paper. Only then were we both able to see the multimillion-dollar solution right before our very eyes.

But here's the question: Why didn't *he* see the solution earlier, before I did? He was the expert, and a super-smart guy. It was probably because he was so caught up in the sales figures, and the personalities involved, and the conflict, and the pressures, and the complexities of the situation. He was too mired in the details, and too close to "see the forest for the trees." And it wasn't until we were able to get a fresh set of eyes on the problem and take the proverbial "thirty thousand-foot view" of the situation that the solution became crystal clear.

I was able to see a solution that he couldn't because, as per the classic Zen saying that I picked up from author Garr Reynolds (*Presentation Zen*, and *The Naked Presenter*): "In the beginner's mind there are many possibilities, but in the expert's there are few."

Or, as George Bernard Shaw once said, "No question is so difficult to answer as that to which the answer is obvious." But it did not become obvious until I sketched it out.

Of course, napkin sketching and figuring things out on the "back of an envelope" have been around for ages, and the idea of drawing things out goes back millennia, to caveman days, even before the written word was invented. But it's only in recent years that the concepts of visual thinking, visual communication, napkin sketching, whiteboarding, etc., have really taken off as practical, recognized, and learnable business skills suitable not just for artists, but for anyone and everyone.

Think about these questions: How would you explain your job using a napkin sketch? If you had to, could you draw a picture that would simplify the complexity of your company's business model to a potential customer or investor? Or illustrate a step-by-step process to train a new employee? On a job interview, would you be able to visually tell the story of your career history (the who, what, when, where, why, and how) in a visual and compelling way?

If so, you just might find that a picture truly is worth a thousand words…or, as in the Southwest Airlines example, many millions of dollars.

In Review

The Big Lesson: In the future, when trying to communicate in a situation wherein words alone may not do the trick, think about how you can leverage the power of drawing—both to conceptualize your idea, and as an effective way of communicating it to others.

The Big Question: What's a challenge you are currently facing that might benefit from your "sketching it out"?

Your Big Insight:

Your Big Action:

CHAPTER 5

A Love Letter to Horrible Bosses

"The worst is not, so long as we can say 'This is the worst.'"

—WILLIAM SHAKESPEARE; *King Lear*, Act 4 Scene 2

So, there I am, sitting at my desk typing up a memo when, all of a sudden, I hear my boss's office door swing open behind me. As I turn around to see what's going on, I instinctively duck to avoid the object flying at my head. A box of pens hits the wall above my desk and breaks open, spraying twelve brand-new blue Paper Mate medium ballpoints in all directions.

My boss had just thrown a box of pens at me.

"What the hell?" I exclaimed.

My boss picks up one of the scattered pens from my desk and shoves it in my face.

"What does this say?" she asks.

"Paper Mate."

"No, next to that, you idiot."

"Medium point."

"And what kind of pen do I use?"

"Fine point."

"So, if you know that I always use a fine point pen, then why the hell am I standing here holding a medium point?"

"Because the office supplies guy must have sent up the wrong ones…"

"I don't want to hear any of your excuses. You always have an excuse for everything! Just pick up all of these pens, put them back in the box, and exchange them for the right ones. If you can't even handle something as simple as ordering a box of pens, maybe you better start looking for another job!"

Office door slams. End of scene. And cut.

No, that was not a scene from a movie. That was a scene from early in my career.

And while it happened a long time ago and I can laugh about it now, the pain and humiliation of working for a toxic boss like that still lingers all these years later.

I was working as an administrative assistant at the time for one of the major TV networks out in Hollywood. I won't say which one, but it had a "C," a "B," and an "S" in its name. And my boss was an absolute lunatic. Condescending, sarcastic, mentally abusive, passive-aggressive, always pissed off, constantly in panic mode, incredibly insecure, and completely incompetent. Add it all up and that makes for a deadly combination. The opposite of a "BFF" (Best Friend Forever), she was my "BFH" (Boss From Hell).

When thinking back on all the obnoxious and horrifying things she did to me, getting a box of pens thrown at my head was just the tip of the iceberg. Looking back now at the "Abuse Log" I kept at the time (I'm not kidding, I still have it), it is unbelievable how much I endured while working for her. The greatest hits included:

- Referring to me as her "boy," as in saying to someone over the phone (and I quote), "I'll have my boy deliver a copy of that script to you."

Bear in mind that I was twenty-nine years old at the time, and 6'4" tall. She was around a year older than me…and a foot shorter.

- Frisbee-ing a copy of a script at the back of my knees while I was walking out the door of her office, saying, "Hey, throw this out for me," even though she had a nice, big paper recycling bin right next to her desk. And, by the way, she always called me "Hey." As in "Hey, shut my door," or "Hey, any messages?" In all the time I worked for her I don't think she ever actually called me by my name.

- Making me stay until 5 p.m. on a Friday of a three-day holiday weekend when everyone else—by official company memo—was allowed to leave at 1 p.m. with their manager's approval. As you can guess, she didn't approve. I was told I had to stay there until the end of the day "in case any important calls came in." None did, since the entire town had, pretty much, shut down for the holiday. Oh, and did I mention that *she* left at one o'clock that day? She did.

- Always saying nonsensical things like, "I need you to type this up as A-S-A-P as possible!!!" To which I would sarcastically mumble, under my breath, "OK…I'll get it done as As Soon As Possible as possible." I don't think she phrased things like that on purpose: I don't think she actually knew what ASAP stands for.

- Any time I asked her if she could explain anything that wasn't entirely clear, she would scream at me, "Why do you have to question everything I tell you to do. *Just do it!!!*" And then, if it wasn't done exactly as she wanted it, she would say, "If you didn't know what you were doing, why didn't you just ask?"

- And when she arrived for work, I would say, "Good morning," to which she would reply, "What's good about it? Another day in this shit hole." And the day would typically proceed downhill from there.

Allow me to go ahead and answer some of the questions you're probably thinking right now:

Q: Why did you put up with all of this?

A: Because my career dream was to someday work for a TV network and, after years of knocking on the door, I'd finally made it in! I didn't quite expect it to be like that...and always hoped it would get better. It didn't.

Q: How did you allow yourself to be treated that way for almost a year? Didn't you have any self-confidence, self-respect, or self-esteem?

A: I did when I first got there. But my boss chipped away at it one day at a time until there wasn't much left.

Q: Did you ever just try sitting down and speaking with her about it?

A: Yes, I did. One day I finally got up the courage, calmly walked into her office and said, "Can I talk to you for a minute? I feel like you're always yelling at me and that whatever I do is wrong. I want to do a good job and I'm happy to do things however you want them done. So, if you could just take the time to explain things a little more clearly and talk to me a little more calmly, I'll be able to do a better job and I think we'll both be happier and more productive."

Q: Wow...that sounded great! So, what did she say?

A: She said (and I quote), "Listen. I spent a lotta years being treated like shit before I got this job. And now it's your turn. If you don't like it, I can call HR right now and have them find a replacement for you by tomorrow. So just quit whining like a little bitch and get back to work."

Q: Hmm. Just for curiosity, was she the only horrible manager you've ever had, or were there others?

A: Unfortunately, there were others. Way too many others. There are a lot of them out there. They're often referred to as "Bossholes."

Q: That's a good one! So many people out there work for bosshole managers. Is there anything someone can do if they find themselves working for someone like that?

A: You can anonymously leave a copy of one of my favorite management books, *The No Asshole Rule* by Robert Sutton, on their desk and hope that they can take a hint. (And, that they don't figure out who left it there.)

Q: Will that really work?

A: Probably not. Unfortunately, most of the bossholes out there don't think they are. And the rest actually seem to enjoy it. I've learned the hard way that there is no cure for this fatal condition—except for leaving it.

Q: As bad as it was to work for all these awful jerks, were there any benefits?

A: Actually, yes: Working for some of the worst bosses to ever set foot on this planet taught me more about management and leadership than any business book or MBA ever could, as I learned from them how *not* to manage and treat people. And for that I thank them.

Q: So, what's the connection between all of these awful bosses you've had and the concept of VisuaLeadership?

A: Well, as I reflected back on all of these terrible work experiences I had earlier in my career, I realized that there was one common, unifying theme…and that was the prevalence of incompetent management coupled with a complete lack of leadership. I realized that leaders are not born but made. And that they are made through learning and practicing the art and science of leadership and management. Moreover, I discovered that one of the most powerful ways to do so is by thinking and communicating more visually. Because when you do, you will be able to get people to see what you're saying. And if they can see what you're saying—and are inspired by your vision—together you can move mountains.

Q: Lastly, if you were to compose a letter to all of those horrible bosses you've had, what would you write?

A: Great question! I would write:

Dear Bosses From Hell:

*Thank you for teaching me how **not** to manage and lead people. Thank you for showing me how to destroy people's morale and diminish their confidence. Thank you for showing me how to de-motivate and uninspire. Working for all of you left me with so many great horror stories to tell and motivated me to go out there and learn as much as I could about managing and leading, in pursuit of a better way. And I've finally found it: VisuaLeadership is that better way. And if it were not for you, I probably would not be where I am today. So, for that I thank you, and I'll never forget you...though I wish that I could.*

Love always,

Todd

In Review

The Big Lesson: Having a horrible boss is...well...horrible. And it can make your life miserable. The key is to try to learn as much as you can from the situation, and to do what you can to try to improve the working relationship. Unfortunately, however, in many cases, the only solution to the situation is leaving it.

The Big Question: Who are some of the *worst* bosses you've ever had? And who are the *best*? What did you learn from each of them? In the future, when your people are asked to think of their best and worst bosses *they've* ever had, what can you do to end up on the first list, rather than the second?

Your Big Insight:

Your Big Action:

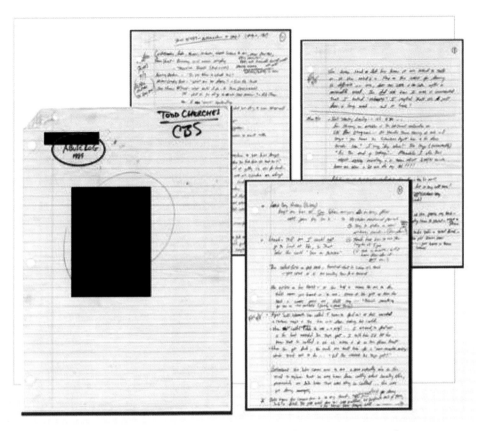

A copy of the "Abuse Log" I kept. Unfortunately, there was an entry almost every single day.

PART TWO

Leading with...Visual Models

Why Models?

First of all, what, exactly, do we mean by a "model?" In brief, a model is a symbolic, conceptual, or physical representation of something. If, as a kid, you ever built a model airplane or a model car, that example might resonate. Similarly, a mental model or a conceptual model is an intangible construct, a representation within our mind of a thing or an idea.

For illustration, a classic model that is familiar to many is Abraham Maslow's "Hierarchy of Human Needs". If you think back to Psychology 101, just the mention of it may trigger a visualization of a five-level pyramid that builds, as follows, from the bottom up: Physiological, Safety, Belonging, Esteem, Self-Actualization. If you are familiar with this model, you may have pictured it in your mind's eye as I was describing it.

Another potentially familiar example: If I were to mention the classic "Time Management Matrix" model (featured in Stephen Covey's *The 7 Habits of Highly Effective People*, and often referred to as the Eisenhower Matrix), you might be able to reconstruct it from memory in your head or on paper...and be reminded of the fact that as a leader, you need to create more time to spend in...which quadrant? (Quadrant 2!)

That's the power of a mental model. It enables us to take a complex concept and place it within a simple visual framework, so that we can not only understand it and, ideally, remember it, but also so that we can communicate it to someone else so that, looking at it, they can say, "I *see* what you're talking about."

Other common business examples of models include organizational charts and stakeholder maps, as well as a company's "business model."

Models can come in all shapes, sizes, and colors, from a four-box matrix, to a circle, triangle, pyramid, staircase, ladder, target, or arrow. We also use process diagrams, affinity maps, mindmaps, and flowcharts, among many others. If, as your project nears completion, you visualize in your mind a "progress bar," that's an example of a mental model (as well as a metaphor...which we'll be getting to shortly).

With the use of a model, we can take the messiness and complexity of a situation and place things within a framework so as to see it more clearly and wrap our head around it. After which, having been able to see it more clearly, we can then make more intelligent and informed decisions. This is not about "putting things (or people) in boxes," it's just a way to simplify complexity in a visual way.

While we don't want to oversimplify things to the point where we lose the subtlety and nuance, using visual models does help us to strip things down to their bare essence for the sake of clarity. Einstein advised us, "Make things as simple as possible, but no simpler." And Leonardo da Vinci stated, "Simplicity is the ultimate sophistication." So when you need to wrap your head around a concept, using a visual model may be just the solution you're looking for. And when someone says, "I know what I'm saying but I just can't explain it," sometimes the best thing you can do is encourage them to sketch it out.

In the *Quartz* article "How Bill Gates Remembers What He Reads" by Kevin J. Delaney, Gates had this to say about the importance and the value of mental models and frameworks: "If you have a broad framework, then you have a place to put everything. So you have the timeline, or you have the map, or you have the branches of science and what's known and what's not known."

Our mental models are, in essence, our "maps of the world," which is why each of us may see the world somewhat differently, as we are each using a different map to navigate the world. However, sharing our maps, and our mental models with others, can help to simplify complexity and increase understanding.

Speaking of maps: I've been driving out to Connecticut to visit my mother-in-law almost every other weekend for the past twenty years. And, yet, I get lost trying to find my way every single time. Either my wife needs to direct me, or I must use the GPS.

Why is it that after twenty years, I still have no idea how to get to my mother-in-law's house? (And no mother-in-law jokes, please; she's wonderful.) The reason, I recently realized, is simply that I have no "mental map" of Fairfield, Connecticut. I just don't know where anything is, I don't know the names of any of the streets, I never recognize any of the landmarks, and I never have any idea of which direction I am going. While my wife grew up there (and therefore knows the area "like the back of her hand"), I grew up in Queens and Long Island, New York. So I can find my way around those parts with my eyes closed.

But in the state of Connecticut, I am a stranger in a strange land. Which just illustrates, with a real-life example, the value and the power of our mental maps, and how they impact our ability to navigate in different spheres—not only literally and geographically, but in all areas of our lives.

All of the models in this next section are ones that I created to use in my coaching practice, as well as teaching and training others to use. If a particular model works for you, great! If not, you can use the model as a starting point and then modify it to better fit you and your situation. Or, alternatively, there are millions of other models out there. In fact, a list of forty of my favorites can be found in the appendix of this book! The point is, you have many options...and it's up to you to find the ones that fit you best and add them to your VisuaLeadership tool kit.

With that said, in this section, you'll find a model that will make decision-making as easy as "ABC." You'll see how increasing your influence is just a matter of "putting your 'CAP' on." And you'll be introduced to some of my other most valuable management, leadership, and personal productivity models on topics ranging from learning and leading to enhancing your passion, increasing your power, and improving your presentation skills.

I hope that this small selection of models presented here will help to give you some new ideas, lead you to discover some innovative solutions, and inspire you to venture forth to explore and discover all of the many other visual models that are out there.

As Buckminster Fuller said: "You never change things by fighting against the existing reality. To change something, build a new model that makes the old model obsolete."

CHAPTER 6

ABC Decision-Making Tool

"You don't need more time. You just need to decide."

—SETH GODIN

There is very rarely only one right or perfect choice for anything. A good decision tends to be about making the best possible choice, based on the information you have available, from among multiple viable options. Think job candidates, or vendors, or smartphone options, or wines, or anything else. And, having too many options, instead of being a good thing, can result in a state of being overwhelmed and analysis paralysis as you get caught in an internal stalemate of stress and indecision. (For more on why this is, I recommend the book *The Paradox of Choice* by Barry Schwartz, or you can watch his TED talk of the same name.)

One of the best and simplest ways to make a good decision (again, not a "perfect" decision, as there is no such thing; it always comes down to trade-offs) is, first, to narrow your options to three good ones. And to help do this visually, see my "ABC Decision-Making" tool below.

"A-B-C" Decision-Making Tool

Part 1: The Issue	Name of Issue/Problem/Challenge/Opportunity: _____ Description: _____ _____ _____ _____ _____ Desired Outcome/Result/Goal/Objective: _____

Part 2: Your Options	Idea/Option A		Idea/Option B		Idea/Option C	
	Name: _____		Name: _____		Name: _____	
	Description/Features: _____		Description/Features: _____		Description/Features: _____	
	Pros (+)	Cons (-)	Pros (+)	Cons (-)	Pros (+)	Cons (-)
	•	•	•	•	•	•
	•	•	•	•	•	•
	•	•	•	•	•	•
	•	•	•	•	•	•
	•	•	•	•	•	•
	Notes/Comments:		Notes/Comments:		Notes/Comments:	

Part 3: Your Decision	Decision/Recommendation: Option ____ Reasoning/Rationale/Explanation: _____ _____ Notes: _____ _____ _____

Big Blue Gumball

Part 1: Issue—As you'll see, the first step is to identify the issue, problem, challenge, or opportunity by (a) naming it, and (b) describing it, as well as (c) writing down your desired outcome. In other words, what is the problem you are trying to solve (that is, "I need to hire a new assistant"), and what does success look like (that is, hiring the best possible candidate).

Part 2: Options—The next step (and this is not always easy!) is narrowing, from the pool of often unlimited possibilities, three good, viable options. When I say good and viable, that means that none is bad or wrong; they are all sufficient to meet your needs, and you're just trying to identify the best one.

For each option, A, B, and C—(a) name it and (b) describe it in terms of its relevant characteristics and features, so as to distinguish it from the other options. Then, list the relative Pros (advantages, benefits, strengths) and Cons (disadvantages, gaps, costs) for each option. Then make a note at the bottom, summing up your subjective assessment based on those relative pros and cons.

40

Part 3: Decision—Again, there is no "right" decision; there is only a "best" decision, based on your understanding of the situation and your interpretations of the factors involved. Write down the option you selected (A, B, or C), along with your reasoning/rationale/explanation for it. Doing so will help you wrap your head around your thought process, as well as assisting you in effectively articulating your decision to others. When someone (that is, your boss, or a client) sees that you've gone through this rigorous process of analysis and assessment, it helps you to make your case and gain their buy-in.

Additionally, this tool is extremely helpful for group decision-makings, as each person involved can go through this process independently prior to presenting their recommendations. This eliminates the groupthink that often happens in meetings and allows everyone time to think through their positions. An added benefit is that you will get the best out of the more introverted members of your team who tend to want and need more solo time to process their thoughts, without being overshadowed or outshouted by their more extroverted colleagues.

In Review

The Big Lesson: Using a tool like this provides a structured format and a linear process that will enable you to capture information, get your thoughts out of your head and onto paper so that you can see and communicate them more efficiently and effectively.

The Big Question: What is a decision you (or your team) need to make wherein this tool might come in handy?

Your Insight:

Your Action:

CHAPTER 7

Put Your CAP On:
Assessing and Enhancing Your Confidence, Assertiveness, and Presence

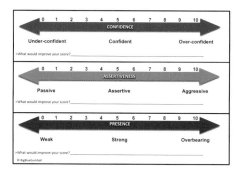

've learned from experience—the hard way—that one of the key differentiators between those who succeed and those who don't, or those who are chosen and those who aren't, can be summed up in three words: confidence, assertiveness, and presence—or, what I collectively refer to as your "CAP." At its most basic, "confidence" has to do with how strongly you believe in yourself; "assertiveness" is about your ability to express yourself; and "presence" has to do with how you are perceived by others. We'll go into more detail on each of these areas shortly...as well as exploring a variety of ways of quickly boosting your abilities in all three areas.

In essence, CAP is about having the confidence, the assertiveness, and the presence to speak up and to speak out. To try new things. To take chances and risks. To fall and to fail. To fail and to learn. To seize opportunities and to act before the window of opportunity slams shut on your fingers. To be resilient enough to bounce back from adversity without embarrassment or shame. To be bold enough to do, as the first black congresswoman Shirley Chisholm of Brooklyn once advised: "If they don't give you a seat at the table, bring a folding chair." And to be willing to push yourself well beyond your comfort zone and into the "Zone of the Unknown."

Years ago, when I was part of a six-person consulting team, the supervisors routinely rotated the team leadership role for each leadership program we delivered. Yet, time after time, I was repeatedly passed over as the team leader. For nearly a year I waited and waited for my name to be called, yet it never was. Finally, one day, frustrated and somewhat angry, I got up the courage to ask why I was never chosen. Can you guess what the response was?

It was, simply, "Because you never asked."

"Would you like to lead the next project?" my supervisors asked me.

"Yes, I would," I humbly replied.

"Done," they said.

Simple enough. It felt good to finally be asked (though if I'd advocated for myself sooner it wouldn't have taken that long).

This was a powerful lesson for me, as I hope it will be for you. And that is this: **People are not mind readers.** If we want something, we need to say so. To paraphrase the New York City subway system, "If you want something, say something." While it is always nicer to be chosen without having to ask, to be recruited without having to apply, that doesn't always happen. And when it doesn't happen, we have to make it happen. That's where confidence, assertiveness, and presence come in. The following exercise will help you to "put your 'CAP' on."

1. **Confidence:** How would you rate your overall confidence on a scale of zero to 10…from "Under-confident" to "Overconfident"?
2. **Assertiveness:** How would you rate your overall assertiveness on a scale of zero to 10…from "Passive" to "Aggressive"?
3. **Presence:** How would you rate your overall presence on a scale of zero to 10…from "Weak" to "Overbearing"?

Next, take a look at each of your ratings and ask yourself: What would improve your score?

Please perform this assessment now, before reading below. Rating yourself should only take about sixty seconds, and the follow-up question should only take a minute or two.

OK…welcome back.

If you notice, one of the keys to this assessment is that unlike many assessments, a "10" is *not* the best! When it comes to these three qualities, too much of "a good thing" can work against you, as one's greatest strength, when overdone, can turn into a potentially fatal flaw. You want to be confident, but not overconfident. You want to be assertive, but not so aggressive that it's a turn-off. You want to have presence, but not be overbearing. Which reminds me of the saying that when it comes to your presence (both in terms of real life and on social media), you should "drip" on people…but not "drown."

Since we just established that a "10" in each category would, actually, be a negative, what would you say is an ideal score? I think that question is subjective, and only you can decide, but I think that somewhere in the 7-to-8 range would be a good target. But that would, of course, depend upon a number of factors including (but not limited to) your personality, your position, your function, and your situation. Speaking of which, you might also score yourself differently outside of work than you do when you are at work.

One of the many different exercises I incorporate into my "CAP" workshops is asking people to submit their Confidence, Assertiveness, and Presence scores to me anonymously, and then I plot everyone's scores on one master chart on the wall. These were the self-evaluations. I then had them score one another—again, anonymously—to see if there was a difference between the self-scores and the other-scores. And what would you guess we found?

In brief, people tend to score themselves much lower in all three categories than everyone else scored them. This indicated to me that while some people come across to their peers as confident, assertive, and possessing presence, these individuals did not, necessarily, see themselves in that way.

One time I was brought in by a client to help a group of their most experienced, senior-level executives to increase their influencing skills. They were all subject matter experts in their field, but were all extreme introverts, personality-wise. And their bosses wanted them to have greater impact.

And to have that impact, they needed to enhance their "3 Vs": "Visibility, Voice, and Value."

VVV (or the 3 Vs): Visibility, Voice and Value

To build your personal brand, gain credibility, enhance your executive presence, increase your influence, get a "seat at the table," and be seen as a leader, it's beneficial to keep in mind, and to develop, your 3 Vs:

- Visibility is about *if* you are seen, and *how* you are seen by others.
- Voice is about *if* you are heard, and *how* you are heard by others.
- And Value refers to the extent to which you are perceived as making a significant contribution to your workplace.

The challenging aspect of this model is that it is entirely subjective and based upon the perceptions of others. The good thing, however, is that it is entirely within your control to develop your ability to enhance those perceptions in all three of these areas. (One way to do so is with my PowerDial featured in Chapter 19.)

Think about it: When you think of people who have confidence, assertiveness, and presence, and whom you perceive as having visibility, voice, and value—who are the people who come to mind…and why? These can be people real or fictional, famous or not, living or dead. What qualities, characteristics, or traits do these individuals possess? And are these traits innate/inherent or learned/developed?

In her book *Confidence: How Winning Streaks and Losing Streaks Begin and End*, Rosabeth Moss Kanter states, "Confidence isn't optimism or pessimism, and it's not a character attribute. It's the expectation of a positive outcome." So, if you reframe your definition of confidence in this way, it opens the door to anyone being able to immediately enhance their confidence, simply by changing their mind-set. Or, as Eleanor Roosevelt put it, "You can often change your circumstances by changing your attitude."

When it comes to confidence, there are three types: Self-Confidence, Other-Confidence, and Leader-Confidence. Your self-confidence is the type we typically think of. But, also important, is your ability to make other people feel confident in you. And, as a leader, one of your key responsibilities is to be able to instill confidence in others. From a leadership perspective, it's difficult to make others feel confident in themselves if you don't feel and exude confidence yourself. So, just like negativity, confidence and positivity are contagious. And people can sense it. So exuding confidence, being assertive when assertiveness is needed (especially when it's on behalf of your people and your organization), and displaying presence are three of the keys to effective leadership.

In regard to presence, you'll notice that I, specifically, did not refer to it as "executive presence" for the following reason: For many (though, of course, not all) people, the term "executive presence" often conjures up the image of a 1960s "Man in the Gray Flannel Suit"—for example, someone like Don Draper in the classic TV drama *Mad Men*.

That association limits us, though, as it's a new world now, a world of diversity, inclusion, and belonging in which "presence" can come in a wide variety of sizes, shapes, styles, and colors. So, when I ask people (of all types) the question, "When you think of people who have "presence," what words come to mind?" here are the top twelve characteristics typically mentioned, what I now refer to as…

"The Twelve Cs of Presence"

1. **Charisma**: They have that "special something" that draws people to them.
2. **Clarity**: They are able to simplify complexity, so as to be understood.
3. **Collaboration**: They foster an environment of partnership and teamwork.
4. **Commitment**: They are dedicated to producing results.
5. **Communication**: They are skilled at expressing themselves.

6. **Composure**: They stay cool under pressure.
7. **Conciseness**: They understand that "less is more."
8. **Confidence**: They project an air of positivity and success.
9. **Connectivity**: They build and maintain a valuable network of relationships.
10. **Cooperation:** They influence people to buy into and execute their ideas.
11. **Core Values:** They act in sync with their convictions.
12. **Credibility**: They are believable and trustworthy.

Bear in mind that you do not need to have every single one of these traits in order to have presence, so you can just pick and choose to focus on the ones that matter most to you.

Lastly, one of the most powerful confidence-building tips I've picked up over the years is the three-word phrase, "Act as if." In other words, when you are about to deliver a presentation, get up there and "act as if" you've done it a thousand times before. When you are about to step up to bat in a baseball or softball game, "act as if" you are the best hitter on the team. When you are walking into a job interview or a sales meeting, "act as if" you are the solution to their problem. When you are in a classroom or meeting, "act as if" you have the right answer and raise your hand with confidence.

This is not about trickery or self-deception; this is about positive self-talk and boosting your self-confidence by being your own best cheerleader. Your preparation is the key to setting yourself up for success; but it is your "A&E"—"Attitude and Enthusiasm"—that will put you over the top. As the psychologist William James said, "If you want a quality, act as if you already have it."

To sum up, while your internal level of confidence, assertiveness, and presence is based on your own self-perceptions, others may "see" you in an entirely different way based on their perceptions, and their assessment, of your visibility, voice, and value. The good thing, as mentioned, is that who you are and how you come across is completely developable and entirely up to you. Take it from me: As someone who was formerly an extreme back-of-the-room and behind-the-scenes introvert with low confidence, little assertiveness, and almost no presence—I am living proof that you can change yours, along with others' perceptions of you, by changing what you say, how you say it, how you look, and how you act...and those factors are all 100 percent within your control. Just keep in mind that these changes do not happen overnight, but over time.

In Review

The Big Lesson: Being aware of—and working to boost—your self-confidence, assertiveness, and presence is one of the most valuable things you can do to increase your visibility, have a greater voice, and be perceived as someone who adds tremendous value.

The Big Question: How can you boost your confidence, assertiveness, and presence? If you do, what might the payoff be?

Your Big Insight:

Your Big Action:

CHAPTER 8

Cycle of Learning and Development

© BigBlueGumball

To be a more effective learner—as well as a more effective teacher, manager, leader, or coach—it is useful to keep the above framework in mind, as this Learning and Development model will show you how to keep the wheel of learning turning, as you cycle through the Emotional, Intellectual, Developmental, and Behavioral phases.

Speaking of "keeping the wheel turning"…if you were a teenager learning, for the very first time, to drive a car, you would need to be:

1. **Emotionally** ready, in terms of your desire and willingness to learn how to drive.
2. **Intellectually** open to learning what you need to know, from reading the driver's manual to learning how to put the key in the ignition and step on the gas and brake pedals.
3. **Developmentally** open to putting the knowledge you've gained into practice on the open road.
4. **Behaviorally** ready to develop "driving a car" as a new skill.

Similarly, in the workplace, learning starts with the "**Emotional**" component. Even in today's world in which "the robots are taking over," we are still, primarily, dealing with human beings most of the time. And humans have emotions. They get hungry, tired, hot, cold, stressed, anxious, overloaded, and overwhelmed. They can be engaged, partially engaged, or disengaged. They can be motivated or demotivated…or anywhere in between, on any given day. They can be in a good mood or bad, open or closed.

We can't forget or underestimate the human element when managing and leading, or training and coaching. People have to want to learn, feel a need to learn, realize and accept that they don't already know everything, and be ready, willing, and able.

Once they are in a mind-set that is receptive to learning and development, the next phase is the "**Intellectual**." This component is about the acquisition of knowledge in the form of information. And this information can come from a wide range of sources, from articles and books and videos to real-world experience. The 70-20-10 rule, developed by McCall, Eichinger, and Lombardo of the Center for Creative Leadership (CCL), suggests that, at work, 70 percent of a person's learning comes from first-hand work experience, 20 percent comes from peer-to-peer learning, and just 10 percent comes from formal training and coaching. So, while many employees expect their companies to train and develop them, the reality is that the personal responsibility for one's professional development lies within each of us.

Following the knowledge gained during the Intellectual stage is the experiential learning that occurs during the "**Developmental**" stage. This is where we put ideas into practice and learn through doing. As I always say, the true value of knowledge is not in its accumulation, but in its application. This is where you put your ideas into action to gain wisdom through firsthand experience.

And the last phase is the "**Behavioral**." This is where, as a result of possessing a positive, open attitude toward learning, pursuing knowledge, and gaining experience through real-world applications, we build new skills and habits.

But don't forget that this model is a cycle for a reason. And the reason is that we need to keep the wheel turning—maintaining a positive attitude, continuing to seek new knowledge, continuing to practice, and continuing to gain new skills. As many have said, the future of work is about learning, unlearning, and relearning; for in an ever-changing world, if we're standing still, we're falling behind…because everyone else is charging full-steam ahead. Or, as Marshall Goldsmith put it in the title of his terrific book: *What Got You Here…Won't Get You There.*

In Review

The Big Lesson: To keep learning and growing, be sure to pay attention to all four stages of the cycle.

The Big Question: How can you use this model to take your skills to the next level?

Your Big Insight:

Your Big Action:

CHAPTER 9

Delegation Decision-Making Matrix

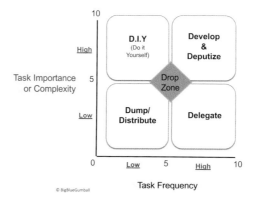

"The single greatest cause of failure in managers is their inability to effectively delegate."

—J.C. PENNEY

If "management" is the practice of getting things done through and with other people, then "delegation" is the process by which managers transfer work to others in order to do so.

The Latin root of the word delegation is "*de legare*," which means "to send away," as in sending someone away or dispatching someone to represent you and to act on your behalf. In essence, that's what delegation is all about. Through the act of delegation, managers assign to someone else certain tasks, projects, duties and/or responsibilities for which *they* are ultimately responsible, along with the associated authority to make the necessary decisions and take the necessary actions to achieve a desired objective.

In order for a delegation to be successful, managers must provide the employee with a sense of ownership and empowerment, along with both the responsibility for completing the task and the accountability for successfully achieving the desired result.

As a manager—especially a new manager or supervisor—one of the most difficult decisions to make is whether, to what extent, and how to delegate a task to one of their people.

To help simplify this complex decision, and make deciding just a bit easier, this framework known as the "Decision-Making Matrix" is here to help.

The Decision-Making Matrix tool is based on two dimensions: For any task or project being considered for delegation, the manager should consider: (a) How important and/or complex is the task, and (b) How frequently is this task or project going to occur?

Here's how this framework works:

1. DIY: Beginning with the upper left quadrant, if a task or project is either relatively Important or highly Complex (that is, between 5 to 10 on a 10-point scale), and it is something that is either a one-time or a not-very-often occurrence, you may just want to decide to Do It Yourself (DIY). With either no time to spare and/or no margin for error, you are probably the best person for the job. You know it will be done right and, most likely, delivered on time. Why take a chance of something going wrong under these circumstances? Also, with the high level of complexity, it would probably take some time to explain and train someone else to do it; and why take the time to do that when, based on the low Task Frequency, this kind of project doesn't come up very often?

2. Dump/Distribute: Moving on to the lower left quadrant, if there's a task that needs to be done that has a low level of Importance (therefore, a low level of risk) and/or a low level of Complexity (meaning it's pretty simple to do), and it's just a task that needs to

be done infrequently, for lack of a better word, you can just kind of "Dump" it on someone else.

3. I know it doesn't sound pleasant; the bottom line is that it gets a task off your plate and onto someone else's. For example, if you need a large quantity of copies made, or a huge stack of data input, you can just give it to someone else to do. This will get the job done, by someone other than you, so you can focus on more important things. And what is Distributing? It's basically dividing a larger job up among multiple people. Again, this is for situations in which you don't care who does the task or project…as long as it's not you.

4. Delegate: The lower right quadrant is for tasks and projects that are relatively low in Importance and/or Complexity, but they happen fairly frequently. For these tasks, because they are going to come up somewhat often, you want to be a little more strategic in terms of matching the right person to the job, and the job to the person. The subtle, but key, difference between "delegating" and "dumping" is that with the act of delegation comes more responsibility and a higher degree of ownership, along with greater autonomy in terms of how the task or project will be carried out. When you delegate to someone, and train them to do a job, it enables you to step away without having to do much supervision or micromanaging. You may probably want to establish deliverables and deadlines, and be there for support when needed; but, ultimately, you are assigning a person a job, and getting out of their way so that they can do it.

5. Develop & Deputize: Lastly, the upper right quadrant is for tasks and projects of high levels of Importance and/or Complexity, and they happen pretty often. For these jobs, you may want to invest significant time in developing the person (that is, through training, coaching, etc.) who will be handling these responsibilities. Because of the nature of these tasks, you'll want the person

to gain as much experience and skill as possible, as quickly as possible. Additionally, because the person working in this box will, very likely, need to be of a higher level of proficiency than those in the other boxes, you may want to empower them with greater leadership responsibilities, "Deputizing" them to take greater ownership, along with a commensurate high level of accountability. When someone is at this level, it may be useful to keep in mind this quote by General George S. Patton: "Never tell people how to do things. Tell them what needs to be done, and they'll surprise you with their ingenuity."

6. Drop Zone: One other aspect of this model to point out is the Drop Zone. Falling right in the middle, it's very easy for a task to fall into the Drop Zone if the decision and/or the distribution of work is not executed properly or communicated clearly. If you think that you successfully delegated an assignment, but the other person doesn't recognize that or is not clear on what to do, that's the Drop Zone. If someone thinks you asked them to do something, but you ended up deciding to just do it yourself and there ends up being a duplication of effort, that's the Drop Zone.

7. Using a baseball analogy (yes, again), it could be called, "I got it, I got it. You take it." This is what it's called when two fielders each think that the other one is going to catch the fly ball or pop up, and neither does...so the ball ends up dropping to the ground for a base hit. Or, the other occurrence, in which both fielders try to catch the ball at the same time and end up crashing into each other...in which case not only does the ball once again end up dropping to the ground for a base hit...but both players often end up getting injured in the process. Neither option is good. And they both result from poor communication leading to a failed delegation, landing you in...the Drop Zone.

To make the best use of this model, it helps to start by thinking through Who, What, When, Where, Why, and How questions in this order:

1. What is the task or project that needs to get done?
2. Who is the right person to do it?
3. When and Where will this need to be done?
4. How should this best be done?
5. Why is this the best way to go?

Thinking through these six questions will not only enable you to make your decisions more effectively, it will also aid you in anticipating the needs of the delegate who will be performing the work. This way, when you're ready to make the hand-off, you're doing so in the best way possible to set the person up for success.

Lastly, one of the toughest choices for a manager to make is regarding how hands-on or how hands-off they should be. On the one hand, you don't want to micromanage; on the other hand, you don't want to abdicate. It's like teaching someone to drive: They won't learn if you don't take your hands off the wheel and your foot off the brake pedal. But they also won't learn if you just toss them the keys and say, "See ya!" So, it is entirely a judgment call.

Ultimately, once you've done everything possible to set the person up for success, it then comes down to trust. If you trust the person you delegated to, you need to eventually step away (as difficult as it may be at times) and allow your employee to spread their wings and fly.

As Theodore Roosevelt said, "The best executive is the one who has sense enough to pick good [people] to do what he wants done, and the self-restraint to keep from meddling with them while they do it."

When a manager evolves into "a leader," he or she realizes that in order to empower your people, you must be willing to give up some of your own power. And though it is not easy to give up control (as well as ego), as they say in *Spider-Man*, "With great power comes great responsibility." And one of the biggest responsibilities of any manager is growing their people through the act of delegating to them.

If you think about it, where would *you* be today…if no one ever delegated to you?

In Review

The Big Lesson: A lot of managers think that delegation is simply saying to someone, "Here...I need you to do this for me." But there's so much more to it than that. It's a strategic process, and using a framework like the Decision-Making Matrix will help you to delegate more efficiently and effectively.

The Big Question: What are your biggest challenges when it comes to delegation, and how can using a model like the Decision Matrix help you to delegate more successfully?

Your Big Insight:

Your Big Action:

CHAPTER 10

The Five Levels of Proactivity

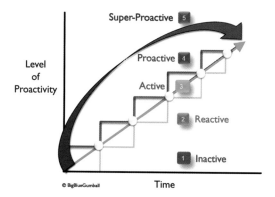

Do you wait for things to happen…or do you make them happen? Do you find yourself stalling for the perfect time to take action…or do you make "now" the right time?

Do you always find yourself one or more steps behind and playing catch-up…or do you go about your business feeling confidently and comfortably ahead of the curve?

Whether we're talking about your personal life or your career, one of the most overlooked keys to success is the level of "proactivity" at which you tend to operate…and live.

Life and work are filled with daily barriers, obstacles, and challenges that stand in the way of getting things done. For example:

- **Ineffective Time Management and Prioritization:** With so much on your plate and so little time, you don't even know where to start.

- **Lack of Focus:** Trying to juggle so many things at once, you are all over the map.
- **Procrastination:** Putting aside the things we *should* be doing, for the things we'd *rather* be doing.
- **Perfectionism:** Not knowing when good enough is good enough.
- **Fear, Doubt, and/or Lack of Confidence:** Feeling paralyzed by indecision or inaction.
- **Waiting for Lightning to Strike, or for the Muse to Come**: A nice way of saying you're waiting for a kick in the pants.

There are probably other factors as well. But if you look at this particular list, what all these reasons (excuses?) have in common is that they are all *internal*…and, therefore, all within our control.

How Proactive Are You?

Here is a simple-yet-powerful model that I call "The 5 Levels of Proactivity." Let's explore it from the bottom up to see how you can work your way up from being Inactive, to Reactive, to Active, to Proactive, and, ultimately, to Super-Proactive:

Level 1: Inactive. At this level, something is needed from you…and you do nothing. Absolutely nada. Zero. Zilch. For whatever reason, you decide to take no action at all. Maybe the problem or request will just go away by itself. But it probably won't.

Level 2: Reactive. At this level, something is needed, and you respond. This is, actually, a good thing! So, congratulations—there was a fire and you put it out. The only problem is if you are constantly in reactive, fire-fighting mode, you are always at least a step behind. After a while, as the speed of needs and expectations increases, you may fall so far behind that you are unable to catch up. And then people are constantly waiting for you, getting frustrated and impatient…until they decide to look elsewhere.

Level 3: Active. When you are at this level, you are keeping up with demand, giving people what they want and need, in real-time, when they need it, and meeting expectations. Things are going well, and you are keeping up with the pace. The only problem is that when you are just keeping pace, you are not getting ahead. At this level, there is no time or space for growth. You're getting things done, but you're either treading water or standing still. And in an ever-changing world, if you're standing still, you're falling behind.

Level 4: Proactive. Now we're getting somewhere! At this level you are not only keeping up with the pace but setting the pace and staying a step ahead. You are not just putting out fires, you're preventing them. You are not just meeting expectations, you're exceeding them. Anticipating others' needs and expectations, you are thinking on your feet, doing your homework, looking down the road, putting yourself in the shoes of your customers, fostering an environment of growth and development for yourself and others, and taking control of your destiny. Remember that the root word of "pro-act-ivity" is "act"—and when you are in this mode, you are ready, willing, and able to act!

Level 5: Super-Proactive. Now you are not just *setting* the pace…you are leading! With a vision of the future, you are thinking not just one step ahead, but many steps ahead. This is where innovation happens, this is where paradigms shift, this is how you drive change and blow people away. This is where you develop your professional brand and reputation as a subject matter expert, or the "guru of," or "the go-to person for" whatever it is that you do. The leaders of the future are those who are able to meet the demands of today while consistently anticipating and exceeding the needs of tomorrow. You anticipate what people want and need before they even realize it. You are a visionary. You are a thoughtleader on "the Future of Work." And as Peter Drucker famously said, "The best way to predict the future is to create it."

That's the model in a nutshell. Now let's bring it to life with a simple, practical, real-life example:

Let's say it's January 1st and you decide you want to get in shape for the summer.

If you're **Inactive**, you don't do anything about it. You procrastinate, you say, "It's only January. I can wait a few months to get started."

If you're **Reactive**, you'll work out if someone else drags you along to the gym, or you'll eat better if someone else shops for healthier food and places it in front of you. But you are not in control, and you are not taking responsibility, taking initiative, driving change, or owning the behavior necessary to achieve your desired outcome. In short, if you're always a step or two behind, you are never going to get ahead.

If you're **Active**, you'll get off the couch and work out if the mood hits you, and you'll have an occasional low-calorie fruit juice or water rather than a soda. And you'll replace that Big Mac with a salad. Your intentions are good, you're taking baby steps, and you're trying, but it's sporadic and undisciplined, you're making decisions in the moment, and you don't really have a plan.

When you're **Proactive**, you make a plan—a structured, formalized, written plan—and you stick with it. You put a process in place and set a quantifiable goal of working out x days a week—no excuses. Your diet plan includes the sacrifices you're willing to make…and you keep those commitments without fail. You follow through and you follow up. You make real behavior changes and track the results, with no excuses and no exceptions. Drucker said, "If you can't measure it, you can't manage it"…and you're managing—and leading—yourself in the direction of your goals.

And what would being **Super-Proactive** look like? It's about having a longer-term time horizon and thinking multiple steps ahead. It's about imagining the possibilities and anticipating the future, including the potential obstacles that may arise down the road. Perhaps thinking and planning beyond the summer, into the fall, winter, spring, and maybe even into the following year. You're continuously leveraging the power of visual thinking, while acting with a big picture and long-term vision of the future in mind.

So that's just one example. How might *you* use this model to be more proactive in leadership and in life?

How important is proactivity? In Stephen Covey's classic book, *The 7 Habits of Highly Effective People*, "Be Proactive" is Habit #1. That's how important it is.

In today's always-on, global, digital world, it's not easy being proactive; it takes time, attention, energy, discipline, and, yes, vision. It's far more common to always be a step behind and playing catch-up than to be one or more steps ahead. But the good news is that the decision to be more proactive is entirely up to you and completely within your control. And it's never too late to get started. As Confucius said, if you need shade, "The best time to plant a tree was twenty years ago; the next best time is today."

So, while being more proactive—and more super-proactive—may involve making some radical changes and taking some substantial risks, as the saying goes (continuing with the tree metaphor): Sometimes we have to go out on a limb…because that's where the fruit is.

In Review

The Big Lesson: Being proactive starts with being more aware, followed by pushing yourself to do things sooner rather than later. It's about having a vision and a plan, and then taking the steps necessary, sooner rather than later, to make that vision a reality.

The Big Question: What are some things that you can do to be more proactive—and even more super-proactive?

Your Big Insight:

Your Big Action:

CHAPTER 11

The Five Types of Feedback

A number of years ago, a player on the Yankees struck out five times in one game. Afterwards, in the post-game TV interview, a reporter asked the manager, Joe Torre, "What are you going to say to him?" Torre answered: "I'm not going to say *anything* to him. He knows he struck out five times. I'm going to write his name in the lineup and see how he does tomorrow. Now, if he does it again, then we're gonna need to figure out what's going on."

I really loved Torre's response to his player's bad night. Way too often, too many bosses—in baseball and in business—tend to jump the gun and overreact, instead of simply looking at an episode of underperformance as an aberration. What is the purpose of feedback, anyway? Is it to vent our frustrations by hitting people over the head? Or is it to provide insight that lets someone know how they are doing for the purpose of future improvement?

Back when I worked as an administrative assistant out in Los Angeles early in my career, I was on time for work every single morning. After several months of perfect punctuality, however, I had a bad week of car trouble that resulted in my getting to work about a half hour late three days in a row.

On that third day, instead of asking me what what's been going on (again, this episode of my being late was an exception, not a pattern), upon my arriving at work my boss just started screaming at me in front of all my coworkers (and I quote), *"I don't know what the hell's going on with you, but if you can't find a way to start getting here on time, you better start looking for another job!!!"*

In case you were wondering, yes, that's the same boss who had previously thrown a box of pens at my head. And, yes, I probably could have and should have talked to her about my car problems earlier in the week, but I was just too terrified to ever speak to her. It wouldn't have made a difference anyway.

When someone on your team slips up, it's good to keep in mind this Rule of Three: The first time something happens, assume the person had good intentions and this was a one-time occurrence. You may want to just let it go. The second time, make a mental note of it and perhaps ask the person if everything's OK. The third time: now there's a pattern and an issue to be dealt with.

Of course, this "three strikes" rule won't apply to every situation. For example, if there's a safety issue, or an integrity violation, or irreparable damage caused by the mistake in question—that may be a "Rule of One" situation. This is a judgment call that a manager must make. But the Rule of Three is a good guideline to follow to avoid knee-jerk reactions, and to allow you time to pause and think how best to handle the situation.

When we think of giving and receiving feedback, the image that most often comes to mind tends to be that of a manager providing feedback to his or her employee to let them know how they're doing. And it could be either positive or negative, as in, "Nice job on your TPS report!" or

"We have a problem." But feedback is, of course, not just something that managers do!

We all give feedback all the time—up, down, and across—both in the office and outside of it. When the waiter asks, "How was everything this evening?" and you say, "Great, thanks!" or "The food was awful, the music was too loud, and your prices are too expensive," that's feedback.

So, when providing feedback, it's important to be clear, intentional, and purposeful regarding who we are giving feedback to, our relationship with that person, the type of feedback we are providing, and its potential impact on the recipient. And to help you to deliver feedback most effectively, I recommend keeping in mind what I call the Five Types of Feedback: Highlighting, Reinforcing, Developmental, Corrective, and Disciplinary.

1. **Highlighting**—Catching someone doing something right and pointing it out for the purpose of acknowledgment.
   - "Hey, great job on that presentation—you were awesome!"

2. **Reinforcing**—Similar to Highlighting, only taking it to the next level by providing more specific and concrete details/examples, as well as encouraging the person to keep doing what they're doing.
   - Hey, great job on that presentation—you were awesome! Your proposal was really interesting, your slides were creative, and you did a really effective job of delivering it. Keep up the great work!"

3. **Developmental**—Pointing out positive performance…along with opportunities for growth and improvement.
   - "Hey, great job on that presentation—you were awesome! Your proposal was really interesting, your slides were creative, and you did an effective job of delivering it. Keep up the great work! Next time, you might be even more effective if you were to incorporate some interactivity by engaging your audience in a conversation. I think that might help you to gain buy-in for your ideas."

4. **Corrective**—Like Developmental, but with the focus on what's been done wrong so as to explore how the person can improve going forward.

   - "Overall, you did a pretty good job on your presentation, but some of the slides were difficult to understand, and certain other parts weren't entirely clear. What are your thoughts on what you might do differently next time?"

5. **Disciplinary**—Like Corrective, only more serious; for example, if or when dealing with an ongoing problem, poor attitude, lack of effort, negligence, an integrity or safety violation, etc.

   - "We need to talk...."

Ideally, of course, a feedback conversation should be a dialogue rather than a monologue, an opportunity to sit down with someone and ask how they thought they did, prior to our providing them with our take. We need to consider the Who, What, When, Where, and Why, in order to determine the How. In other words: Who is the person and what is your relationship to or with them? What is the nature of the feedback? When and Where are the right time and place to have this conversation? And Why, what is the purpose of the feedback—what are you trying to accomplish? The answers to all of these questions will then determine the How.

For example, sometimes it makes the most sense to provide feedback publicly in real time, in the moment; and other times we need to have a more private and confidential conversation. But the bottom line is that if we want feedback to be done well, and to go well, we need to be aware of the situation and the individual, and take the appropriate action in the right way, in the right place, and at the right time.

"My manager gives me way too much feedback!" said no employee ever. No matter how much feedback a manager gives, it often feels, to many people, that it's not enough. Leaders need to be aware that in the absence of feedback, it is human nature to fill that void of silence with negativity. So, one of a leader's most important responsibilities—and privileges—is to set their people up for success by letting them know how they are doing and how they can do better.

Providing feedback without real, specific, concrete examples, though, is not very helpful. Without the specifics, the recipient may not be clear on exactly where they went wrong or how they can improve. And even if the feedback message is positive and constructive, you still want to be specific to reinforce what the person did well and should continue doing. Using the "Stop, Start, Continue" process, and/or the Feedback Sandwich method (both discussed in other chapters), are excellent ways to help you formulate and then deliver your intended message in an effective way.

On the subject of being specific when providing feedback, here is an important point to keep in mind: I hear a lot of people deliver feedback messages along the lines of "You are *always* late," or "You *never* return my emails." But I caution you to avoid the use of broad, sweeping generalizations if you want your feedback to be taken seriously and credibly. People rarely do anything "always" (100 percent of the time) or "never" (zero percent of the time). The truth is, typically, somewhere in between.

The same holds true for using words such as: usually, generally, mostly, occasionally, sometimes, often, frequently, and rarely. For example, you have more credibility if you say, "Over the past month you have arrived late [that is after 9 a.m.], fifteen times out of the twenty work days." That is more quantifiable and indisputable—and gives you more credibility—than telling someone that they are "always" or "usually" late. Similarly, saying, "Out of the last ten emails I sent to you, you only responded to two of them," that also carries more weight than saying, "You frequently don't respond to my emails." So, the next time you are about to make a broad generalization that someone may dispute, remember to ask yourself the question, "What percentage of time is 'always'?"

Lastly, when is a single rose more valuable than a dozen roses? When it is given any day of the year other than Valentine's Day, a birthday, or an anniversary. Similarly, a lot of managers reserve all their feedback comments for mid-year or end-of-year performance review meetings. The most valuable feedback that you can give, however, is that which you deliver any other day of the year. When there is an opportunity to correct a mistake, help someone do something better, or to catch someone doing something right, those are perfect—and often unexpected, but greatly appreciated—feedback opportunities. Though this metaphor has in some ways become a cliché, the truth is that feedback is, indeed, a gift...and one that could, potentially, if well-delivered with positive intentions, change the course of someone's life. And, while receiving feedback is sometimes difficult and uncomfortable—and, at times, even embarrassing or painful[1], if we reframe feedback as a gift, we will welcome it rather than discard it. For, like any physical gift that we may receive, we can either cherish it or toss it in the trash. But either way, we should give some consideration to the thought behind it. And, even when it's a message that we may not want to hear, there may be some hidden value there.

If you were about to go on stage to deliver a presentation, and your fly was open, you had toilet paper stuck to your shoe, and spinach (or, for me more likely, chocolate) in your teeth—wouldn't you rather know than not know?

In Review

The Big Lesson: When you are about to deliver feedback to someone, it will be more effective if you start by asking yourself what type of feedback you are giving, who you are giving it to, and what your intention is.

The Big Question: What are some situations in which using the five types of feedback model can help you to be more effective?

Your Big Insight:

Your Big Action:

---

[1] I refer you to David Rock's "SCARF" model discussed in his book, *Your Brain at Work*.

CHAPTER 12

Future Self: Two Questions
That Can Forever Change Your Life

This one is barely even a model; it's more of a mantra. It's simple and straightforward, yet asking yourself these two questions before making any decision or taking any action—whether big or small—can dramatically change your life, as it has changed mine.

I have a post-it note stuck to the front of my calendar so that I see it at the start of each day (as well as a copy that I carry around in my wallet). It simply says, "Future Todd."

This idea originated from a refrigerator magnet I once saw in a store (that's a whole book idea in and of itself: "Life Lessons from Refrigerator Magnets"!). The magnet said:

"Do Things Today That Your Future Self Will Thank You For."

And, from that—for when I need an even stronger, more forceful reminder—I came up with this alternate version:

"Don't Do Things Today That Your Future Self Will Blame *You For."*

Hence, my "Future Self" approach to work and life involves my asking, for decisions big and small: Will my Future Self *thank* me for what I am about to do? Or *blame* me?

It's easier said than done (as many important and difficult things are). But when you remind yourself, before acting, to briefly "hit the pause button" and be mindful of your future self in the present, you're more likely to make better decisions and avoid doing things that you could potentially regret later on.

To illustrate, here are three brief examples—two hypothetical (partially based on recent coaching conversations), and one of my own personal stories:

Example #1: Say you receive an email from your boss, or a colleague, or a client that, for lack of a better way of putting it, pisses you off. Feeling defensive, your instinct is to start pounding away at your keyboard to let them know what you really think.

But before you do, you can hit the pause button and ask yourself: If I send this email, will my Future Self *thank* me or *blame* me for what I am about to do?

It's amazing how well this simple technique works. And where I find it really comes in handy is with social media. Think about how many hours of your life you may have wasted engaging in Facebook, LinkedIn, or Twitter battles with people (including complete strangers!) where, other than releasing steam, it didn't really accomplish anything. Rather than letting your "Present Self" complain about your "Past Self," you could have had your previous "Present Self" envision how your "Future Self" would react. And then act accordingly.

Example #2: Say you just got accepted into a prestigious graduate program overseas that would involve you quitting your dream job, giving up your cozy apartment, putting a long-term relationship on hold, and leaving your friends and family for two years. An introvert by nature, this would be a huge, scary, and risky move that would push you way beyond your comfort zone…and, yet, it sounds as if this would make for a life-transforming adventure. When you ask yourself the question immortalized in the *Clash* song, "Should I Stay or Should I Go," ask yourself: which option will your "Future Self" thank you for?

Example #3: Three years ago, after outgrowing the waistband on all my pants, with my wife's help I went on a diet and exercise program that helped me to lose thirty-six pounds in three months. And I am proud to say that (even though it is a daily struggle even to this day), I have been able to keep the weight off ever since. How? By asking myself the "Future Self" question multiple times, every single day, including every time I am faced with temptation, or not in the mood to do my daily thirty minutes on the treadmill.

If you were to ask me what my all-time favorite song is, I would probably have to say, "the Mister Softee ice cream truck theme song." I've been mindlessly lured in by that siren song many times in the past while walking the streets of New York City. But now, when that tune starts to call my name, I pause…and I visualize whether my "Future Self" (aka "Future Todd") will thank me or blame me for the decision I am about to make. Thankfully, I have programmed myself to drown out that Mister Softee theme song by humming in my head the classic Bacharach and David tune, "Walk on By." And that's what I do. (Most of the time.)

In Review

The Big Lesson: Before you do anything that you might possibly regret later—for example, reactively sending out an impulsive email, turning down a life-changing opportunity, or overeating—ask yourself whether your "Future Self" will thank you or blame you for this decision.

The Big Question: What are some choices or decisions you've made in the past—in work or in life—that you are thankful that you made, and what are some that you now regret? How might asking the two "Future Self" questions earlier on have influenced the choices that you made? And how can you use these questions to make better decisions in the future?

Your Insight:

Your Action:

CHAPTER 13

Head, Heart, Hands, and Feet

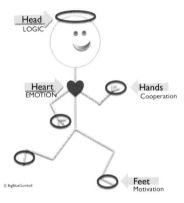

We often hear about leaders aspiring to "capture the hearts and minds" of their people, but what does this actually mean? To capture someone's "heart" is to, metaphorically, appeal to their emotions. To capture someone's "mind" is to appeal to their sense of logic.

This "hearts and minds" metaphor goes all the way back to Aristotle's modes of persuasion, or rhetorical appeals, which consisted of *Ethos* (appeal based on the character and credibility of the speaker), *Pathos* (appeal to the emotions and feelings of the audience), *Logos* (appeal, via facts and evidence, to the audience's sense of logic and reason), and *Kairos* (appeal to one's sense of urgency…as in, "Now is the time").

Similarly, the "Head, Heart, Hands, and Feet" model can be used in a variety of ways, from clarifying one's thoughts to managing people to influencing others to take action.

For example, when confronted with having to make a decision, you can ask yourself: When thinking about the facts, what is my "head" telling me? Emotionally, what is my "heart" telling me? Who can I join "hands" with to work together on this? And what is my motivation?

To illustrate, let's say that you are preparing to deliver a sales pitch to a potential new client. This model will remind you to think about the following four questions: What data are you going to present to them? (Head.) What are their core values and what they are passionate about? (Heart.) What do they tend to look for in a strategic partner? (Hands.) And, based on who you will be meeting with, what is going to motivate them to say, "Yes, let's do it!"? (Feet.)

Or, when on a team, you can identify a topic, issue, challenge, or question that your team is working on, and use this framework to find out the following from each member of the team:

1. **Head:** Logically and objectively, what is your "head" saying about this topic? This involves a focus on logic and reason, facts and figures.

2. **Heart:** Emotionally and subjectively, what is your "heart" telling you? This involves a focus on people's feelings, sense of empathy, and compassion.

3. **Hands:** How are we going to join "hands" in working together on this? This involves people's inclinations towards community and collaboration, and sense of teamwork.

4. **Feet:** What is our motivation to take action? This involves people's individual motivators, what they care about, their passions, and sense of purpose.

While all of these questions could, of course, be explored without the use of this visual metaphor, using "Head, Heart, Hands, and Feet" as a guide will provide you with both a visual structure and a simple visual checklist to ensure that you pay attention to all four of these crucially important areas.

In Review

The Big Lesson: The "Head, Heart, Hand, and Feet" model provides a powerful visual leadership framework for fact-gathering, communicating, managing, and influencing, by focusing on the four key areas of information: logic, feelings, teamwork, and motivation.

The Big Question: How can you use these four key components to frame a challenge you currently face?

Your Insight:

Your Action:

CHAPTER 14

The Hierarchy of Followership: Is it More Important to be Liked, Admired, Respected, or Trusted?

We all want to be liked.

But if you had to decide among being liked, admired, respected, or trusted—which would you choose?

If you could only pick one, would you rather have a boss that you liked, that you admired, that you respected, or that you trusted?

What about if you are a manager or HR recruiter interviewing potential job candidates. Could you, would you, hire someone who you trusted to do the job but didn't necessarily like on a personal level?

These terms are, of course, not mutually exclusive. Ideally we'd all like to be—and associate with—someone who possesses all four of these highly positive qualities.

But what about when they come into conflict with one another? Which trait or traits would you most like to be perceived as having? And whose lead would you be most likely to follow?

Let's say that you were assigned to a project team with four other people:

1. Alan is someone you really **like** on a personal level. He's a good guy, friendly, fun, personable, and you enjoy being in his company. But he's kind of a class clown who others often make fun of, so you don't really admire that people don't take him seriously, respect, or trust him on a professional level.

2. Betty you don't really like that much on a personal level, as she's not really that friendly or warm towards you. But you **admire** her impressive background, advanced degree, and career accomplishments. As she doesn't treat you or others with respect, you don't have much respect for her in return and are not really sure if you trust her.

3. Chris is not that friendly either, and you don't really admire that he got his job as a favor through a personal connection, leapfrogging over others who'd been here longer and were more deserving. But you **respect** that he has overcome numerous personal and professional obstacles to get as far as he has in his career despite these setbacks.

4. And Diane is someone who, upon first meeting, you don't really like, admire, or respect based on what you've heard about her through the grapevine. But she is super-smart, has an amazing, unparalleled track record of success, and you **trust** that when it comes to getting things done, compared to everyone else on the team, there's probably no one better.

Based on the above descriptions, if you had to elect a team leader from this group (that is, someone other than yourself), who would it be—and why? Is it the person you most like, admire, respect…or trust?

Sometimes as leaders we need to make tough decisions that not everyone's going to like—or like us for. And, while it is nice when people admire us for our past accomplishments, that's all it is: a nice-to-have. Most importantly, we want people to respect us—our intelligence, our judgment, our integrity, etc.—and, ideally, to trust us.

But what is "trust" anyway?

In my leadership workshops and classes, when we discuss the most important characteristics, traits, and qualities of effective leaders, the word "trust" inevitably comes up near the top of the list. But what, exactly, do we mean by it?

When you look up the word "trust" in a dictionary, there are numerous definitions, but they all basically have to do with "belief" and/or confidence. Belief that someone or something is reliable, good, honest, effective, etc., along with the assured reliance on the character, ability, strength, or truth of someone or something.

From a word origin perspective, "trust" and "truth" have the same root and are both related to the concept of "belief." Below are some questions that drill down into the notion of trusting someone:

- Do you believe that this person is telling the truth?
- Do you believe that this person will follow through on what they say they are going to do?
- Do you believe that this person will follow up with you as promised?
- Do you believe that this person will keep their commitments?
- Do you believe that this person can be held accountable for meeting or exceeding expectations?
- Do you believe, from a leadership perspective, that this person is someone you would voluntarily choose to follow?

Assuming that, from a leadership perspective, trust is essential to creating followership, what can *you* do to gain the trust of others?

The best way to gain others' trust…is to be "trustworthy." That's obvious. It means exhibiting the qualities that you would want in a job candidate, a teammate, or a leader. Among the descriptors most often mentioned when surveying people in my workshops, these are the key behaviors one needs to exhibit in order to gain the trust of others:

- Be truthful
- Be transparent
- Be authentic
- Be accountable
- Take ownership

- Keep promises
- Follow up
- Follow through
- Do what you say
- And say what you do

So, the next time you are deciding whether you trust someone enough to hire, to work with, to follow, or to develop a relationship with, the above criteria provide for a pretty good checklist. And if someone is missing any of these characteristics, well, that could be a red flag.

Similarly, when looking in the mirror, while everyone wants to be liked, while it is ego-boosting to be admired, and an honor to be respected, ultimately, the key to building relationships, gaining followership, and to being seen as a leader is to build trust.

In Review

The Big Lesson: There are many different definitions of leadership that have to do with creating and communicating a compelling vision, building followership, having influence, and more. But, when you step back and look at what many of these definitions have in common, it comes down to one key quality: building and maintaining trust.

The Big Question: What do you do, can you do, and should you do to build your "trustworthiness" and to gain the trust of others?

Your Big Insight:

Your Big Action:

CHAPTER 15

In Defense of the Feedback Sandwich

I am a *huge* fan of Wharton professor Adam Grant. I always love his work and greatly enjoyed (and try to live by the philosophy of generosity espoused in) his book *Give and Take*. However, I have to say that I must respectfully disagree 1,000 percent with the position he takes in his blog post and video entitled "Stop Serving the Feedback Sandwich," wherein he rails against what I consider to be a highly effective feedback technique.

I happen to be a huge proponent of the Feedback Sandwich. Why? Consider this example: Say I wrote a blog post explaining why I advocate for this feedback method and I received the following two feedback comments from people:

The first one says: "The Feedback Sandwich sucks!"

While the other says: "Regarding the Feedback Sandwich approach, I can see your point regarding its merits. It's important to note, however, that this method is not appropriate for all situations and, when misused, can often be ineffective and counterproductive, and may actually undermine your intentions. You are correct, though, that in many cases, when used appropriately and skillfully, there's tremendous value in pointing out what someone's done right and done well, before pointing out what they've done wrong (or could have done better)—and then ending on a positive note."

If you were me, which of these two comments would you prefer to receive? Which do you think would be more powerful, impactful, and effective? And if you're the deliverer of the feedback, which approach would give you more credibility?

While both critics express a counter-position, the first example (basically, "You and your opinion suck") is what many people, including a lot of bosses (and, of course, online commenters!) do: They just slam you or flame you with their opinion of why you're wrong.

The second is an example of the Feedback Sandwich.

The Secret Recipe: How to Use the Feedback Sandwich

In brief, this technique is referred to, metaphorically, as a "sandwich" because the feedback (the "meat" of the message) is delivered to the recipient in between the use of cushioning (the "buns") to lead in and soften the blow on one end…and to provide positive reinforcement on the other. This model is composed of four parts:

1. The **top bun** represents starting on a positive note, for example: "Nice job on your presentation. I really thought your content and delivery were great."
2. The **lettuce** represents your transition, for example, a pause, or a phrase like: "One area of improvement might be…"
3. The **meat** represents the main substance of your feedback message: "While I really liked your content and your delivery, I thought that your PowerPoint slides could use some improvement—and here's how…"
4. And the **bottom bun** represents your close, which might be something like: "Again, overall, I thought you did a really great job…and if you can improve your slides, I think your next presentation is going to be even better!"

The above feedback message can be delivered in a brief 30-second comment, or over the course of a 30-minute conversation. In fact, it is often preferable—and most productive—to *ask* the person how *they* thought they did, prior to offering them *your* opinion. But, again, if you were on the receiving end, wouldn't you rather hear what you did well… prior to hearing what you could have done better? Or would you be happy to just receive the blunt-and-to-the-point criticism that the Feedback Sandwich-bashers seem to be advocating: "Here's what you did wrong… now go fix it."

Why I Think the Critics Are Wrong

Like any tool, technique, or methodology, the Feedback Sandwich is not intended for all occasions. That's obvious. But when used by a skilled person, with the right recipient, at the right time and place, in the right situation, and in the right way, I strongly believe, from firsthand experience—on both the giving and receiving ends—that it is a tremendously productive and effective way to deliver feedback.

While the most common examples of giving feedback often tend to concern a manager providing feedback to a direct report, we all are continuously giving feedback to other people all the time. Even something as simple as responding to a waiter who asks how everything was is providing feedback. For example, "The food was delicious, as always. We did want to mention, though, that we thought the music was a little too loud—which made it hard to talk. But, overall, we enjoyed our dinner and we thank you for your wonderful service this evening." Right there is an example of using the Feedback Sandwich approach to deliver your message in a polite, productive, and most likely, receptive way.

That's why it's so mind-boggling to me to hear experts in the field bash this entire model outright. I've heard the model referred to as a "Compliment Sandwich," a "B.S. Sandwich," and a "Crap Sandwich." And, yes, when used improperly, it is indeed! But, in short, the people who denigrate, discount, and disregard this model in its entirety might want to take a fresh look at it from another perspective. The Feedback Sandwich is simply a tool—like a hammer or a screwdriver; and, like any tool, is not meant for all purposes and all occasions.

And when it is misused, as in this example, of course it is not going to be effective, or appropriate: "Hey I really like your new haircut! By the way, you're the worst employee I've ever had. And you're fired. But, again, you look really nice today. Give me a call when you find a new job and we'll grab some lunch!"

The "buns" need to be genuine, sincere, productive, and directly relevant to the issue you are providing feedback on! It's not supposed to be a "compliment" (hence, not a "Compliment Sandwich"), and it's not about flattery or sugarcoating—or making it easier on yourself as the deliverer of the message. It's about conveying your feedback in a way that is most productive, most effective, and—to continue the metaphor—most "digestible" for the recipient.

That's a key point to keep in mind: as the feedback-giver, your feedback is about the other person; it's not about *you*. Therefore, ask yourself before delivering your feedback: is the purpose, delivery style, and wording of your message intended to beat the person over the head, or to help them to improve their performance? And is the manner in which you are delivering the feedback—to this person and in this situation—going to achieve that objective?

Leadership guru Marshall Goldsmith suggests that maybe we need to shift our emphasis from "feed-back" to "feed-forward." In other words, we can't undo the past; so why dwell on it? Or beat the other person up over it? All we can do is learn from it and move on, by focusing on what we can do differently and better next time.

Additionally, regarding the "fluffiness" criticism (that is, that using cushioning detracts from your main message), the "thickness" of the "buns" needs to be proportionate to the person and the situation…while taking into consideration your relationship with this person. Some people need and prefer a lot of cushioning, while others just want you to "give it to me straight" (that is, a more "Radical Candor"-type approach, to reference the book of that same name by Kim Scott).

Sometimes saying "Great job!" is all that is needed to start and finish with. But in most cases, more specific and detailed feedback comments (including evidence and examples) are essential if you truly want to make the feedback meaningful and productive.

When the Sandwich Approach *Doesn't* Work and When You *Shouldn't* Use It

So when is the Feedback Sandwich *not* recommended? In *many* situations! For example, if someone really screwed up, of course you are *not* going to use the Feedback Sandwich: "Billy, you're a good boy and we love you very much. But we've asked you numerous times not to play with matches, and now you've burnt down our entire house and destroyed everything we own. So again, we love you, but you need to be more careful from now on so you don't burn our house down again in the future." Or, "Peter, you're a good guy and one of my favorite employees. But I've noticed that lately you've been falsifying all the data in your TPS reports. So I'm gonna need you to stop doing that, OK?"

When it comes to integrity or policy violations, safety issues, and/or serious or recurring performance problems, of course you are not going to "sandwich" your feedback; you are going to be blunt, serious and direct: "Peter, we have a serious problem here"; or, "Billy, sit down…we need to talk." In those situations, you would omit both buns and get right to the meat. Cushioning your message here would be completely unnecessary, inappropriate, and entirely ineffective.

Similarly, there are situations where it might make more sense to start with the top bun and deliver the meat but leave off the bottom bun altogether. For example, "I appreciate your effort and thank you for your hard work; however…this is the third time this mistake has happened and now we have a serious problem that needs to be addressed…."

As you can see, there are a variety of ways to make use of the various elements of the Feedback Sandwich. Though seemingly simple to understand, there's an art and science to mastering its usage. And just because it's not a one-size-fits-all solution (what is?), in my opinion, critics of the Feedback Sandwich are wrong to suggest that we should do away with this incredibly powerful and effective management/leadership/coaching tool altogether. I've been on both ends of it, and I've received feedback with and without it; and all I can say is that despite any research or opinions to the contrary, in real life, when done right, it simply works.

Do's and Don'ts

Here's a simple and common work situation in which it's clear that the Feedback Sandwich would be a proper and effective approach for a manager to take:

Let's say you asked one of your people—a relatively new employee—to write a proposal and then show it to you before sending it out to a client. Upon reading it, you find that the person worked hard on it, did their research, and got all the facts right. The problem is that in their haste to get it to you, they didn't take the time to proofread it, and so it contains a number of small grammatical errors and minor typos. So how do you deliver this feedback message? You could just bluntly say (as the critics suggest), "I read your proposal and it's filled with errors. You need to fix it." Or you can be sarcastic and obnoxious (as many bosses are) and say something like, "Have you ever heard of spellcheck?"

Alternatively, you could use the Feedback Sandwich: "Thanks for getting this to me so fast—I really appreciate it. Good job on the research and the writing. However, I spotted a few typos and grammatical errors, so I need you to proofread it, correct the mistakes, and get it back to me within the hour so we get it out before the end of the day. When we're sending something out to a client, speed counts—but it's equally important to make sure that it's perfect and presentable before it goes out the door. But as this was your first time, overall, you did a really nice job."

Simple and straightforward, it gets your point across regarding the necessary corrective actions, powerfully delivers your message, keeps the relatively minor mistakes in perspective, and—often overlooked, but equally important—restores the employee's confidence and morale in spite of the (again, minor and easily-fixable) errors. As the manager, it's important to ask yourself: is the purpose of the feedback to slam the person for what they got wrong, or to acknowledge what was done well, fix the problem, and help them to improve going forward? The Feedback Sandwich does all that and does it well.

"It Sucked": A Real-life Case Study

Earlier in my career, when I worked for one of the major TV networks, my boss's boss asked me on a Friday to write up "coverage" (a review and recommendation report) on a new pilot script and get it back to him on Monday. (He was asking me because my boss was out on vacation.)

Excited to be given this first-time opportunity and wanting to make a good impression, I spent all weekend on it and had it on his desk by first thing Monday morning. When Tuesday afternoon rolled around and I still hadn't heard anything back yet (as we know, silence is often the worst kind of feedback), I knocked on his door and said: "Hi Jack, I was just wondering if you had a chance to read my coverage." Rummaging through a pile of papers, he finally found it, glanced at it, and then frisbeed it across his desk at me, hitting me in the shins. "Yeah," he said. "It sucked."

As he went back to doing what he was doing before I interrupted him, and with the report I was previously so proud of now resting on my shoe tops, I meekly bent down, picked it up, and limped back to my desk with my tail between my legs, crushed and demoralized. I thought I had done such a good job, but I left work that day wondering if I should start exploring new career possibilities.

The next day, though, I still felt like I needed to get some feedback on what I had done so wrong. And I figured I had nothing to lose. So when 6 p.m. rolled around, after most others had left for the day, I somehow got up the courage to go to his office and knock on his open door again:

"Hey, Jack, do you have a minute? I was just wondering what was wrong with the coverage I wrote—I thought I had done a pretty good job." His response: "You did a great job! Your writing is terrific—it's always terrific—and you had some really great insights. I just really hated the script. But, your report itself was fine."

Um…maybe he could have said that initially…before I almost packed up my bags and quit? In retrospect, what he gave me the first time was the meat. The second time, he provided the same exact meat…but he presented it in the form of a sandwich: a Feedback Sandwich. So, although the outcome was the same (he rejected the script I was recommending), the validation of my work made me feel a million times better, and left me eager for the next opportunity to show what I could do.

That's the power of the Feedback Sandwich in action.

So while there are many different feedback techniques out there, all with their respective pros and cons, the Feedback Sandwich is just one way—a powerful and effective way—to get your message across when appropriate—which is much of the time. Think about it. If you are on the receiving end, would you rather someone take a hot, sizzling, greasy burger off the grill and place it in your bare hands…or would you rather they neatly and gently present it to you between two nice, fluffy buns?

In Review

The Big Lesson: Consider using the Feedback Sandwich method, when appropriate, to deliver your feedback in the most effective way.

The Big Question: Think about various times that you've either received feedback or given feedback to someone else, how effective it was, and whether the Feedback Sandwich method was used. When might you use this approach in the future…and when would it not be the most effective way?

Your Big Insight:

Your Big Action:

CHAPTER 16

The Learning/Enjoyment Matrix

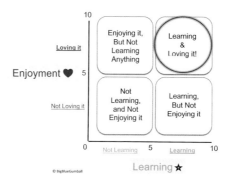

Isn't it nice when you get to spend time doing what you love, loving what you are doing, and learning something in the process? Think about the best learning experiences of your life. Times when you were not only learning but enjoying the experience as well. It could have been while taking a class or workshop, reading a book or article, watching a video or TED talk, or working on a project. It could have been at work, at school, or anywhere else in life.

When you are "Learning and Loving it" (upper right quadrant) you are fully engaged, time flies by, and you can describe your situation either as being "in the zone," "in your element," or "in a state of flow." In these situations, we can't wait for it to start, and hate for it to end. Wouldn't it be great if we could spend most of our time in this quadrant?

Alternatively, sometimes we spend time doing things from which we're not necessarily learning anything, but we're enjoying (upper left quadrant). And there is, of course, absolutely nothing wrong with a little mindless entertainment, escapism, and fun. We all need that.

But what about when we're supposed to be learning, but not necessarily enjoying it (lower right quadrant)? You know, those times where we're disengaged and bored, struggling to understand, and exhaustedly struggling just to get through it. And, yet, despite the pain and suffering, little by little, you are learning something new, and growing. Do you keep forging ahead…or do you quit?

In fact, the reality is that although it is nice when we are enjoying the learning process, oftentimes our biggest breakthroughs occur when we are *not* having fun and struggling through the learning process. Keep this in mind when the going is tough, as you may start to notice improvements and see the light at the end of the tunnel.

Lastly, what about when you're engaged in something where you are neither learning anything nor enjoying it (lower left quadrant)? What then? And, what if it's not a $14.95 paperback book that you're bored with, but a hobby you were trying out that you've made a costly investment in, a project you've been working on, a relationship you are heavily invested in, or even your current job or career? Then what? And how can this model help you figure out what you should do?

The "Learning/Engagement Matrix" model is intended to make you more aware of where and how you *are* spending your time, compared to where and how you *should be* spending your time. In some ways this framework parallels the Time Management Matrix (aka the Eisenhower Matrix, featured in Covey's *The 7 Habits of Highly Effective People*), as well as my "Passion/Skill Matrix" model featured in this book. Framing your time in terms of this model—not just at work, but outside of work as well—will increase your sense of awareness and make you feel better about what you are doing at any given moment.

For example, if you are learning something and enjoying yourself, great! If you are enjoying what you are doing, but not learning anything, that is fine, if you are "off the clock" and in relaxation mode. However, if you feel that you should be doing something more productive, this awareness will prompt you to shift gears and gain focus.

In Review

The Big Lesson: When you hit the pause button to think about how you are spending your time in any given moment by framing it in terms of whether you are learning something and/or whether you are enjoying what you are doing, this model will help you to be more consciously aware and to make more productive use of your time.

The Big Question: When and how can you use this model to use your time more productively, while feeling better about it?

Your Big Insight:

Your Big Action:

CHAPTER 17

The Passion/Skill Matrix:
Do What You Love, and Love What You Do

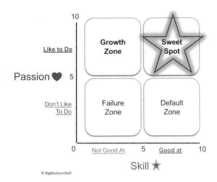

"People do best…what they like best to do." That's an old adage by Frederick W. Taylor, the original efficiency expert and management guru who wrote his *Principles of Scientific Management* way back in 1911. Seems obvious, doesn't it? And yet, so many people hate their jobs. So why is that? What's going on?

Think about your hobbies. You know, the things you do for fun. Whatever it is, whether it's playing a sport, a musical instrument, practicing a craft, or whatever, you probably do it for at least one of the following two reasons: you're good at it and/or you enjoy it. Otherwise, why do it?

If you love doing something, let's say, playing the guitar or the piano or drums—even if you're not very good at it—you're going to pick it up and "fiddle around" with it, spending your spare time practicing, and watching and listening to others play, all in the hope of getting better.

Even if you're not that great and know you're probably never going to play in a band, you still do it because it's fun.

Similarly, if you're good at something, even if it's something like balancing your checkbook, you may not love doing it, but since you're skilled in math and it comes quick and easy to you, you don't really mind doing it. Or maybe you do?

What about something that you love doing *and* you're good at? Now you've hit the magic bullseye: your passions and your skills are in alignment! Let's say you love playing tennis and you discovered years ago that you're pretty good at it. Most likely, with this combination of passion and skill, you enjoyed watching tennis on TV to see how the pros do it, didn't mind hitting a tennis ball against the wall for hours on end, and got a rush from playing every chance you got. Over time, your skills grew. And as your skills grew, so did your confidence, which led to you taking on tougher challenges, practicing more, winning against better and better opponents, having fun competing and winning, and enjoyed your increased success. No, you're probably never going to qualify to compete in the U.S. Open, but you're at a level you're proud of and enjoy as you keep working on taking your game to the next level.

Now, what about when you are stuck doing something that you are not good at, and do not enjoy doing? How successful do you think you are going to be? Probably not very. And, yet, this describes a lot of people's jobs.

So how does this happen?

Here's how it happened to me: Many years ago, I had been out of work for a while when I was offered an amazing job as the VP of Business Development and head of the New York office for a leading west coast interactive agency. I was so honored to be hired by, and excited to be working for, this innovative company that I couldn't wait to take on the challenge of helping them to grow their east coast business.

But once the initial excitement wore off, the job itself ended up being much tougher for me than I ever anticipated. I started just around the time of the dot-com crash when finding new business instantly became a tall order. And, unfortunately, I quickly discovered the hard way that I did not possess either the ability or the personality type required to succeed in this kind of role—especially in this exceptionally tough market environment. And, so, as time went on and as I continued to fail, my stress level rose, and I enjoyed the job less and less, until I could not even bear to get up for work in the morning.

If you've ever had a job that you didn't like *and* that you were not good at, you know what I'm talking about. Through nobody's fault but my own, I was set up to fail every single day, and I just wanted out. When I eventually got laid off, despite my intense feeling of loss—as I loved the company and the people, especially the CEO—it ended up being a huge relief.

In almost every job, there are going to be aspects of your role that you enjoy doing and those that you don't. There are going to be things that you are good (or even great) at, and things that you are not. So, the key to success lies in finding a position that strikes the right balance.

For example, in my current role running a management and leadership consulting, training, and coaching firm, I love and excel at the consulting, training, and coaching part. But there are also aspects of my job that I don't love and that I am not that great at (for example, the financial and the technology functions). So, what to do about it? What would *you* do about it?

Well, that's where looking at yourself and your job through the lens of the Passion/Skill Matrix model comes in handy. Since you probably care more about how *you* could use this model to assess your situation than worrying about me and mine, let's take a look at it this way:

1. Make a list of all the different things you do on a regular basis within your job: all the tasks and responsibilities that come with your role, and then break these tasks up into these four categories:

- Things you are *good* or *great* at;
- Things that you are *not*;
- Things that you *like* or *love* doing; and
- Things that you *don't*.

If you like to quantify things, you can even score each item on a scale of 1–10 (with 10 being the most positive) from "I'm terrible at it" to "I'm amazing at it" and from "I hate it" to "I love it."

2. Next, draw a four-box matrix like the one above (or you can use the worksheet shown at the end of this chapter), and place each of these items in one of the four boxes. For example (depending on your type of job), let's say you are good at and enjoy writing; put that in the upper right quadrant. If you enjoy designing PowerPoint slides, but are not that great at it, put that in the upper left. If you're good at generating Excel spreadsheets, but don't enjoy it, put that in the lower right. And if you hate public speaking and feel that you are not good at it, put that in the lower left.

Now, let's look at the four-quadrant matrix to ask the "So what?/So that!" question to discover how you can this model to be more successful:

Your **Sweet Spot** (upper right quadrant)—The things that you Like/ Love and are Good At: If you have a lot of items listed in that box, you're incredibly lucky! Try to spend as much time as possible on these things. This is where the intersection of your skills and your passions lie, and where you have the greatest potential to leverage your strengths and go from good to great. When you're working on things that fall into this category, time flies, ideas flow, your energy is high, and you're in your element...so spread your wings and fly!

Your **Growth Zone** (upper left quadrant)—The things that you Like or Love to do but are *not* great at...yet: These are your primary developmental opportunities. Why is that? Because if you have a passion for something, or even a curiosity, and you feel that you may have an aptitude or potential here, you are more likely to work at it by learning more about it, studying, practicing, trying, even failing, and seeking training and coaching in these areas. Einstein once said, "Anyone who has never made a mistake has never tried anything new."

If you're passionate about something, keep working at it! You never know how far you might get unless or until you try. And notice the powerful difference between saying "I'm not good at this" vs. "I'm not good at this...yet." By simply adding that simple word "yet," you open the world of possibilities.

Your **Default Zone** (lower right quadrant)—The things that you Don't Like to do, but are Good at: Perhaps they are things that you used to like doing, or things where you just became the "go-to" person for by default because it comes naturally to you and everyone knows it. Perhaps people think that you enjoy it.

For example, as a former English major, people always gave me things to proofread and edit because they knew I was a decent writer; but that didn't mean I wanted to be everyone's proofreader! Well, being good at something that you don't like doing is a great developmental opportunity—for someone else! Here's where you might be able to outsource, delegate, or take on the role of a mentor or coach to help someone else develop *their* skills in this area. This is a win-win opportunity that will help someone else to grow while freeing you up to do other things...so that you can spend more time "above the line" in your Growth Zone and Sweet Spot.

Your **Failure Zone** (lower left quadrant)—And, lastly, the things that you Don't Like (or Hate) to do, *and* are Not Good at. This is your Failure Zone...and you need to do whatever it takes to get out of this box as soon as you can. Again, we all have aspects of our jobs that we may not love, and may not be great at, but if you are spending a lot of time doing things that fall into this box, you are setting yourself up for a whole lot of pain and suffering. Take it from me, as I've been there (numerous times).

If you're in a job that you really, truly dislike and that you are really, truly not good at—and don't see a way to either improve your performance and/or find a way to not hate what you're doing—then you are not doing your employer any favors by continuing to function in this capacity. Sometimes we stay in jobs just for the paycheck, but it's really hard to sustain this state of being over the long haul. And it's eventually going to take its toll on your physical and mental health. So, whatever it takes, you need to try to get yourself out of this box as soon as you can, in any way you can.

Question: Is it possible to turn something from your Failure Zone into a Sweet Spot? Of course! Your Failure Zone could, potentially, be your greatest area of opportunity! By definition, the items in your Failure Zone are those that you are not good at and don't love. But do you not love these things because you are not good at them? If you improved, might you begin to enjoy them more? And if you enjoyed them more, might it be possible that the momentum could help you to transition into a different quadrant?

Say you identify something as belonging in your Failure Zone because you are not good at it and don't like it. But what if you tried…and got better at it? And once you got better at it, you didn't hate it quite as much. And now that you don't hate it as much, you are willing to try it again, and with more and more experience you find yourself inching your way up, in this area, out of the Failure Zone until it now—magically—ends up in your Growth Zone!

From there, once you've broken through the box you had put yourself in, could this potentially gravitate across into your Sweet Spot? Only time will tell…but it is entirely within your power to make it happen…if you are willing to be open to the world of possibility. Think about it: How many of your Sweet Spot skills were once part of your Growth Zone; and, prior to that, your Failure Zone? My guess: probably *most* of them!

Here's *my* real-life example for illustration:

Around twenty years ago, I was working for one of the country's top management training companies as a program manager, in charge of overseeing our mini-MBA program. My job was to schedule and to supervise the external consultants who delivered the workshops; and my place was always behind the scenes and at the back of the room. As an extreme introvert and bookworm my entire life, I traveled all around the country with these superstar trainers and watched in envy and awe as they wowed our workshop participants with their knowledge, confidence, poise, and stage presence. And though I sometimes fantasized about my being up there in front of the room, I knew it was just a pipedream. When it came to public speaking, I was both terrified of it and terrible at it. All through school—from grade school to graduate school—I was always the student who sat way in the back of the room. At work, the dynamic wasn't much different.

Until one day…when everything changed.

I was at a luxury resort in Hilton Head, South Carolina, setting everything up for a senior-level leadership program that would begin the next morning. The participants were to be a group of twelve small-company CEOs, and I wanted to ensure that everything would go smoothly. As I always did, I arrived the night before so as to get things perfectly set up for the trainer, who would arrive the next morning.

Only the trainer *didn't* arrive that morning. He had been sick the night before, overslept, missed his early-morning flight, and wouldn't be arriving until later that evening—after the end of the first day of the program. So, in a panic, I called my boss back in New York, asking, *"So what do we do???"*

"We only have two choices," he said. "We could cancel the program, be completely embarrassed, and lose thousands of dollars along with our reputation." He paused. *"Or…"*

This is when I started feeling faint, as I sensed what was coming: "Or… *you'll* have to deliver the program."

Wait. I'm sorry…What?

"You know the contents of this program inside and out," he argued. "So what's the problem?"

What's the problem?! I thought. *Are you kidding me?*

Anyway…long story, short: I did it. I delivered that first day of the three-day program all by myself. Despite the fact that I had never—and I mean *never*—spoken in public before, let alone facilitated a leadership program for a group of twelve CEOs. The attendees (knowing the full story, which I confessed to them) greatly appreciated it…and assured me that, together, we would get through that first day. In fact, in many ways, those twelve leaders collaborating to help get *me*—and to get us *all*—through that first day—may have been the greatest leadership lesson of all. When the instructor finally arrived later that night, all was right with the universe. The program ended up being a complete success.

When I got back to New York and had a chance to reflect on everything that had happened, and my first public speaking experience, it hit me that I actually wasn't that bad. And, to be completely honest, I didn't hate it.

In fact, to my utter shock, I even kind of enjoyed it. And with that experience, my "Public Speaking" score of a 0/0 (zero/zero) got nudged up, just a notch, out of the depths of my Failure Zone. Though public speaking wouldn't enter my Growth Zone for another five years, or become one of my Sweet Spots for another five years after that, it provides a living example of how, if this could happen for me, it could happen for anyone.

How does this story relate to the power of visual thinking? For years—both at school and at work—I would sit way in the back, envisioning what it would be like for me to be the one up there on the stage and envying those with the courage to get up there. However, when the time finally came, wherein I had no other choice but to take that gigantic leap, it was due to my having visualized it in my mind's eye so many times before that enabled me to do it for real when I had to. And, for me, that was my greatest personal example of how "seeing the invisible" before it happens can enable you to "do the impossible" when the opportunity comes.

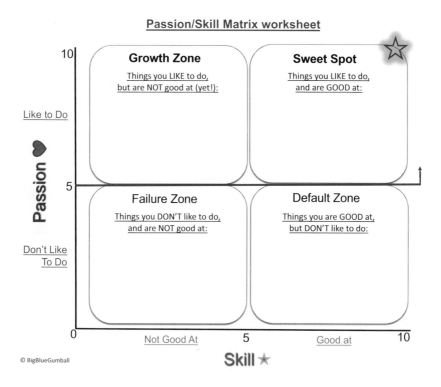

Passion/Skill Matrix worksheet

Growth Zone	**Sweet Spot**
Things you LIKE to do, but are NOT good at (yet!):	Things you LIKE to do, and are GOOD at:
Failure Zone	**Default Zone**
Things you DON'T like to do, and are NOT good at:	Things you are GOOD at, but DON'T like to do:

Passion ♥ — Like to Do / Don't Like To Do

Skill ★ — Not Good At / Good at

© BigBlueGumball

In Review

The Big Lesson: If you really sit down to reflect on your current role relative to this model and where you are spending your time, you can dramatically enhance your potential for success.

The Big Question: What percentage of your time at work (and in life) are *you* spending in each quadrant? And how can you use this model to spend as much of your time as possible "above the line"?

Your Big Insight:

Your Big Action:

CHAPTER 18

The Pizza Slice Approach to Difficult Conversations

As I mentioned earlier, one of the most valuable things that models and frameworks help us do is simplify complexity and help us visualize the messiness of the realities that surround us. And one of the key areas of complexity in most of our lives is the network of people who surround us. Which is why having a mental map of the key stakeholders can really come in handy, particularly for strategizing around necessary but difficult conversations.

And what do we mean by "stakeholders" by the way? A stakeholder is anyone around you who, as the word literally states, "holds" a "stake" (that is, a vested interest) in you and/or in what you do. I often speak in terms of the words "impact and influence"—so these are the people whom you impact through your words and/or actions, and/or whom you need to influence in order to get things done…and vice versa. In essence, there are interdependencies here wherein your work affects theirs, and their work affects yours.

Take the Stakeholder Map (which is, basically, a miniature org chart… with *you* at the center) and write in the names and titles of all of your key players. If needed, you can always sketch out an expanded version on a larger piece of paper. Doing this exercise will enable you to then visualize the interrelationships of all the people in your sphere of impact and influence. This will assist you as you think about how anything you say or do may impact someone else in the world around you. Most immediately, it is typically your boss, your peers, and your direct reports. But your actions can extend far beyond this immediate network.

One way to use this Stakeholder Map is to use it in combination with other models—for example, the PowerDial (Chapter 19).

One other way to use it is with the classic model known as "RACI." For any task or project, you can make a list of: Who is *responsible* for executing the task (or various pieces of it)? Who is *accountable*, that is, who ultimately "owns" it? Who needs to be *consulted*, that is, checked with? And who needs to be kept *informed*? If you use your Stakeholder Map while filling out your RACI spreadsheet, you can ensure that you don't inadvertently leave anyone out.

Back to difficult conversations. Your Stakeholder Map provides value by helping you prepare for difficult conversations that you may need to have with those around you. Those difficult conversations can run the gamut from a talk with your boss (or with your boss's boss), a challenging conversation with a peer or direct report, or with a client or vendor.

Here's an example of how I use this framework with my coaching clients:

1. Looking at your Stakeholder Map, what is one difficult conversation that you need to have? Write down the name of the person, along with the details of the situation.
2. What, from your perspective, makes this conversation "difficult"?

3. If you had to have this conversation right now, without any preparation, what would you do and say? And what would be your desired outcome?

Performing this visualization exercise will help you envision how this conversation might unfold before you put yourself in that situation. It will help to make a difficult conversation less difficult—and increase your odds of achieving a successful outcome—by playing it out in your mind, before anything comes out of your mouth.

To help you think things through, I recommend using this "7 P's Difficult Conversation Checklist":

1. **Preparation:** What do you need to do to get ready to have this conversation (including gathering the facts and data; clarifying your position and your desired outcome; making sure that you are in a proper frame of mind; determining the ideal time and place to hold the conversation)?

2. **Person:** Who is the individual with whom you will be having this conversation? What is their personality? Style? Status? Relationship with you? Prior history? Receptivity? Can you anticipate their reaction/response?

3. **Points:** What are the key messages you want/need to communicate? What supporting evidence are you going to provide? What are you going to leave out?

4. **Purpose:** What is the intent of the conversation—that is, what do you want, need, or hope to get out of it? What is the desired outcome or change? What outcome do you think the other person would like to see happen?

5. **Plan:** When, where, and how do you intend to have this conversation? (Try mentally envisioning the setting and circumstances.)

6. **Practice:** Whether on paper, in your head, out loud, or in a role-play with someone, it's valuable to envision how this conversation might play out. Are you prepared for all possible reactions and responses?

7. **Perspective:** How difficult do you expect this conversation to be (for example, on a scale of 1–10)? What is the worst thing that might happen? How can you prepare for the worst...while setting yourself (and the other person) up for the best?

Additionally, you can also use the Three-Legged Stool in Chapter 22 as a tool for thinking through your conversation. For, as in any conversation that you are initiating, you will want to think about:

- How are you going to **Open** (what is the very first thing you are going to say to kick the conversation off)?
- What are you going to **Say** (and not say)?
- Are there are examples, stories, or metaphors you may want to use to help make your case?
- How are you going to **Close** (what is the final thing you want to say, and how are you going to say it to maximize your impact)? Do you have a well thought-out "call to action"?
- When the conversation is over, what do you want the other person to think, feel, know, and do?

While this seems like a lot of work and a huge investment of your valuable time, what will the cost be to you if it does not go well?

As Cervantes wrote, "To be prepared is half the victory."

In Review

The Big Lesson: Creating a Stakeholder Map is a valuable way to visually map out the key people and relationships in your world so as to help you to maximize your impact and influence. And using the "7 P's Difficult Conversations Checklist" in combination with your Stakeholder Map will help you to think through what you want (and don't want) to say, as well as how best to say it so as to increase the odds of getting the outcome you desire.

The Big Question: What difficult conversations do you need to have, and how can you use this model and process to increase your odds for success?

Your Big Insight:

Your Big Action:

CHAPTER 19

The PowerDial: The Power to Change... to Get the Power You Need

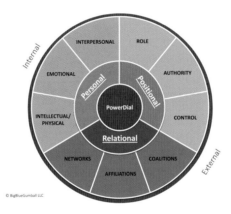

One of the main reasons we often hesitate, procrastinate, or fail to take action is because we feel as if we lack power. When out of work or stuck in a dead-end job, or struggling to get others to buy in to our ideas, or feeling ignored or overlooked, it can seem as if we have no leverage at all.

But guess what: You have a lot more power than you think!

Getting anything done, especially in the business world—whether convincing someone to hire you, to fund your project, or to fund your proposal—requires the ability to influence others.

As Gregory Berns, the author of *Iconoclast: A Neuroscientist Reveals How to Think Differently*, wrote: "A person can have the greatest idea in the world...but if that person can't convince enough other people, it doesn't matter." And to convince other people of something—to influence them—requires confidence and power.

But what is "power" anyway? One way to describe it is as the ability or potential to allocate resources, make and enforce decisions, and/or to impact and influence others.

If you think about electricity, for example, the wall socket represents only "potential" power. It is only after plugging something in that we see that potential come to life to produce results. So the big question is: How do you turn your potential power into performance to maximize your productivity and to produce results?

To see how, let's take a deep dive into the BigBlueGumball PowerDial model:

As you can see, your power comes from three different sources: **Personal** power; **Relational** power; and **Positional** power.

So right off the bat, the point to be made is that we're not dealing with an "either-or" situation. It's not a question of either having power or not, but a matter of how much power you have, and how you might reap the power potential from each of these three distinct sources:

1. Your Personal power refers to *who you are, what you know, and what you can do.*
2. Your Relational power relates not to *what* you know, but *who you know* and, in some ways the even more important question of *who knows you.*
3. And the third area, Positional power, is about just that—your role or status or position. It relates to what you *do*, what you *have*, and what you have control over.

So, although people tend to speak about "power" as if it's a single entity or quality that you either have or you don't, you can now see that power comes from a variety of sources, each of which can be leveraged, developed, and grown.

The next important thing to notice is that Personal power is internal—it comes solely from within you. The other two, Relational and Positional power, are external, as they are related to, or dependent upon, other people or other factors outside of yourself. So while enhancing your Positional power will have a longer-term time horizon, and the Relational power area will also take some time to develop as it involves building and strengthening your relationships with other people, the Personal power areas are entirely within your control.

Let's, now, take a deeper dive into this model to show how you can use it to boost your confidence and increase your influence.

1. Your Personal power is derived from three areas: the Intellectual/Physical (your knowledge, intelligence, talents, skills, and strengths); the Emotional (self-awareness, emotional intelligence, attitude, passion, and confidence); and the Interpersonal (your personality and people skills).

2. Your Relational power comes from your Networks (connections and access); Affiliations (memberships, associations, and friendships); and Coalitions (teams and partnerships). In other words, who you are personally connected to, have access to, can receive support from, and partner with.

3. Your Positional power comes from your Role (title, rank, level of seniority); Authority (degree of empowerment); and Control (of resources, as well as degree of dominance, and veto ability).

To gauge where you currently have the most power (and the least), and to measure your progress as you set out to develop and leverage your strengths in all or some of these areas, you might want to make a list of how you rank in each of these areas (using specific examples to make it real), and then score yourself in each area on a scale of 1–10. This will enable you to track your progress as you enhance your strengths in each area.

Towards that end, thinking about your Personal, Relational, and Positional power self-assessment—and reflecting on your core strengths and key areas of development—ask yourself: what is *one* action you can take within the next week to increase your power? And then think about how you might enhance your power over the next three to six months.

To help you to kick-start your confidence, take a look at the sample PowerDial Action Plan below for some sample action items.

As the novelist Alice Walker once said, "The most common way that people give up their power is by thinking they don't have any." But the good news is that, with the help of the PowerDial, the power to increase your power is entirely within your hands.

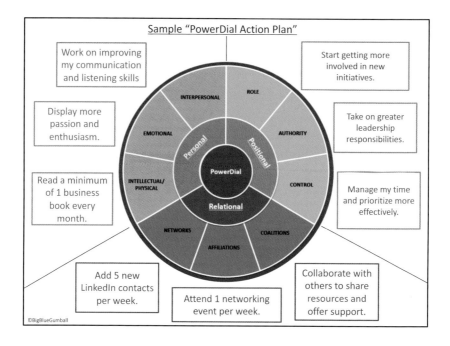

Sample "PowerDial Action Plan"

Work on improving my communication and listening skills

Start getting more involved in new initiatives.

Display more passion and enthusiasm.

Take on greater leadership responsibilities.

Read a minimum of 1 business book every month.

Manage my time and prioritize more effectively.

Add 5 new LinkedIn contacts per week.

Attend 1 networking event per week.

Collaborate with others to share resources and offer support.

©BigBlueGumball

In Review

The Big Lesson: Rather than thinking you either have power or you don't, reframing what it means to have power—by breaking it down into these nine categories—can help you to increase your power and, thereby, enhance your ability to impact and influence others.

The Big Question: Looking at the PowerDial Action Plan, what are some steps you can take—both short term and long term—to incrementally increase the amount of power you have?

Your Big Insight:

Your Big Action:

CHAPTER 20

Stop, Start, Continue, and the Magic Wand

Out of all of the various tools in my executive coaching tool kit, the Stop, Start, Continue, and the Magic Wand visual model (and metaphor) is one of the simplest and most valuable—both in terms of creating awareness and improving performance. Best of all, it can be used in a wide range of scenarios and for a wide variety of purposes.

For example: Prior to meeting with a new coaching client for the very first time, so as to make that first session the most productive, I email them a self-reflection questionnaire containing these five not-so-simple-to-answer questions:

1. **Five Words:** What are five words you would use to describe yourself (at work)...and why?
2. **Continue (yellow light):** What are three things that you do regularly that feel productive and that you would advise yourself to keep doing? Why?

3. **Stop (red light):** What are three things that you do that you feel would be in your best interest to stop doing? Why?

4. **Start (green light):** What are three things that you're not currently doing that you'd like to start doing? Why?

5. **Magic Wand:** If you could wave a magic wand and immediately change *just one thing* for, or about, yourself at work, what would it be? Why?

While these are not easy questions to answer, they serve as a powerful self-reflection and introspection instrument to help the individual look in the mirror. Framing these questions using the colorful "traffic light" and "magic wand" metaphors serves to help both the coaching client and me to mentally code these questions in a visual and memorable way. And kicking off the coaching engagement with these questions helps to open the door to the coaching engagement and gets the initial conversation off to a running start.

By the way, in case you were wondering, though it is more mellifluous-sounding to say, "Stop, Start, Continue," I typically begin with Continue first, so as to capture the positive behaviors, or the things that seem to be working, prior to moving on to the things that may need to change.

This five-question model can also be used, within a coaching engagement, as a 360-degree assessment by asking the client's supervisor, direct reports, and peers these questions about him or her. For example, "When thinking about Art Vandelay, what are five words you would use to describe him, and why? What are three things that you would recommend he Continue, Stop, and Start doing, and why? And if you could wave a magic wand to help him to be more effective and successful, what would you magically change for or about him, and why?

I have often used these five questions as part of a team assessment to explore and discover how a team is doing and what needs to change.

Additionally, I use it within my coaching engagements to solicit feedback from my clients on how they feel the coaching is going and what, if anything, I may need to change.

I also use it in my NYU class to solicit midterm feedback from students on what is working and what, if anything, they would like to see changed.

And deploying this exercise doesn't need to be a whole formal process. You can just use it informally and conversationally, as in a feedback or debrief conversation, by asking someone, "What do you feel went well?" (yellow light). "What do you feel didn't go as well?" (red light). And, "What would you do differently next time?" (green light).

And, most importantly: For yourself as a self-reflection tool, you can ask yourself these five questions and consider what's working and what's not. And you can even ask these same questions of those around you as a quick, simple, and powerful way to gain insights into your behaviors and your performance.

One thing, though: Although I pose the fifth question using the visual metaphor of the "magic wand," the reality is that, unfortunately, there *is* no magic wand. The "magic" comes from taking the insights you've gained from the other four questions and then doing the hard work that it takes to make a positive change.

In Review

The Big Lesson: Using the five simple questions in the Stop, Start, Continue, and the Magic Wand model is a quick, powerful, and visual way to gain self-awareness and feedback that you can then use to make positive changes.

The Big Question: Are you brave, and honest, and self-aware enough to ask and answer these questions about yourself? And are you brave and willing enough to solicit this feedback about yourself from others?

Your Big Insight:

Your Big Action:

CHAPTER 21

Ten Types of Visual Thinking

When I worked in the TV industry out in Hollywood earlier in my career—first in comedy program development at Disney, and then in drama program development at CBS—it was interesting to observe the process by which an idea for a TV pilot eventually became a TV series (if the originators were incredibly lucky, considering the odds were about a thousand to one).

The process producers used when trying to develop an idea for a show went as follows:

First, the producers would sit around coming up with numerous possible concepts—as many as they could—after which they would need to narrow the list to the best ideas. Sometimes they would take various elements of the different ideas (that is, storylines, or characters) and combine them together to come up with a new and better idea. They would then assess the concepts to determine how good the ideas were and if they were worthy of developing further.

In the course of doing so, they had to make sure that the ideas were original and could be pitched as something new that TV viewers hadn't seen a million times before. Some of these ideas involved taking an idea that already existed and putting a new spin on it; others involved coming up with a brand-new idea that, perhaps, hadn't ever been done before; and other times—most risky of all—someone would pitch an idea that could, potentially, reinvent the industry.

In a nutshell, I just walked you through the following ten different types of visual thinking:

1. Divergent Thinking (expansion)
2. Convergent Thinking (contraction)
3. Integrative Thinking (connection/synthesis)
4. Analytical Thinking (dissection)
3. Critical Thinking (interpretation)
4. Creative Thinking (new/original ideas)
5. Innovative Thinking (new/original applications)
6. Evolutionary Thinking (progressive)
7. Revolutionary Thinking (ground-breaking)
8. Paradigm-shifting Thinking (radically new point of view)

What distinguishes these as visual thinking techniques is that at each stage of the process, the developers would need to envision what the show would look like in terms of the Who, What, When, Where, Why, and How. They would need to create and develop the characters, often with preliminary suggestions for the cast (Who); come up with a plot (What); determine the time (When) and place (Where) in which the show would be set; figure out the storyline (Why); and the type of production (How).

In order to do this, they would need to picture what the show would look and feel like in their own mind's eye, and then try to communicate their vision to others in such a way that everyone else could "see" it in *their* mind's eye as well.

As for how the Ten Types of Visual Thinking work, let's take a closer look [Note: The Ten Types of Thinking is *not* a linear, sequential process even though I am describing the different types, in order, for explanatory purposes.]:

1. **Divergent Thinking** (expansion): Starting with the seed of an idea, with this type of thinking the goal is to expand on the initial idea to come up with as many different ideas as possible while suspending criticism or judgment. This type of thinking is often called Green Light Thinking, Green Hat Thinking, or ideation. As ideation guru Bryan Mattimore (author of *Idea Stormers*, and *21 Days to a Big Idea*) would tell us, idea generation is all about leveraging external stimuli to serve as a catalyst for new ideas.

2. **Convergent Thinking** (contraction): Next, you take all the various ideas that you came up with and narrow them to the best ideas, often by using some of the other types of thinking on the list.

3. **Integrative Thinking** (connection/synthesis): With this type of thinking you come up with brand-new ideas by combining some of the best elements of multiple ideas. This could be described as two plus two equals five…or ten.

4. **Analytical Thinking** (dissection): This is about (for lack of a better metaphor) "cutting open" an idea, as you would a frog in a high school biology class to explore its inner workings (something that I needed to run out of the room during, before I got sick to my stomach; but I digress).

5. **Critical Thinking** (interpretation): This type of thinking is personal and subjective. It's about expressing our biased opinions based on the information at hand combined with our own personal experiences.

6. **Creative Thinking** (new/original ideas): This type of thinking is about putting on our metaphorical thinking hats to come up with new, original ideas.

7. **Innovative Thinking** (new/original applications): This type of thinking is about taking the creative ideas that were generated and exploring real-world applications. While many people use the terms "creativity" and "innovation" interchangeably, I love this definition from the book *Leading Innovation* by Brian McDermott and Gerry Sexton: "Innovation is the value-added application of a creative idea." In other words, you can come up

with a million creative ideas, but it's not officially an innovation until you implement it and it adds value.

8. **Evolutionary Thinking** (progressive): This type of thinking involves building on something that already exists. A slow and incremental progression.

9. **Revolutionary Thinking** (ground-breaking): This type of thinking involves coming up with something completely new.

10. **Paradigm-shifting Thinking** (radically new point of view) And, lastly, this type of thinking involves coming up with something so new and different that it radically changes the game, creates a new set of rules, and opens an entirely new world of possibilities.

Einstein was once quoted as having said, "You can't solve problems using the same kind of thinking you used when you created them."

Knowing that there are different types of thinking—ten, in fact—that you can employ at different times and in different situations, enables you to think, generate ideas, analyze situations, solve problems, and make decisions in a whole new and exciting way.

In Review

The Big Lesson: Knowing that there are different types of thinking that you can use opens a world of possibilities.

The Big Question: Which of the ten types of thinking do you tend to use? And which ones might help you to be an even more effective visual thinker in the future?

Your Big Insight:

Your Big Action:

CHAPTER 22

The Three-Legged Stool Communication/ Presentation Model

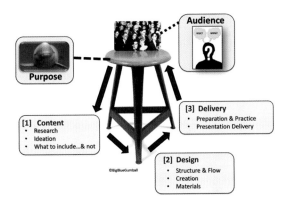

While I could write an entire book just on the topic of designing and delivering more effective communications or presentations, I just want to briefly introduce you to our Three-Legged Stool model as a useful way to think about doing so more visually.

Metaphorically, one way to think about any communication or presentation is as a stool with three legs. Just as a stool with less than three legs would tip over, a presentation for which you do not consider all three elements (Content, Design, and Delivery) will most likely topple as well.

Taking it from the top...

Any and every communication, of any kind, should begin with the two core questions: What is my Purpose? And who is my Audience? This applies to any message from a one-on-one conversation to a speech for a hundred thousand people.

So, in this stool metaphor the "seat" represents your Purpose, the foundation on which your Audience will sit, and the point at which all three legs of the stool come together to support it.

Regarding your audience, you can envision every individual audience member having two thought bubbles floating over their head. And the two thoughts they are thinking, in regard to your message, are: "WSIC?" and "WIFM?"—which stand for "Why Should I Care?" and "What's In it For Me?" If your listener is not interested in what you have to say, and/or if they don't "see" the benefit, then why should they want to pay attention to you?

And, speaking of paying attention: When delivering any message, it helps to keep "AIDA" in mind. No, not the opera or the musical. AIDA is a classic marketing acronym, which comes in just as handy as a communication or presentation checklist, and it stands for Attention (or Awareness), Interest, Desire, and Action. In other words, when formulating any message, you need to think about:

1. How are you going to capture and hold your listener's Attention (and create Awareness)?
2. How are you going to pique their Interest on an intellectual level?
3. How are you going to get them to Desire (that is, want) to know more, on an emotional level? and
4. How are you going to get them to change…or take Action?

In regard to your Purpose, you need to be clear on the *why* behind your message. Why are you delivering this message, and why are *you* the best person to do so? In other words, what is the "reason" behind your communication? If you're not clear on the answer to that question, how can you expect your audience to be?

If you take a look at the above model, you'll see that this step in the process is visually represented by an aquatic sea animal. No, it is not a dolphin; or a whale. It is a porpoise. Why? Because, as I said earlier, every presentation needs to have a porpoise…and this is the "POP," or the "Porpoise Of your Presentation"!

Yes, you may be groaning and cringing right now (I can see it; *and* you can probably tell that I get my sense of humor from my father); however, with this corny pun forever—and visually—etched in your memory, you will, most likely, never forget it. When communicating any message in any medium, it all starts with your ~~porpoise~~ purpose.

Now that you're clear on your audience and your purpose, you can proceed with the three-step process represented by the three legs of the stool: Content, Design, and Delivery. In brief…

1. **Content:** Research, Ideation, and What to Include and What Not To. During this phase, with your audience and the purpose of your communication clearly in mind, you need to do your homework, generate ideas relative to what you are going to talk about, and (perhaps the hardest part) decide what to include, and what to leave out based on the various constraints involved (the biggest of which is time; others include your audience's attention span, areas of interest, etc.).

2. **Design:** Structure and Flow; Creation; Materials. Once you've identified your content, the second leg of the stool involves figuring out how you are going to structure and sequence your content. Using visual thinking techniques (such as mindmapping and storyboarding) is an effective way to visually organize your content so as to be able to "see" how your message will "look" and feel. Also involved in this step of the process: (1) determining how you are going to open and close your presentation, (2) deciding what examples and metaphors you are going to use, what stories you are going to tell to bring your message to life, and (3) what physical materials you may want or need to create (that is, documents, PowerPoint slides, etc.).

3. **Delivery:** Presentation Preparation, and Preparation Delivery. And, finally, the third leg of the stool involves preparing and practicing for the delivery of your message, followed, ultimately, by the delivery of your message to your audience. The author Cervantes wrote, "To be prepared is half the victory," and no truer

words were ever spoken. Most people don't prepare and practice nearly enough. And a big part of your preparation process should be using visual thinking to "envision" in your mind's eye the "Who, What, When, Where, Why, and How" of your presentation. In other words: What you will say, and How you will say it; When and Where you will be saying it; Who you will be saying it to (your audience); and, of course, Why you are saying it (your purpose).

Again, this Three-Legged Stool model could make for an entire book (or workshop), but I just wanted to briefly introduce you to this visual/metaphorical framework to provide you with an overview of this powerful mental model that—if you use it as a guide and a checklist—will dramatically enhance your ability to more effectively design and deliver any communication or presentation in the future.

One other valuable mental construct to keep in mind when developing any message is our "Three E's": Educate, Engage, and Excite model (along with the accompanying Three I's):

- **Educate** is about asking yourself, "At the end of this communication, what do I want people to know…and how can I best 'Inform' them?"
- **Engage** is about asking yourself, "How am I going to gain people's 'Interest' by capturing and holding their attention?"
- **Excite** is about asking yourself, "How am I going to 'Inspire' people, through my message, to go out and do something differently?" In other words: what is your "call to action"?

In Review

The Big Lesson: The Three-Legged Stool and the Three E's are two valuable models to help you mentally frame and structure any communication or presentation.

The Big Question: How are you going to use this visual framework to more effectively get people to see what you're saying?

Your Big Insight:

Your Big Action:

CHAPTER 23

Bonus Model: Purpose, Way, Impact (PWI)

While all of the models contained within this book are my own original content, I wanted to add this brand-new model by my friend
JP Laqueur and his partner Steve Goodwin of BrandFoundations. Their
rocket model is bound to really "take off"…and, as such, I wanted to be
among the first to share it with everyone.

Their "Purpose, Way & Impact: A Three-Stage Rocket to Clarity and
Growth" model is their next-generation version of the traditional Vision,
Mission, and Values model that we've all been using all these years. In
brief, as they say in their description, "Rather than rehash a comparison of
these old terms, we think it's time to retire the Mission, Vision, and Values
framework entirely in favor of a new model that we believe is more intuitive, easier to remember, and more useful to leaders and employees alike."

The analogy they propose is that of a three-stage rocket[2]. (See illustration opposite.)

To BrandFoundations, there is no more important or more differen-
tiating foundation for an organization than having a clear and powerful
expression of these three areas:

1. **Purpose:** why you exist, and the change you are trying to bring
   about (the Why);

---

[2] Used with permission from JP Laqueur.

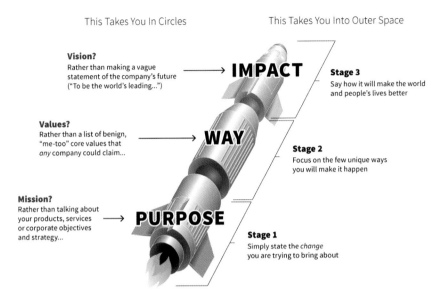

Way: the unique ethos and behaviors that characterize the way you operate, the few unique ways you will make it happen (the How); and

Impact: the ultimate impact you make on society, your statement declaring how you will make the world and people's lives better (the What).

What I also love about this innovative visual model—in addition to its simplicity and its intuitive nature—is that it's not a model limited to organizations. Individuals too can create their own personal Purpose-Way-Impact statements to help formulate their thoughts and guide their actions into the future.

For example, here's mine:

1. **My Purpose:** Is to help make the world a better place…one leader at a time. And, to me, *everyone* is a leader in one way or another—even if they're just managing and leading themselves.
2. **My Way:** Is through my innovative approach that I call "VisuaLeadership," which is all about leveraging the power of

visual imagery, mental models/frameworks, metaphor/analogy, and visual storytelling to manage and to lead.

3. **My Impact:** In so doing, I am contributing to helping people to maximize their own—and others'—performance, productivity, and potential...in leadership and in life.

In Review

The Big Lesson: The Purpose-Way-Impact model is a new and future-oriented visioning model that will help you—and your organization—clarify how you will make your vision a reality in the future of work.

The Big Question: How will creating your own PWI statements help you to turn your vision into a reality?

Your Big Insight:

Your Big Action:

PART THREE

Leading with...Visual Metaphors. *Why* Metaphors?

I was recently watching a TV news interview in which they were discussing global warming. One of the scientists commented that the melting of the polar ice caps was "a canary in the coal mine" and that we will potentially experience a "domino effect" as sea levels continue to rise, adding that we face an environmental crisis of "Titanic proportions."

While the use of three different metaphors within sixty seconds may not be a world record, it *does* serve to illustrate how often metaphors are used as part of normal, daily conversation—typically, without our even realizing it. So this one example was just, yes...the tip of the iceberg.

For example, take a look at the titles of various blog posts. I think you'll find that a majority of them incorporate the use of metaphors, not only as a creative attention-getting device but as an effective and memorable way of communicating the post's central idea.

The same goes for many books. In case you were wondering, the best-selling management book *Who Moved My Cheese* has absolutely nothing, whatsoever, to do with a search for missing dairy products. Nor does the classic *Harvard Business Review* article, "Management Time: Who's Got the Monkey?" have anything to do with locating a missing primate.

If I were to tell you that this book covering visual thinking and visual communication is **rooted** in the idea that thinking in pictures will help you to be a more effective leader, that I wanted to **plant this seed** in your mind by providing you with numerous examples as illustration, and that if you **branched out** into this area, I would be willing to **go out on a limb** and bet that if you start incorporating visual imagery, models, metaphors, and stories into your repertoire it will immediately **bear fruit**...I think the power of metaphor, in leadership and in life, even if you have never really thought about it before, will become immediately apparent.

What, exactly, *is* a metaphor...and what is a metaphor for? In the most simple and basic terms, a metaphor is a figure of speech in which we use one thing (typically unrelated) to explain something else. For example, if I were to say, "My luve is like a red, red rose/That's newly sprung in June..." (quoting the classic poem by Robert Burns—and, yes, that's how he spelled "love" way back then), I am taking an abstract concept (new love) and using a familiar physical object to visually illustrate and explain what it's like. It's difficult, if not impossible, to picture in one's mind an intangible concept such as love; but one can easily envision the comparable beauty and newness of a just-bloomed "red, red rose." So, whether you send someone a poem, or text them a red heart icon, your metaphorical message should, hopefully, come through loud and clear.

Similarly, if I were to verbally tell you a story that begins with the words, "It was a dark and stormy night," that auditory description will get translated in your "mind's eye" into a visual image that you can see, feel, and experience. That's the power not only of visual thinking but of visual communication. We use visual language to transfer ideas and images from our head into someone else's so that they can "see" what we're saying.

And why use metaphors instead of just describing something literally? Because a good metaphor serves to make the unfamiliar familiar, the intangible tangible, the abstract concrete, the complex simple, the confusing clear, and the invisible visible. Which is why metaphor is one of the most powerful visual thinking and visual communication methods available. And metaphor is not just within the purview of poets and songwriters, but of all of us. They are all around, hiding in plain sight.

For example, if you think about it, when we talk about...

backing up our data to "the cloud"…it's not literally stored up in the sky;

using a computer "mouse"…it's shaped like one, but is not, actually, a rodent;

saving a "folder" or a "file" to your "desktop"…you are using neither a real file or folder, nor the top of an actual desk;

"cutting and pasting"…there are no scissors or glue involved;

your computer having a "virus"…it may be "infected," but it is not, literally, sick with disease;

opening a new "window" on your computer…will not, actually, let in any fresh air.

This list goes on and on and on…and these are just a few computer-related metaphors that we commonly hear and use so often that we don't even realize they're metaphors. What others can *you* think of? For example, when we talk about "white-collar" and "blue-collar" jobs, that's a metaphor. When we talk about work/life "balance" (as in a scale), job "burnout" (as in a candle), or receiving a "pink slip" when getting laid off (are those actually even used anymore?), those are all metaphors. And every CEO in America talks about their company's "secret sauce"— the magical ingredient that differentiates them from the competition. But unless you're McDonald's and you're talking about a Big Mac, it's a metaphor.

And the next time you look at your smartphone, take a close look and see how many apps and icons are visual metaphors! Just for a few examples: the camera, the calculator, the compass, the notepad, the old-fashioned telephone receiver…and email (do you need to put a stamp on that little "envelope"?) When it comes to social media, as far as I know, there is no actual "book" at Facebook, Twitter does not involve actual birds, and YouTube does not involve any actual "tubes."

Speaking of "windows," by the way: Many years ago, when I was interviewing for my job at Liquidnet (I'll talk more about that later), I met with their consultant extraordinaire, Angelo Valenti. Part of our conversation went like this:

Angelo: "I have a question for you: Do you do windows?"

Me: "You mean, like, Microsoft Windows?"

Angelo: "No. I mean do you "do windows"? [pause] "As in, when needed, are you willing to roll up your sleeves and get out the Windex and paper towels?"

Me: "So...you are, *literally*, talking about actual windows?"

Angelo: "Yes, that's exactly what I'm asking."

While he was, literally, asking me if I was willing to do manual tasks if necessary, he was also, metaphorically, inquiring as to whether I was willing to do whatever it took to get the job done. His creative and memorable use of metaphor in this situation had tremendous impact on me, and still resonates all these years later. Think about it: What is the equivalent of "doing windows" in *your* line of work?

When using metaphors, it's important to keep in mind that while a familiar one will serve to clarify, an unfamiliar one will result in the exact opposite effect by confusing and, potentially, alienating your audience. If you know baseball and I comment that your presentation was a "home run" or a "grand slam," you'll understand it's a huge compliment. If you don't know baseball, however, you may not know if I'm praising or criticizing you.

For instance, in one of my NYU classes, I used the expression, "sounding like a broken record." If you're a Baby Boomer who grew up knowing what it sounds like to have a phonograph needle stuck in the groove of a scratched record album, you will immediately understand the reference. However, if you were a millennial student who never personally had to endure that extremely annoying life experience, you might interpret this expression the exact opposite way—as this particular student did—and assume that my reference was a positive one, related to "breaking an Olympic record"...and, perhaps, even, the winning of a gold medal for it.

I guess I could call this an example of a "Metaphor Fail." But it was a valuable lesson...and, as my wife always reminds me, I should remember to focus on "the donut"...and not "the hole."

In summary, we tend to process and understand new information relative to what we already know and understand, as well as where and how this new information fits into our "mental map."

So when using a metaphor or an analogy to explain a concept by saying to someone, "It's kind of like this..." you are helping them to "connect the dots"—and helping people to connect the dots is one of the most valuable things a leader can do. For, as the Greek philosopher Heraclitus wrote, "A wonderful harmony arises when we join together the seemingly unconnected."

Tying this all back to visual thinking and visual communication, the use of metaphor and analogy can not only help us to clarify understanding and get our idea across, but also mentally transport us to another time and place. The poet William Wordsworth wrote about the concept of "emotion recollected in tranquility," or our ability to reexperience something simply by reflecting on it in our mind's eye. One of the classic and most powerful examples and illustrations of this principle can be found in the closing stanza of his poem "I Wandered Lonely as a Cloud" (in this case, an *actual* cloud; not the "server" kind):

> For oft, when on my couch I lie
> In vacant or in pensive mood,
> **They flash upon that inward eye**
> Which is the bliss of solitude;
> And then my heart with pleasure fills,
> And dances with the daffodils.

Intellectually, we all know that a human heart cannot "fill with pleasure"...as the pleasure center of the body is located in the brain; nor can the human heart literally "dance." And, yet, if you've ever had this, or a similar experience, you know exactly what he is talking about.

In his *Poetics*, Aristotle wrote: "The greatest thing by far is to be a master of metaphor; it is the one thing that cannot be learnt from others; and it is also a sign of genius, since a good metaphor implies an intuitive perception of the similarity in the dissimilar."

So, from a leadership perspective, whether you are "*giving* someone a fish," or "teaching them *how* to fish," think about how you can leverage the power of metaphor so that you—and the people you lead—will not only "eat well tonight"...but for the rest of their lives.

With that being said, in this section we'll explore how "seemingly unconnected" references to black socks, pink spoons, a yellow ball, and more can help you to lead more visually, in work and in life, by leveraging the power of metaphor.

CHAPTER 24

Black Sock Decision-Making: One Simple Way to Help Simplify Your Life

There was a time when I was traveling for business almost every single week. That meant packing for three or four days on the road at a time and figuring out which suits and shirts and ties I was going to wear. Then I'd have to choose the perfect pair of socks to match each outfit.

This may seem trivial, but I had about thirty different colors and varieties of dress socks in my drawer to choose from, each with different designs, patterns, stripes, and shapes. Every time I got to this dreaded stage of the packing process, I would get more and more bothered by what an annoying, useless, and royal time-waster it was. One day, as I sat there staring deep down into the abyss of my sock drawer, I came to the realization that something had to change.

So, I made a potentially life-altering decision: I would switch to wearing nothing but solid black socks from then on. That very next day, I went down to Macy's in Herald Square and bought eighteen pairs of the exact same plain, black dress socks. Guess how many of my clients ended up noticing? None. And yet, how much time, energy, and stress did I immediately eliminate by making this one simple change? Tons!

By now, you've probably figured out that this chapter—and the Black Sock Decision-Making principle—isn't really about hosiery at all. It's about stepping back and finding ways to simplify the complexity in our everyday lives and exploring the possible ways to reduce—by even *one*—the dizzying number of decisions we need to make on a daily basis.

Think about it: How many decisions did you have to make today before you even left for work this morning?

- What time to wake up?
- Which toothpaste to use?
- What to wear?
- What to have for breakfast?
- What time to leave for work?
- What route to take?
- What's on your to-do list for today?
- Where to start?

Now imagine how much easier and less stressful your morning would be if you could eliminate just one single decision (or, perhaps, even more) from your list, simply by reconsidering your options and streamlining your decision-making process.

In one of my favorite TED Talks (and books), *The Paradox of Choice*, psychologist Barry Schwartz explains "why more is less," and how having *too many* options is actually too much of a good thing. And in one of my favorite visual thinking-related books, *Presentation Zen*, the brilliant Garr Reynolds encourages us to seek ways to turn complexity into simplicity—in our communications and in our lives—by looking for ways to strip things down to the "essential."

Yes, the ability and the willingness to see things with new eyes and to differentiate the essential from the nonessential requires both mindfulness and time. But it will end up saving time in the long run, helping you to focus, be more purposeful, make better decisions, become less stressed, and ultimately change your life for the better.

So keep in mind these three classic quotations:

- "Our lives are frittered away by detail; simplify, simplify."
  —*Henry David Thoreau*
- "Make things as simple as possible, but no simpler."
  —*Albert Einstein*
- "Simplicity is the ultimate sophistication."
  —*Leonardo da Vinci*

And remember that the more decisions in your life that can be standardized, systematized, automated, and/or eliminated, to the point where you don't even need to think about them anymore, the more you can free your time—and your mind—to focus on the things at work, and in life, that truly matter.

That, in a nutshell, is what the principle of "Black Sock Decision-Making" is all about:

Simplifying your life...one day—and one sock—at a time.

In Review

The Big Lesson: The principle of "addition by subtraction" has, seemingly, been around forever. But it takes a conscious commitment of time, effort, and focus to "Stop and Think" about how you can be more efficient, and more effective, through the power of reduction, elimination, and simplification.

The Big Question: In what areas of your life can you apply the "Black Sock Decision-making" principle to achieve better results?

Your Big Insight:

Your Big Action:

CHAPTER 25

The Elephant in the Room

A few years ago we were hired by a New York-area financial services company to design and deliver a six-session leadership development program for a group of around thirty of their managers. This engagement was memorable for two key reasons:

First, when we met with the head of HR, we were told in advance that the CEO was not a big fan of training in general, and management training in particular. But he (the CEO) said that he was open to the possibility, so agreed to meet with us. Waiting for him to arrive, we had our whole sales pitch ready to go when he poked his head into the room, stood there in the doorway, and said:

"I have to get to this other meeting, and I only have two minutes. So I just wanted to ask you one question: I think management training is complete bullshit. Tell me why yours is any different."

Wow. To be honest I don't even remember what we said, but it must have been convincing because he turned to the head of HR and said, "OK, if you want to do it, it's up to you." And off he went without even a goodbye.

So one of the lessons I took from this episode was that no matter how prepared you are, you just never know what's going to be thrown at you. You need to over-prepare, be prepared to be unprepared for anything, and—even when put on the hot seat—respond to any tough questions with poise, presence, and confidence.

A few weeks later, after having partnered with our HR client to custom-design the program, we were all ready to get started. The participants were looking forward to it, and so were we.

But, just before we were about to start our very first session, we all received some news that threw a monkey wrench into our plans: the company was being acquired. This huge and shocking piece of news came out of nowhere—and would impact every manager sitting in front of us. Rumor was that some of jobs would be moving to the Midwest, a few positions would remain where they were, and the rest would be eliminated altogether. So no one in the room had any idea what the future held for them, and the decisions would not be made or announced for a while.

This made it very difficult for Steve (my brother/business partner) and me to open with our usual, enthusiastic, "How is everyone…welcome to our program!" We did our best to deliver the training as planned, but it was obvious that people's attitudes ranged from distracted and disengaged to resentful and angry. Not at us, but about the situation; still, it made our job extremely difficult and uncomfortable. And it became obvious that it would be impossible to continue to act as if everything was business-as-usual with this gigantic "elephant in the room."

So…what to do? What would *you* have done?

Well, rather than pretending that the elephant wasn't there, we decided to hit the metaphorical "pause button," put the agenda aside, and shine a big, gigantic spotlight on it.

We acknowledged that, yes, this happened…and that it was unfortunate. In his classic book, *Good to Great*, Jim Collins referred to this approach as "confronting the brutal truth." The acquisition was the new reality, and no pretending or ignoring it would make it go away. So we reframed the situation in this way:

"This training was originally intended to make you a better a manager and leader at *this* company. However, regardless of whether you are staying or going, by the end of these six sessions you will be a more efficient manager and a more effective leader *wherever* you will be working! In fact, if you end up being one of the people who will be leaving, this training will make you even more marketable as a manager and leader than you are today."

That simple acknowledgment, and reframing, of the situation changed everything. Not for everyone, but for most. And while it, understandably, took a while to get everyone to focus, once they did, they were able to reap the benefits of the experience.

At first it seemed as though the timing of the training couldn't have been worse. But the reality was that, for the people in the room who eventually bought into it, the timing couldn't have been more perfect.

In Review

The Big Lesson: When there is an "elephant in the room," instead of pretending it's not there, shine a light on it and figure out what to do about it, because it will, most likely, not disappear on its own.

The Big Question: What are some of your big "elephants in the room" that need to be addressed sooner rather than later?

Your Big Insight:

Your Big Action:

CHAPTER 26

Leadership Lessons from Donna the Deer Lady

Have you ever wondered why they always put Deer Crossing signs on the busiest, fastest, most trafficked, and most dangerous stretches of highways? Why are we telling the deer that it's OK for them to cross in the middle of an interstate, instead of moving these signs to areas with less traffic, thereby recommending to them that they cross there instead, where it would be much safer for everyone involved?

These excellent, thought-provoking questions were posed during a radio call-in show back in 2012 by a woman in Fargo, North Dakota— who soon became known as Donna the Deer Lady. On the surface these questions completely make sense. And her suggestion is a really great one.

That is, until you realize—as Donna eventually did…after the radio hosts explained it to her—that these signs are not intended for *the deer*… but for *the drivers*.

So, what this teaches us (among a number of other things) is that while signage can be an effective means of visual communication, it may not work in all situations.

However, it does raise a good point: Just as deer are going to pretty much cross wherever they want, regardless of where we place the signs, there are many situations—in work and in life—in which we try to change people's behavior instead of us adapting to *their* preferences, wants, and needs.

For example, one of the classic and most common human nature/user experience examples is this one: When you build a school campus, you can install walkways, post "Keep Off the Grass" signs, and try to enforce "the law"…only to get annoyed when people start cutting across the grass to get from Point A to Point B. *Or* you can wait to see how the foot traffic naturally flows, and then construct the paths to adapt to the routes that people prefer to take.

Similarly, in the workplace, you could lock yourselves in a room and come out a few hours or days later with a statement of the new, official company Mission, Vision, and Values…while declaring, "Effective next Monday, our new culture will be as follows…."

Or, you can take a look at your employees, figure out what kind of culture you currently have, and what kind of culture you—*and they*—want. And then involve them in the process of creating it. There's a classic business expression that you can either have "culture by design…or culture by default." But I think the most productive and effective company cultures I've seen are those that are, yes, designed…*not* in a vacuum, but taking into consideration the desires, the wants, the needs, and the personalities of the people within your organization.

For example, you could implement a strict, inflexible "No Working from Home" policy, which might then encourage someone to lie about being sick (thereby encouraging them to violate one of the company's core values regarding honesty and trust) when they may need to work from home one day—for example, to take care of a sick child.

Or, you can institute a more flexible and employee-friendly policy that states, "While our company guidelines are that we require employees to work here in the office, if there is an occasion in which you need to work from home, please speak with your manager and, if it's not an issue, we will be happy to do what we can to accommodate your request." Of course, not every type of job is suitable to this type of allowance, but if it is…then, why not?

Just as deer are going to cross wherever *they* want to, regardless of where *we* put the sign, human nature is human nature. And the world—and the workplace—is changing. We can try to force people into the old ways of doing things by stating, "This is the way it's always been done," but as managers and leaders, that may not get us what we want and need in the long run. For as long as Gallup's been doing their employee engagement surveys, the numbers have not budged. Only about one-third of the workforce is engaged while two-thirds remains disengaged and just showing up to do their job for the paycheck and then heading home. What is it going to take to someday flip this ratio to two-thirds engaged?

My feeling is that we need to create workplaces that are more employee-friendly, where there are fewer oppressive and draconian policies, along with better leadership—and leadership development—not only from the top down, but from the bottom up. I was eating lunch in a diner in midtown Manhattan recently, and I couldn't help overhearing—since I was eavesdropping—the conversations going on at the four booths right across from me.

At all four—and I'm not exaggerating—at *all four*—everyone was complaining about their bosses or (and I quote from one of the tables) "the idiots in senior management." So why is this? With all the resources available—management and leadership training, executive coaching and mentoring, books, articles, blog posts, videos—why is there still, in this day and age, so much bad management and such a lack of leadership going on?

I've been working for…well…without revealing my age…a long time. And one day I sat down with my résumé and listed every single manager I've ever worked for, rating them on a five-point scale from Great Boss to Horrible Boss. And the results revealed the following bell curve:

Great Bosses: 10%

Good Bosses: 20%
Average Bosses: 40%
Bad Bosses: 20%
Horrible Bosses: 10%

Exercise: How does *your* list of managers compare? If it's better than mine, my congratulations; if it's worse, my condolences.

The above breakdown translates into the fact that—from my own, personal, subjective experience and perspective—only 30 percent of my managers were good-to-great bosses, while 70 percent were not... and worse. Part of this is a result of my having worked for many years in the entertainment industry—a business notorious for the core values being: money, power, ego, and control. And these values influenced who ultimately was promoted into management roles, as well as the style in which they managed. And it was all about "management." "Leadership" wasn't even on the radar. This was one of the top reasons that I eventually left that business entirely...even though it was originally, as previously mentioned, my dream career.

Bad bosses are definitely not exclusive to the entertainment industry. Being a manager is a skill, like any other. And, as we all know, being a strong individual performer or producer in any given field or function does not in any way indicate that you would make a good manager/leader in that area, just as being a great athlete in a sport does not guarantee that you will make a great manager or coach in that sport. In fact, the opposite is very often true, and the list of examples in support of this contention is a mile long.

Getting back to how we can better engage employees by adapting *to* them, instead of trying to bend and twist human nature and present needs and expectations to fit company policies that may no longer work or make sense, to me one of the best lessons comes from Dan Pink and his terrific book *Drive: The Surprising Truth About What Motivates Us.*

In his book (and excellent accompanying TED talk), Pink hits the nail on the head when he identifies "Autonomy, Mastery, and Purpose" as the three key factors that encourage and enhance employee engagement and motivation. He reveals that people need to have fewer restrictions so that they have the freedom to do their job in the way that works best for them (Autonomy); people want and need to be continuously learning and growing so that they can develop into their best selves (Mastery); and they need to know and to feel that the work they do matters (Purpose).

This reminds me of that classic story about asking two bricklayers what they're doing. One replies flatly, "I'm laying bricks...what does it look like I'm doing?" The other replies enthusiastically, "I'm building a hospital, or a school, or a cathedral." Two workers doing the same job. One is simply task-focused. The other is passion- and purpose-driven. Which of those two will be more engaged, more productive, more proud, and around longer? Which of these two will have a more powerful and positive impact on others around them? Which one is more likely to be a leader?

Keeping this story in mind, what can you do to get the most and the best out of people...including yourself?

So, what does Donna the Deer Lady have to do with all this? Well, from a leadership perspective, we can put up all of the "road signs" we want and try, to no avail, to get the deer to change their ways...or we can see what the deer naturally want, need, and do, and then modify our world to set them—and us—up for success. Leaders who fail to realize this may just end up stuck and standing there like a deer in headlights.

In Review

The Big Lesson: While we can try to force individuals to change their ways, sometimes the best solution might be to consider changing ours.

The Big Question: What are some examples from your life that this story makes you think about?

Your Big Insight:

Your Big Action:

CHAPTER 27

The *Little Pink Spoon*: How to Give 'em a Taste and Leave 'em Wanting More

One of the great pleasures of life is popping into a Baskin-Robbins and trying out a few different flavors with those little pink spoons. Who doesn't love those little pink spoons! Between you and me, 90 percent of the time I just end up getting Rocky Road anyway, but it's always fun to taste a few other flavors before ordering my cone.

If you think about it, though, why is Baskin-Robbins so willing to give away their product for free? Of course, it's simple and obvious: they hope that by giving us a free taste, we'll end up buying a cup or a cone or a pint or a gallon. So they gladly give away millions of little pink spoonfuls in order to make many millions of dollars more in return. It's the same reason movies show trailers, cosmetics companies give away free samples, and car dealers offer test drives: people want to try before they buy.

So, with this concept in mind, how might you apply the Little Pink Spoon principle in your life? In other words, how can you give people a "free taste" of what you have to offer and leave them wanting more? Here are my three "show-ems":

1. Show and Tell

No, "show and tell" is not just for kindergarteners. For example, verbally telling an interviewer how your background qualifies you for the job is one thing; visually *showing* them is another. As research has shown, vision triumphs over all other senses. John Medina states in his fascinating book *Brain Rules* that when people *hear* information, three days later they'll remember 10 percent of what they heard; but if they *see* it, they'll remember 65 percent of what they saw.

So what can you do to become more memorable? As we've been discussing all along: Be more visual! Bring stuff along to the interview with you that you can show. Samples of work you've produced, reports or PowerPoint presentations you've created, photos of projects you've worked on, awards you've received, copies of articles or blog posts you've written. Even if the interviewer doesn't take the time to read or even look at what you brought, just holding it up and showing it to them makes it real…more real and tangible and credible than just telling them about it.

Additionally, just having these samples handy (even if you don't show them to anyone) is a great, kinesthetic way to remind yourself of the real-life stories you can use when asked, "Tell me about a time when…" or "Give me an example of…." Holding these items in your hands will naturally bring back a flood of memories and feelings from that time and place and enable you to deliver your stories with the details as fresh in your mind as if it just happened.

Note that even if you are not, technically, an "artist" (though as Seth Godin always says, no matter what it is that you do, "your work *is* your art!"), it doesn't mean that you can't put together a "portfolio" of your career accomplishments. As Dan Pink reminds us in the title of his book, *To Sell Is Human*, we are all "in sales," even if what we are selling is ourselves. And since so few people outside of the design world tend to think of creating a visual portfolio of their work, your proactivity and creativity in doing so will definitely help you stand out from the crowd.

2. Show Them That You Can Do It

While job interviews, sales pitches, and presentations can sometimes feel more like one-way interrogations than two-way conversations, there are things that you can strategically and proactively do to turn an awkward discussion into an engaging dialogue that better demonstrates your capabilities. Ultimately, what you want to do is to get the "interviewer" or "customer" to transform their perception of you from a generic "interviewee" or "vendor" to a "partner" by getting them to actually *envision* you working there.

One way of doing this might be to ask the person to provide you with an example of an actual, real-world business challenge that they are currently facing—one that you would be dealing with if they were to move forward with you. And then, by taking off your "interviewee" or "sales" hat and putting on your "employee" or "consultant" hat, you can transition the conversation from an interview into a solution-finding meeting…thereby demonstrating your capabilities. In many ways, asking insightful questions is just as valuable as providing thoughtful responses.

In fact, years ago when I was hired at Disney, I asked my new boss why he had hired me over the other candidates. His response was: "Because you asked the best questions." Again, you may not be able to solve all the person's problems right then and there, but you'll be perceived as someone who is ready, willing, and able to get to work.

3. Show Them That You Really Want It

It's one thing to show that you can *do* it; it's another thing to demonstrate that you really *want* it. I once interviewed for a job that, on paper, I was totally perfect for. After I didn't get the offer, I contacted the hiring manager to ask if he might be willing to offer me any feedback on why I wasn't chosen. His response: "In terms of qualifications, I thought you were great. But it didn't seem to me that you were that enthusiastic about this position. We need people who are passionate about working here." Lesson learned: people aren't mind readers, so make sure they know how much you want the job (assuming, of course, that you really do).

Secondly, here's a question to consider: Are you willing to work for free? Of course, you need to earn a living and don't want to undervalue yourself. But just as you might want to taste a new ice cream flavor before purchasing a whole cone, the prospective employer or customer might be on the fence about hiring you, or might not yet be ready to make a permanent offer. So one way to show what you can do and how much you really want it is to offer them a "free sample." It's not always possible, but what if you could start out as a volunteer or an intern, or in a temp-to-perm situation, or on a consulting or project or trial basis?

This might not be an option, but it never hurts to be creative and open to exploring out-of-the-box possibilities as a way of getting your foot in the door! And once you have one foot in the door, that second foot is now just one step away.

So, as you prepare for your next interview, client meeting, sales pitch, or presentation, think about how you might give people a "little pink spoon-sized taste" of who you are and what you have to offer. And, if all goes well, they'll want all of you…with a cherry on top.

In Review

The Big Lesson: Give people a sample of what you have to offer, and leave them wanting more.

The Big Question: How can you give people a sample of what you have to offer to get them to buy in to what you're selling?

Your Big Insight:

Your Big Action:

CHAPTER 28

Making the Bed:
How Overcoming Procrastination
Will Make You More Productive

Photo credit: Ethan Sherbondy

(D)isclaimer: Just for the record, I wrote a version of this chapter as a blog post two years before Admiral William H. McRaven's now-famous commencement address, and book, entitled *Make Your Bed*. Just sayin'.)

I really hate making the bed.

I know it's such a small and trivial thing, but it's one of my least favorite things in the world. Yet it must be done every single day. So, like other things that people don't like to do, I often put it off. I'll do everything else first and save it for last. Or avoid doing it altogether.

But what's the result of this behavior?

I'm thinking about it. I'm dwelling on it. I'm dreading it. It's hanging over my head and distracting me as I try to go about doing other things. And until it's done I can't move on with my day, because I know from experience that the only thing worse than having to *make* the bed is coming home at the end of the day to the sloppy mess of an unmade bed.

So, what's the solution?

Make the bed immediately! Right away. Now. As soon as possible. Start on it before your feet even hit the floor. Before you even have a chance to think about it! And before you know it, the bed is made. And then you can move on to the more important things without it hanging over your head all day long.

And what does this have to do with…well…anything?

Ask yourself this question:

What are the "unmade beds" in your life?

The things on your to-do list that are hanging over your head, the things that are always on your mind? The things you have to do, need to do, or dread doing? The things that you have been putting off for whatever reason? The things that should be done? The things that need to be done? The things that, if you did them, would impact other things on which that first thing depends? The things that would make a difference? The things that really matter? Unmade beds can take a lot of forms.

Why do we delay?

It could be because of busyness (or bus-i-ness), distraction, fear, lack of knowledge, lack of skill, lack of motivation, or any other number of other reasons that people procrastinate, including the universal excuse: lack of time.

But we all have the same twenty-four hours a day, the same 525,600 minutes that everyone else has. Why does it seem as though some people are able to do so much more with those limited and precious minutes than others? Is it self-discipline? Determination? Willpower? Good habits? The ability to focus? The ability to prioritize? The ability to avoid or eliminate distractions? The ability to overcome fear? The ability to just get things done? (And not just *any* things, but the right things!) There are a million possible reasons. But the bottom line is this:

No one wants to *hear* excuses…they only want to *see* results.

Look at your list of New Year's resolutions from two years ago, and then compare it to the resolutions you made at the start of this current year. Is there anything from the previous year's list that you haven't even gotten around to starting yet? My bet is that there is.

The key may be to narrow your list, prioritize by what's most important, and focus…really focus on what's important, rather than always being hijacked by what's urgent. Too often, we make too many commitments and spread ourselves too thin. We set way too many lofty, ambitious ("un-*smart*") goals. And what happens? We end up getting none of them done. As Henry David Thoreau famously wrote, "Simplify, simplify." (Although if he *really* wanted to "simplify," he could have just said it once.)

So instead of trying to do a million things, just pick one. One *big* one. And really, really focus…which reminds me of this acronym that I once saw on a refrigerator magnet (author unknown):

To "FOCUS" is to "Follow One Course Until Successful."

I'd been working on this book you now hold in your hands for at least ten years. By the time I finally sat down to write it, after getting a publishing contract, I had accumulated over two thousand (yes, more than two thousand!) printed and handwritten pages of notes and ideas.

But it was not until last year—when I actually got the contract and was given a deadline—that this long-time vision of becoming a published author finally became a reality.

In short, for so long, this book was the biggest unmade bed in my life.

But if it was, for so long, my single highest career-related priority, what took me so long to finally make it happen?

The reality is that—despite the best of intentions and the highest of hopes—sometimes "life" just gets in the way. And before you know it, another year has gone by. I know we've all been there. And sometimes things happen—not, necessarily, when they're "meant" to happen, but when we're ready to *make* them happen; that is, when the timing becomes right.

One classic definition of "luck" is "when preparation and opportunity meet" (you can visually picture that saying as a Venn diagram of interlocking circles if you'd like). And I believe that when you are prepared to be *ready*, you will make your own luck if you proactively seize the opportunity when it comes along.

Case in point: After my friend and former Liquidnet colleague Bill Maw published his book, *The Work-Life Equation,* he kindly introduced me to his agent, Ken Lizotte, of emerson consulting group. I spoke to Ken, thought he was great, and said that I would get back to him to continue the conversation when I was "ready."

Two years later, I made a new friend at the Leadership Forum at Silver Bay up in Lake George, New York: a guy named Rob Salafia, from Boston, who was in the process of writing his first book, entitled *Leading From Your Best Self.* After I mentioned that I, too, was working on a book, he kindly offered to introduce me to his agent. His agent's name? Yes… (drumroll please…) Ken Lizotte!

That was the universe telling me: "That's it. No more procrastinating. It's time to finally 'make that bed.'"

While it would have been nice to have gotten this book out into the world a few years sooner, I think that getting it released in the year 2020 has a certain symmetry to it as, for a book about being more "visual," the year "2020" just feels kind of…well…perfect.

In Review

The Big Lesson: While it sometimes feels like things will happen when they are "meant" to happen—that is, when the timing is right—determining when the timing is right is, in actuality, somewhat within our control. And if we proactively take steps that will increase our odds of success, we will be better equipped to seize the moment when a "door of opportunity" opens.

The Big Question: What is the biggest "unmade bed" *in* your life that would have the greatest positive impact *on* your life…if you could find a way to make it happen? And, once you determine what that thing is, what steps can you take to increase your odds of turning this "vision" into a reality?

Your Insight:

Your Action:

CHAPTER 29

Management vs. Leadership in Metaphors

"Management is about doing things right;
Leadership is about doing the right thing."
"Management is about efficiency;
Leadership is about effectiveness."

—PETER DRUCKER

I hear a lot of people using the words "management" and "leadership" interchangeably. However, although these words are interrelated, these terms describe two very different things. In some ways two sides of the same coin, to me the maxim that sums it up best is this: "Manage the Process…and Lead the People."

Out of all the many thoughtleaders out there who have explored this topic, to me, John Kotter of Harvard Business School does the best job of defining and describing the subtle-but-important distinctions. In brief,

Kotter talks about how these are not different *positions* or different *people*, but different *functions*, each with its own characteristic activities. When we're dealing with short-term, day-to-day tasks, execution, and getting things done, those are management-related activities. And when we're dealing with bigger-picture, longer-term strategic and people-related activities, that's the focus of leadership.

Of course, I'm simplifying here, but as Kotter describes it, the intended outcome of management-related activities is order, stability, and results…while the outcome of leadership-related activities is change. Hence, the paradox—and the inherent conflict—of simultaneously trying to produce stability and change at the same time.

I've found that one of the most thought-provoking and eye-opening ways to explore this crucial topic is by posing these four essential questions:

- What is "management"?
- What is "leadership"?
- What's the difference?
- Why does it matter?

I've found that one of the best and most interesting ways to wrap our minds around and explore the subtle-but-important distinctions between "management, managing, and managers" vs. "leadership, leading, and leaders" is through the use of examples, analogies, and metaphors. Please note, as you think about distinguishing between these two terms, that there are, indeed, some gray areas of overlap—it is not black and white. As you read through the list below, you'll see some examples are simple and straightforward, while others may require some thought—and, perhaps, even lead to some debate. But let's see what you think after seeing the table on the next page.

With these definitional differences in mind, and with the acknowledgment that "management" and "leadership" are not, necessarily, positions or titles, but *functions* with distinct areas of focus, the question then becomes, "Why does it matter"?

VisuaLeadership

MANAGEMENT	LEADERSHIP
Doing things right	Doing the right things
Efficiency	Effectiveness
Present	Future
Short-term	Long-term
Micro view	Macro view
Small Picture	Big Picture
What and How	Who and Why
Detail-focused	Idea-focused
Internally-focused	Externally-focused
Hard Skills	Soft Skills
Operational	Organizational
Tactics	Strategy
Execution	Planning
Pushing	Pulling
Delegation	Coaching
Things	People
Quantitative	Qualitative
Tangible	Intangible
Practical	Visionary
Risk-averse	Risk-taking
Rational	Emotional
Problem-solving	Opportunity-seeking
Analytical	Conceptual
IQ	EQ
More of a Science	More of an Art
Evolutionary	Revolutionary
Skeleton and Head	Head, Heart, Soul, and Guts
"Left brain"	"Right brain"
Fishing	Teaching how to fish
Microscope	Telescope
Playing Checkers	Playing Chess
Focused on the position	Focused on the person in the position
Getting the most out of your people	Getting the best out of your people
Order	Change

To me, the answer is not just a matter of semantics but of success, as understanding the difference will lead to you being better at both managing and leading. How? Primarily by helping to identify what type of problem we are trying to solve, what type of situation we are facing, and whether it requires either a management-based or leadership-based solution.

For example, "hiring and staffing" are management-related functions, while "people development" is a leadership-related activity. With that being the case, it helps to separate the two activities, and know which metaphorical "hat" we need to wear at any given time to successfully perform them. Similarly, "delegation" is a process-oriented management function, while "coaching" the person who we've delegated to is a leadership-related activity.

Another valuable point to keep in mind is that regardless of your title or position, and whether or not you have direct reports, you still need to "manage" and "lead" your own life! Take a look at the words on the list and think about how they apply to you both in leadership and in life. While you are dealing with your calendar, paying your bills, going to work, organizing your world, and getting things done, you are "managing" your life. When you are thinking big picture, long term, strategically, creatively, learning, and growing, you are "leading" your life.

If you think about it, you are the CEO of your life. You are also the COO, the CFO, the CIO/CTO, the CMO, the CHRO/CPO, and the CLO. How?

- As the CEO (Chief Executive Officer), you are responsible for determining your life's vision, mission, values, culture, and strategies…along with motivating and inspiring yourself to turn your vision into a reality.
- As the COO (Chief Operating Officer), you are responsible for all tasks associated with executing your strategic plan (scheduling, planning, project management).
- As the CFO (Chief Financial Officer), you are responsible for all the money-related decisions in your life (budgeting, accounting, financial planning, investments).

- As the CIO/CTO (Chief Information Officer/Chief Technology Officer), you are responsible for all the information and technology-related decisions in your life.
- As the CMO (Chief Marketing Officer), you are responsible for overseeing your personal brand, and marketing yourself to the outside world—both online and offline.
- As the CHRO/CPO (Chief Human Resources Officer/Chief People Officer), you are responsible for all traditional HR-related functions, including handling your compensation and benefits, wellness, compliance, career planning, and performance management and measurement.
- As the CLO (Chief Learning Officer), you are responsible for your own personal and professional development, including training, coaching, mentoring, and setting yourself up for future success.

So, let's revisit our original four questions: What is Management? What is Leadership? What's the Difference, and Why does it Matter? I hope that by having a better understanding of the distinctions between managing and leading, you'll be better enabled to both manage and lead others more efficiently and effectively, as well as manage and lead an even more successful life.

In Review

The Big Lesson: Understanding the important distinction between management and leadership will enable you to do both more successfully.

The Big Question: By thinking about yourself as the C-Suite of your own life, how will this help you to be more efficient and more effective—both now and in the future?

Your Insight:

Your Action:

CHAPTER 30

Mum's the Word

Polonius: What are you reading my lord?
Hamlet: Words, words, words.
Polonius: What's the matter?
Hamlet: Between who?

Do you ever feel like sometimes there are just too many words, too much talking…and not enough action? Don't get me wrong; I love words. (As mentioned previously, I was an English Literature major and have always been an avid reader.) But as the saying goes, when it comes to words, a picture is worth at least a thousand of them. So, sometimes the best thing we can do, as Shakespeare suggested in *Henry VI* (II.i.2), is "seal up your lips and give no words but mum."

With that objective in mind, it's useful to think about where, in your job—or elsewhere in your life—might you benefit from leveraging the power of nonverbals to help get your message across? For, as we know, in addition to our words and tone of voice, our messages are also communicated through our facial expressions, body language, and gestures.

I mentioned one example earlier, in my story about how I used a combination of drawing and hand gestures during my Shenzhen, China theme park installation project, which turned our daily exchanges into an ongoing game of Pictionary and Charades. And I've provided a number of other examples as well. But what others can you can think of? When have you used nonverbals to communicate, and where have you seen others using these techniques?

A few common examples of people using hand gestures or other nonverbals to communicate include the following (suggestion: *visualize* each of these in your mind as I list them):

- sign language interpreter
- mime
- traffic cop directing traffic
- baseball coach flashing signs, or a catcher signaling a pitch
- orchestra conductor with baton
- soldier saluting
- traders on the stock exchange floor
- movie reviewers giving a thumbs-up or thumbs-down sign
- driver using hand gesture to signal a turn
- an umpire or referee using hand signals (that is, "out!" or "touchdown!")
- a teacher using a "shhhh" sign to quiet her students
- scuba diver underwater giving hand signals
- dog trainer using hand signals
- shaking your head to indicate yes or no
- shrugging your shoulders to indicate "I don't know"
- giving someone a "high five"

Numerous studies have been conducted regarding how people inter-pret—and, often, misinterpret—our meaning based on a combination of our words, tone of voice, and body language—especially when they are incongruent or out of alignment. The most famous of these studies was conducted by Dr. Albert Mehrabian. This study is so well-known, and yet so often misinterpreted, misconstrued, and otherwise misused and abused, that I will not even venture to go into it here. But given this chapter's focus, I would be remiss in not mentioning it here. So I did. If you'd like to learn more about Dr. Mehrabian's study and what all the controversy is about, I recommend that you simply look it up by Googling his name and reading the whole story.

The bottom line is: When communicating verbally, it's important to be consciously aware of all three factors—our words, tone of voice, and body language—if we want our message to be clear and understood. For example, if I am picking you up at the airport and say, "*Hey…great to see you!!!*" with a big smile on my face and my arms outstretched in anticipation of an imminent hug, you will know exactly what I'm saying, feeling, and meaning.

Or, if I have been standing at the baggage carousel for the past two hours, impatiently waiting for you and your late-arriving plane, and I say, with an air of sarcasm, "Hey. Great to see you," with a scowl on my face and my arms crossed in annoyance as I gesture obnoxiously towards my wristwatch, you will get a very different message and feeling…despite my use of the very same five-word greeting.

So, whether you are communicating a message with voice alone, through body language, or some combination thereof, the key is to be consciously aware and intentional about how you can combine visual, auditory, and kinesthetic methods to get your intended message across. Especially when communicating in a situation wherein culture, language, accents, noise, or any other internal or external factors might get in the way of your message.

And just one final word of caution: When communicating using gestures and hand signals, be aware that they do not all translate universally into every language and culture. For example, use of the "thumbs up" sign is not recommended in many parts of the world. So you may want to do your homework before making any assumptions.

But one good thing, at least: a smile seems to mean the same thing in every language.

In Review

The Big Lesson: Be purposeful and intentional about using nonverbal visual cues, signals, and gestures in addition to, or in some cases, in place of speaking.

The Big Question: How can you more strategically leverage the power of nonverbals when communicating?

Your Insight:

Your Action:

CHAPTER 31

Play Ball! Twenty Thought-Provoking Coaching Questions from the Baseball Field to Help You Succeed at Work and in Life[1]

For those of us who love the game, baseball is more than just a sport. It's a way of life. A part of our language. A lens through which we view the world. And a training ground for innumerable valuable lessons in leadership and in life. So much so, in fact, that as the French historian Jacques Barzun famously put it, "Whoever wants to know the heart and mind of America had better learn baseball, the rules, and reality of the game…."

For example, when we ponder why it is that more Major League Baseball managers previously played catcher than any other position, the answer to why that is provides us with insights that we might apply to our own workplace. Can you guess the reasons why?

---

[1] Based on: Todd Cherches and Deborah Grayson Riegel, What Would Your Baseball Ask? Business Coaching Wisdom from the Ball Field.

The only position to be facing "outward" rather than "inward," catchers are uniquely positioned to see the entire playing field at once, giving them a singular, big-picture perspective; they are involved in every pitch of the game and need to always be strategically thinking a few steps ahead. Responsible for "calling the game," they often act as the on-field general, and they need to develop the technical skills, the communication skills, and the people skills to handle a pitching staff. In short, they need to be "on the ball" at all times.

All of this trains them to think and to act as a coach, a manager, and a leader. So, with this "catching analogy" in mind, you might ask yourself: What "catcher-type skills" do I need to develop to go from player to leader? What am I doing *today* that's grooming me for *tomorrow*?

Continuing the baseball analogy: In the office you might need to consider such common questions as: Who on my team could I ask to "pinch-hit" for me when I'm too busy or unable to perform; when might I need to "sacrifice" for the good of the team; or when do I, perhaps, need some "relief" in terms of bringing in someone else to help seal the deal and "close" out the win?

When we have two strikes against us—whether on the field, at work, or in life—we need to have the wisdom to know when to bear down, choke up, and just try to make contact rather than swinging for the fences. To be able to recognize the difference between when we're needed to be the hero vs. when what's really needed is for us to just find a way to get on base and let someone else drive us in. "Get 'em on; get 'em over; get 'em in." When you're part of a team, that's what it's all about…in baseball, in business, and in life.

All in all, our great American pastime has, over the course of our lives, "coached" many of us to think about and get better at a wide range of work- and life-related skill sets, including time management, communication, innovation, strategic thinking, management, leadership, teamwork, and so much more—all while enjoying some peanuts and Cracker Jacks (with the hope of finding a good prize inside!).

Both on the field and off, whether we realize it or not, baseball has become an inescapable part of our everyday language:

- "Let's **touch base** next week."
- "That marketing campaign was a **home run**."
- "The new guy is really **on the ball**."
- "I really **struck out** with that proposal."
- "Can you give me a **ballpark** estimate of what it's gonna cost?"
- "That last-minute client request came **out of left field**."
- "Your suggestion was a **grand slam!**"

So even if you don't play professional baseball for a living, or even if you are not a baseball fan, when challenged to "hit it out of the park" in your work or personal life, I encourage you to take a shot at answering the following questions by taking a baseball perspective.

But before you slide head-first into answering the questions below, take a moment to think about some of the key personal and/or professional goals you're currently trying to reach and consider how, by exploring these random questions through a baseball lens, you can increase your odds of circling the bases and scoring the winning run:

- The **First Base** Perspective: What is the first milestone you need to achieve?
- The **Second Base** Perspective: How will you get yourself into scoring position?
- The **Third Base** Perspective: You're almost there; what's next?
- The **Home Plate** Perspective: What is your most immediate goal?
- The **Batter's Box** Perspective: Where do you need to take a stand?
- The **Base Line** Perspective: How will you know if you're going in the right direction?
- The **Outfield Fence** Perspective: What would "knocking it out of the park" look like?
- The **Pitcher's Mound** Perspective: Where could you use a new point of view?
- The **Baseball Bat** Perspective: What tools do you need to get the job done?
- The **Pine Tar** Perspective: What are you going to do if you get in a sticky situation?

- The **Batting Gloves** Perspective: How are you going to get a grip on things?
- The **Baseball Cap** Perspective: How do you keep your head in the game?
- The **Spikes** Perspective: Where do you need more traction?
- The **Baseball Mitt** Perspective: What opportunities can you reach out and grab?
- The **Catcher's Mask** Perspective: What realities do you need to face?
- The **Hitting Coach** Perspective: What adjustments do you need to make?
- The **Third Base Coach** Perspective: What signs do you need to pay attention to?
- The **Pitching Coach** Perspective: Who can help you get ready?
- The **Umpire's** Perspective: What rules do you need to play by?
- The **Fans'** Perspective: Who's rooting for you to win?

While there are plenty more where these came from, these metaphorical questions from the baseball diamond, like a ballpark hot dog, can provide you with some valuable food for thought and help you to focus your attention on some of the key questions you may need to ask. And as you work towards building a championship team and a winning season, it may be valuable to keep posing and seeking to answer these questions as you continue in pursuit of your own Field of Dreams, wherever or whatever that may be.

Play ball!

In Review

The Big Lesson: When it comes to metaphors, few topics are more popular or more common in American English than those from the world of baseball.

The Big Question: What are some other baseball metaphors, not mentioned here, that you can think of? What metaphors from other sports—or other walks of life—are commonly used? And what perspectives and questions might they offer?

Your Big Insight:

Your Big Action:

CHAPTER 32

"Put Me in, Coach" vs. "Put Me in Coach"[2]

Have you ever really stopped to think about the word "coach"? When we're talking about business coaching, what does that word have to do with the other uses of the word "coach" in the English language—for example, flying coach on an airplane or riding in a stagecoach?

Well, as an executive coach—and as a former English major and amateur etymologist (that is, someone who studies the origins of words; not to be confused with an *entomologist*, which is someone who studies insects…which I most definitely do not!)—I decided to look it up one day out of curiosity and was "wowed" to discover that…

The English word *coach* is derived from…

the French word *coche*, which came from…

the German word *kotsche*, which originated from…

the Hungarian word *kocsi*, which is derived from…

---

[2] Source: Various, including The American Heritage® Dictionary of the English Language and Merriam-Webster Dictionary.

the Hungarian city of Kocs (pronounced "coach")…
where the very first horse-drawn carriages were invented in the 1400s!

As the horse-drawn carriage or wagon with spring-suspension, known as the "cart of Kocs" spread throughout Europe during the 1500s, all western languages borrowed the Hungarian town's name to describe this new type of vehicle known as a "coach." At that time, these horse-drawn carriages were the fastest means of transportation most people had ever seen. And by the 17th century, the "stage coach" came into being by making regular, established stops at various stations or "stages" along a given route. And with more and more of these coaches in existence, they eventually transitioned from a conveyance only of royalty and the rich to a more common form of public transport.

So, how did we get from riding in a coach to coaching someone in sports and in business?

Well, the modern usage of the word "coach" for an "instructor, tutor, or trainer" originated at Oxford University in 1848. The notion being that the tutor helped to "carry" or "transport" a student through their exam process—as if they were being metaphorically driven by carriage from one stage to another. Having first appeared as a noun ("a coach"), the word transitioned to a verb ("to coach") soon thereafter.

The use of the word "coach" as applied to an *athletic* trainer, and not just an *academic* one, first appeared in 1860s England in reference to boat racing. Soon it was being applied to "coaches" in all other types of sports, and then, in the mid-1900s, to the world of business. And even with that, the field of business coaching, as we now know it, is still relatively new.

So, in answer to our question: the word "coach" is a metaphor that has its evolutionary origins in the revolutionary vehicle that was invented six hundred years ago as a means of helping to "transport" a person from where they are to where they want or need to get to, more efficiently and effectively than they could on their own: by "coaching" them.

A little bit of (somewhat related) bonus trivia:

As mentioned, I am somewhat obsessed with the origins of all things, but especially the origins of words. I loved discovering the origin of the word "coach," and I hope you did too…as it's a fun and eye-opening trivia question to ask people.

To me, however, the ultimate trivia question is: Where does the word "*trivia*" come from?

The answer: If you break it down, the word, "trivia" is a combination of "tri"—which, of course, comes from the Latin for "three" (as in "triple," "tripod," or "triathlon") and "via"—which is Latin for "way" or "road." So, in ancient Rome, a "trivium" was, literally, "a place where three roads meet." And, what happened at those places—that is, "*trivia*," the plural form—where three roads met? Well, those crossroads ended up being public gathering places where people, coming and going, would sit around exchanging information…some of which was commonplace, unimportant or, yes, "trivial."

So, as you travel forth on your leadership and learning journey, whether flying coach or working with one, remember that ultimately, it's all about successfully getting yourself to your desired destination.

In Review

The Big Lesson: (Among many lessons in this chapter…) Studying word origins—including metaphorical ones—can help us to gain a greater understanding of concepts of all kinds.

The Big Question: Knowing that "coaching" has origins in transportation, how might working with a coach—or, even, coaching yourself—help you to get from Point A to Point B?

Your Big Insight:

Your Big Action:

CHAPTER 33

Remote Control Your Life

Have you ever attended a meeting where someone was droning on and on…and you just wished that you could take a remote control and put them on "mute"? Or, even better, change the channel to another, more interesting discussion?

If you think about that familiar mantra—*accept the things you can't change, have the courage to change the things you can, and possess the wisdom to know the difference*—I've found that one of the best ways to take greater control of your life is to imagine that you have a magical "Life Remote" available to you. Because you *do*. While you can't control everything, here are some of the remote control buttons that you *can* push at various times throughout your day, when needed:

When you wake up in the morning, you need to hit the Power button to start your day. While this will vary for each person, think about what it takes for you to "power up." It could be jumping in a hot shower, having that first cup of coffee or a hearty breakfast, meditating or exercising, reading the news, or listening to music. Whatever it is for you, think about what's going to "empower" and energize you to start your day on full strength.

OK…you get to work and now you're ready to hit the Play button. But you also need to "check your local listings" (that is, your calendar schedule) to make sure you're tuned to the right "channel" and watching the right show at the right time. If you've ever missed a meeting or shown up at the wrong place at the wrong time, you know what I'm talking about.

Let's say you are in that first meeting of the day, and one of your colleagues is delivering a presentation on the latest departmental figures. There are times you may want to use your remote and hit any of the following buttons…

- *Pause:* "That's a great point! Can you hold that thought for a second…?"
- *Record:* "I'd like to write that down so I don't forget it!"
- *Rewind:* "Can you go back a minute and repeat what you just said?"
- *Volume:* "Can you do me a favor and speak just a little bit louder, as we can't hear you in the back of the room?"
- *Fast Forward:* "I see from the clock that we only have about five minutes left. Can we jump ahead to the end so that we can discuss next steps and 'who's doing what by when'?" (As a side tip: ending every meeting (or conversation) by determining and agreeing on "Who's doing What by When" is an effective way to establish accountability and improve productivity. More on that later.)
- *Stop:* "OK, I see that our time is up; see you all next time."

These are just a few examples—using a meeting as a sample scenario—of how you can use the TV remote control as a metaphor for taking greater control of your life. But what are some others?

Do you need to change your Volume by speaking up and speaking out more…or, perhaps, less, by knowing when to stay "mute" and just listen?

Do you feel you are being heard and understood, or might you benefit from hitting the Closed Captions button, or translating your message into another language?

Do you occasionally need to hit the Guide button and ask for help?

Or the Search button to find whatever it is you're looking for?

Everyone's busy, but do you make the time and take the time for your Favorites?

And do you make time to hit the Info button to learn more?

Is it time to change the Channel to a new career?

If you feel like you are always On Demand, do you still find ways to occasionally Power off so as to avoid burnout, or to hit the Pause button, allowing yourself time to relax and to reflect?

Do you need to find a way to Recharge yourself by changing your batteries?

Again, while you can't control everything—especially other people—in a lot of ways we have a lot more power than we think. So it may help to remind yourself on a daily basis that you hold that power right in the palm of your hand.

In Review

The Big Lesson: Act as if you have a magical remote control that gives you the power to take greater control of your life...and know that you have the power to press those buttons accordingly.

The Big Question: What are some areas of your life in which you would like to take greater control...and what buttons can you push to make that happen?

Your Insight:

Your Action:

CHAPTER 34

The Viz-o-Meter

W hen I worked in the TV industry, we used to test TV pilots (that is, the first episode of an aspiring television series) on focus group audiences to see what they thought of them. This assessment process would be one of the factors used in determining whether a show would make it onto the air. So the testing company would recruit random samples of prospective audience members, composed of different demographic groups, to rate the show and provide their feedback.

One of the most common ways of doing this was by using an electronic measuring system in which, while watching the episode, each audience member would hold in their hands a dial similar to the one pictured above. As the show went on, if the focus group member *liked* what they were watching—that is, they were enjoying the situation, or the character, or found the scene entertaining—they would turn the knob on their dial clockwise, to the right, into the Green Zone, which indicated a positive score ranging from 5 to 10, depending on how far they turned it. And if or when they were *not* enjoying what they were watching, they would turn their dial counterclockwise, to the left, into the Red Zone, from 5 down to 1.

So, what does this have to do with…well…anything?

Well, if you think about it, we do this all the time—not just when in a focus group, but in everyday life!

We are all carrying around these metaphorical, visual measuring instruments in our heads—for short, let's just call it a "Viz-o-meter." When we are about to encounter any situation, or person, we start with an unconscious assumption, expectation, or bias, with our dial starting out either in the Red (1-5) Zone, the Green (6-10) Zone, or the Neutral Zone (5.5).

For example: "This meeting is going to be a really boring waste of my time" [2]…or, "I can't wait to watch this speaker's presentation!" [9].

Or, let's say we're interviewing a job candidate, or you're meeting someone for the first time (for example, on a date). Based on what you know going in (for example, from their résumé, or from their LinkedIn or Facebook profile), you already have certain preconceptions. Though we may want to think that we don't—that we are going in neutral and unbiased with no expectations of any kind—as humans, that is very rarely, if ever, the case. Of course, we don't want to be biased, but unconscious or not, none of us starts with a blank slate.

But, regardless of our starting point on the Viz-o-meter, as soon as we meet the person, it is human nature to mentally turn our dial clockwise, in a positive direction to the right, somewhere into the Green Zone—or counterclockwise into the Red Zone. Again, this is just human nature based on our past experiences and expectations. However—and this is one of the most valuable benefits of this metaphorical model—being consciously aware that we are doing this will help us overcome our biases from a diversity, inclusion, and belonging (DIB) perspective. This will help us to realize that—whatever the context—just because a person doesn't "look" like we envisioned doesn't mean that they cannot do the job.

As the conversation goes on, with each positive thing the person says, and with every positive interaction, we mentally turn our Viz-o-meter to the right, while thinking to ourselves, "Wow, this person is really smart," or "That is an excellent point," or "That was really funny," or "I really like this person!"

Similarly, with each thing a person says or does that reflects nega-tively on them—from our entirely subjective perspective—we may turn our mental dial to the left, thinking: "That was not a great response to that interview question. I'm not sure if this person has the experience we need for this role"; or in a dating situation, "Based on that comment, I'm not sure if this person is the one for me."

The value and the power of the Viz-o-meter is that we are already doing this anyway, with every interaction and every experience. So, having this visual metaphor in your head will now make you consciously aware of the fact that you are constantly analyzing, assessing, and (in some way) rating each and every person, thing, situation, interaction, and experience you encounter. It's like when you attend a workshop and they ask you after-wards to fill out a feedback evaluation questionnaire to rate the workshop and provide your comments—only this is an ongoing, never-ending "Life Evaluation" model that we are all always carrying around in our heads.

Think about it: As you were reading this chapter—in fact, as you've been reading this entire book—you've been evaluating it in your mind. You've been mentally turning your Viz-o-meter dial to the right towards the Green Zone during the parts you liked ("This is a really interesting and useful model," or "I like this story—I'll give it a 9!") and, possibly (though I hope not too often!), you may have turned your dial to the left into the Red Zone while reading something that may not have resonated with you. And that's OK! Not everything is for everyone, and nothing is going to be a "10" for all every time.

For example, I once delivered a presentation skills workshop where one of the post-course evaluation questions was, "Was the pace of this workshop too fast, too slow, or just right?" With twelve participants in the workshop, what do you think happened? Four people said "too fast," four said "too slow," and four said "just right." So, what do you do with that? All you can do is realize that everything is subjective, and people experience things through their own "lens" based on who they are and what they want and need at any particular time.

But, again, the key takeaway here is that every single one of us is constantly mentally evaluating everything—even if you're just standing at a fruit stand rating each bunch of bananas ("These are too ripe" [2], "these are not ripe enough yet" [5], "these are perfect!" [10]).

With this visual mental model and metaphor of the Viz-o-meter in mind, you can now be more consciously aware of when you are doing... so as to make better, more informed, more conscious, and less biased decisions.

And knowing, now, that at the same time everyone is also evaluating us on *their* Viz-o-meter, we can think to ourselves, in any situation: "What can I do to get this person to dial it up to 11?"

In Review

The Big Lesson: In leadership and in life, we are constantly evaluating everyone and everything. By using the Viz-o-meter as a mental model, you can be more consciously aware of when you are doing it and make the necessary adjustments to make better and more informed, and less biased, evaluations.

The Big Question: How can you use the Viz-o-meter concept to be more effective?

Your Insight:

Your Action:

CHAPTER 35

Walking the Leadership Tightrope

A few years ago, while watching aerialist Nik Wallenda's teeth-clench-ing, death-defying, and awe-inspiring tightrope walk across the Grand Canyon, I found myself reminded of two other, similar types of daredevil activities to which we can all better relate: living and leading.

While most of us are not literally going to plummet to our death if we make a mistake in our daily lives, as a leader—which includes every one of us, regardless of our official title—it can often feel as if we are all alone in the world, trying to get ourselves and/or our people from point A to point B, hundreds of feet in the air without a safety net.

So what can a Flying Wallenda teach us about the solo wire-walking act that each of us must do each and every day? I'll get to that in a minute.

But first, some of you may be asking, "What the heck is a 'Flying Wallenda'?" For those who may not know, Nik Wallenda, a seventh-gen-eration aerialist from the acrobatic Flying Wallenda family, recently walked a high wire across the Grand Canyon. Yes, you read that right: the Grand Canyon, 1,500 feet above the Little Colorado River Gorge. That's the height of the Empire State Building. In a gusting 35-mph wind. On a two-inch-wide steel cable. With the world watching. And he did it in just under twenty-three minutes. Most of us couldn't walk a perfectly straight line on a New York City sidewalk in perfect weather for twenty-three consecutive minutes. Regardless, while pondering Wallenda's incredible feat, I was struck with these ten lessons that can apply to all of us...in leadership and in life:

1. **You're Not Alone Up There.** Sometimes, when we're out there in the world doing our thing, it can feel as if we're up there all alone on a high wire (and, for some, with the added burden of carrying a bunch of additional people on our shoulders!). But if you surround yourself with a team of people who care about and support one another, and are cheering each other on, it makes the journey much more manageable, and so much more fun. Whether it's creating your own personal Board of Advisors, or just having a trusted mentor, coach, friend, or significant other to talk to, it's important to build a support network that you can rely on.

2. **Know Who to Listen to—and When.** During the walk, Wallenda was hooked up by microphone to his father, who whispered in his ear the entire time, guiding and encouraging him. While that was helpful at certain points, there were also times that he needed to tell his father to, basically, "shut up," so he could focus on what he was doing without distraction. Having a mentor, coach, or advisor is invaluable, but there are certain times when we need to quiet those external voices so that we can concentrate, focus, think, decide, and act on our own. While it's good to seek the input of trusted others, ultimately, decisions need to be made between you and your own inner voice.

3. **There are People Rooting for You...to Fall.** The brutal reality is that there were people who—for various reasons—were waiting, and hoping, and rooting for Wallenda to fail...and to fall. The same goes for each of us who set foot on the tightrope of life. It's

important to know who you can trust, and who you can't. Surround yourself with people who have your back, and separate yourself as much as possible from those who want to hold you back or drag you down.

4. **Don't Look Down, and Don't Look Back.** Once you've begun your journey, move full steam ahead without looking back. Second-guessing yourself only serves to undermine your own confidence and others' confidence in you. And while it's probably a breathtaking view, looking down will only make you dizzy and distract you from reaching your goal. Avoid temptations, distractions, and self-doubt, and keep your head held high as you venture forward with conviction and confidence.

5. **Stop and Catch Your Breath Occasionally.** A few times along the way, Wallenda stopped for a moment. Yes, he just stopped and squatted down. On the wire. To catch his breath. To take it all in. To regroup, recalibrate, and refocus. There are times, even when a deadline is pressing, that we need to hit the pause button, if only for a moment, to take a deep breath and re-center before moving on to the next step.

6. **Keep Your Eyes on the Prize.** Wallenda had one—and only one—goal: to get from one side of the Canyon to the other. That overwhelming sense of purpose and unwavering focus led to his success. Too often, we try to please everyone and do too many things at once. When we do, we end up doing none of them successfully.

7. **Confidence is Key.** Harvard professor Rosabeth Moss Kanter once defined "confidence" simply as "the expectation of a positive outcome." Having faith in yourself, backed up by positive self-talk, will help you to battle the negative voices of doubt and fear (what Seth Godin always refers to as our "lizard brain"). Positivity, hope, and optimism are crucial ingredients to your success. During his walk, Wallenda was talking to himself (as well as to certain

"unseen others") aloud and with enthusiasm, from start to finish. As Henry Ford said, "If you think you can or you think you can't, you're right."

8. **Don't *Start* with the Grand Canyon.** As a seventh-generation aerialist, Wallenda had been working towards this monumental feat practically since birth. From walking on a rope just a few inches above his childhood backyard to walking a tightrope across Niagara Falls the year before, Wallenda's conquest of the Grand Canyon was many years in the making. It's important to dream big, but it's equally important to recognize our limitations, set challenging-but-doable goals, and have realistic expectations. Then, once accomplished, we can incrementally build on those goals and take our game to the next level.

9. **Practice, Practice, Practice.** Cervantes said, "To be prepared is half the victory." Though we like to say that someone is "a natural" or "an overnight success," it is more likely that we failed to notice the behind-the-scenes years of blood, sweat, and tears that led them to that point. Being willing to take intelligent risks and having the resiliency to bounce back from the inevitable setbacks along our journey is what separates those who make it up to and across the canyon from those who don't.

10. **Don't Forget to Reflect, Celebrate, and Share the Success.** When Wallenda finally made it to the other side, after the hugs and kisses and pats on the back, he took a moment—on his own—to walk back over to the lip of the Canyon and reflect in silence on what he had just accomplished. When questioned about the rumors about his next endeavor—a possible high-wire walk between the Empire State Building and the Chrysler Building—Wallenda responded that he just wanted to rejoice in the moment before thinking about the future. Too often, we move on to the next challenge before making the time and taking the time to reflect on and to celebrate our accomplishment…along with recognizing the contributions of the people who helped us along the way.

So as you ponder the incredibleness of Nik Wallenda's amazing feat, I hope the insights gained and the lessons learned will inspire you to new heights.

In Review

The Big Lesson: Lessons in leadership and in life are hiding in plain sight all around us—if we just pause to notice them. And though it may not be televised live for millions of people around the world to see, we are each, every single day, in some way, walking a tightrope across the Grand Canyon.

The Big Question: In what ways is your life and/or your job, at certain times, like walking a tightrope? And how might any of these ten tips help you to make your way successfully across from one end to the other?

Your Big Insight:

Your Big Action:

CHAPTER 36

Yellow Ball Leadership

When I was a little kid I would impress guests with how smart my dog, Coco[3], was.

I would hold up three rubber balls, all the same size: a red one, a blue one, and a yellow one, and then I would throw them across the room—or all the way across the backyard—telling her which one to bring back.

I would say, "Alright, Coco—go bring back theeee…um….*yellow* ball!"

And she would. Everyone was amazed by her brilliance and her obedience. As well as incredibly impressed with how well I trained her.

But the truth was: Whenever I threw those three balls, she *always* brought back the yellow ball. 100 percent of the time. Why? Apparently, just because she wanted to.

The first-ever management consultant, Frederick W. Taylor, once wrote (in 1911), "People do best what they like best to do." And, apparently, that applies to dogs as well.

So, whatever that is for you…go out there and get that yellow ball!

---

[3] Name changed to preserve her anonymity.

In Review

The Big Lesson: If, as a manager, you take the time and make the effort to find out what people are good at, what they like and want to do, and what motivates and inspires them, it will dramatically increase the likelihood that they will succeed.

The Big Question: What is *your* "Yellow Ball"? What's something that you are good at and enjoy doing that, perhaps, others around you may not know about? And, if you are a manager, do you know what each of your employees' "Yellow Ball" is?

Your Big Insight:

Your Big Action:

CHAPTER 37

Your Leadership Weather Report

What's your "leadership weather report" today?
When you walk into a room…

Are you a ***cloud*** of doom, and gloom, casting a dark shadow on everyone, and threatening lightning and thunderstorms…?

Or…are you a burst of ***sunshine*** that lights up the room with warmth and good humor, filling it with a spirit of hope and optimism, positive energy and passion and making people feel good to be around you and glad that you've arrived…?

Are you the kind of manager who makes people feel bullied and threatened and intimidated and scared? Or the kind who encourages and empowers your people, boosting their morale and their confidence, and always seeking ways to help them to maximize their performance, their productivity, and their potential?

Are you the kind of co-worker, teammate, or classmate who's always "looking out for Number One"…or the kind who looks out for others and works to make them better?

Unlike the weather *outside*, the climate you create *inside* is entirely up to you.

In Review

The Big Lesson: Your mood, attitude, and energy are contagious, so it's important to be consciously aware of how your disposition— especially from a leadership perspective—can impact others…in both positive and negative ways.

The Big Question: While it's not realistically possible to be in a great mood *all* of the time, what are some things you can do to inspire others through the power of positivity?

Your Big Insight:

Your Big Action:

PART FOUR

Leading with...Visual Stories.
Why Stories?

I was once delivering a workshop on leadership storytelling for a group of CEOs when one of the participants commented, "I hate storytelling—I'm a terrible storyteller." When I asked him what made him say that, he went on to tell this terrific story about why he thought he was so bad at it.

Looking around the room at the other CEOs who had all started to smile in recognition of what had unfolded before our eyes, I remarked, "Do I have to say it, or would someone else like to?"

Basically, it turned out that this guy was, indeed, a terrific storyteller; he just needed to be reassured of this fact in order to feel confident in his ability to do so.

By the way, the above is an example of a complete story in four simple sentences.

We are all natural storytellers. We tell stories all the time. When we tell someone about our day...that's a story. When you say, "You won't believe what happened to me on the way over here!"...that's a story. When you try to teach your kid something by starting out with, "When I was your age"...that's a story.

Pretty much everything that has ever happened to you in your life is, if you think about it, the basis of a story. And from each of our stories we share a piece of who we are, what we think and feel, and what's important to us. And through the power of story, we can teach, we can change people's point of view, and we can even change the world.

Unlike just delivering facts or data, stories are human, stories are emotional, stories are compelling, stories are engaging, stories are universal, stories are relatable, stories are entertaining, and stories are memorable.

What makes something a story? Aristotle said that it's a narrative that contains "a beginning, a middle, and an end." And what are the components of a story? Basically, a story tends to cover the "5 W's and 1 H": Who, What, When, Where, Why, and How.

In brief, to construct a story, you need to think about Who the characters are (the cast); What happens to them (the plot); When and Where the story takes place (the setting); Why it happened (the message); and How it ends (the conclusion). That's the formula for any story, from a four-sentence anecdote like the one above...to an Academy Award-winning screenplay.

Another way to think about it is that a story has: (1) a Set-up ("Here's the situation"); (2) a Conflict ("Then, what happened was..."); and (3) a Resolution ("Here's how it ended...").

The key, from a leadership perspective, is to use stories purposefully and strategically: to convey information, to connect with people, to influence, and to inspire. One way to think about it is in terms of these "Three E's": Educate (What do you want people to learn and to know?); Engage (How are you going to capture and hold their attention?); and Excite (How are you going to inspire them to act?).

And what do we mean by "visual" storytelling. Basically, it's about using language "to paint a picture with words" (which, by the way is, of course, a metaphor). You can do so using visual images (that is, slides, video, demonstration), or through words alone. Either way, you are taking someone on a journey and sharing an experience in such a way that they are able to "see" it in their mind's eye.

There are many different types of stories, used for different purposes. One type of story is the "Cautionary Tale" whose message is, "Don't let this happen to you." Another related type of story is the "Personal

Failure Story," in which you reveal a mistake that *you* made so that others may benefit. For example, "Let me tell you about the worst mistake I ever made." In order to do so, a leader, must be willing to be authentic and vulnerable.

Modeling this type of storytelling helps to create a climate of "psychological safety" (a term you should definitely look up), in which others will then be willing to share *their* stories, leading to a culture of openness, collaboration, and trust.

One of the most popular types of stories is the "Origin Story." It is human nature to be curious, and to want to know how and where and why things started. That's why origin stories of comic book heroes—from Superman, Batman, and Wonder Woman to Spider-Man, Iron Man, and Black Panther—tend to end up being huge commercial blockbusters when they hit the screen.

So, how can you use this concept from a leadership perspective? You might, for example, share a story about your career journey, which could be anything from how you got started to how you ended up in your current position. Or you might share a story about the history of your company. If you think about it...

Disney started with a mouse.
GE started with a light bulb.
eBay started with a PEZ dispenser.
Amazon started as an online bookstore.
Netflix started with those little red mailing envelopes.
And so on!

So, tell us...what's *your* story?

Once of the best story frameworks I know of is called the PARLA method. This method can be utilized in a whole variety of situations, from presentations to job interviews to coaching conversations. PARLA stands for:

Problem/Situation: Here's what happened (the backstory).
Action: Here's what I, or someone else did.

Result: Here's the outcome (positive, negative, or mixed).
Learned: Here's what I learned (and what you can learn from it too).
Apply: And here's how I use what I learned (and how you can too).

One other skill related to story-*telling* that leaders would benefit from developing and practicing, by the way, is "story-*listening*." As discussed previously, the best leaders tend to be great listeners, and creating a psychologically safe environment in which others are encouraged and empowered to share their stories so that all may learn from them will serve to benefit everyone. As Bill Nye the Science guy once said, "Everyone you will ever meet knows something you don't."

Lastly, one of my top suggestions to help you build up a repository of stories for future use is to start journaling! Whether you do so electronically, or by hand in a notebook (which I strongly recommend, as the act of writing by hand is more kinesthetic), jotting down your stories provides a terrific exercise in capturing your thoughts, ideas, and feelings for future access and retrieval. Moreover, the act of writing them down will encode them in your brain, and having them in a format that you can thumb through and reflect back on will enable to you access them in the future when you are in search of the details of that one amazing story that will make your presentation.

Self-disclosure: I started keeping a journal, just by chance, on the first day of my freshman year of college. And I have not missed a day since. Yes, I've written in my journal every single day for (I hate to admit it) the past thirty-nine years. And I'm so glad I did, as doing so allowed me to reconstruct, in detail, many of the stories contained within this book.

With that, I am excited to share with you the following stories as an illustration of the power of visual storytelling. In each one, I tried to paint a picture with words to capture the time and place, the characters involved, and the leadership lessons learned.

In so doing, my hope is that from *my* stories, *you* will not only take away a variety of valuable insights but will be inspired to formulate your own stories so as to share the wisdom of your experience with others. For, when you think about the Who, What, When, Where, Why, and How model, *you* are the *"Who"* in the story of your life. And, looking to you for leadership, we want—and we need—to hear your stories.

CHAPTER 38

Ego-free Leadership

While I love a great quote from a top business leader, some of the most powerful lessons in leadership and in life can come from anywhere—including a refrigerator magnet. In fact, that would probably make a great book: *Leadership Lessons from Refrigerator Magnets*. Maybe I'll start working on that as soon as I finish this one. Or not.

Anyway, one of the magnets on the refrigerator in my kitchen quotes Robert Brault: "Enjoy the little things, for one day you may look back and realize they were the big things." Similarly, Dale Carnegie once wrote something to the effect of (I'm paraphrasing here): "Some of the things we say and do, *we* may forget a few minutes later; however, the people we say and do them to may remember for the rest of their lives." This applies both to the good things…and the bad.

With all of the many bad bosses I've had and mentioned, it's a pleasure to be able to share a few leadership lessons from a couple of the best. With that, I'd like to share three stories from my amazing and memorable time working as the head of leadership development for the financial services company Liquidnet—the last company I worked for before going off on my own to form my own company.

Story One: "I Need a Snack"

One of the things I loved most about working at Liquidnet was the amazing culture. They flattened the hierarchy by eliminating job titles, had an open-door policy where anyone could talk to anyone at any time—including being able to knock on the glass door of the incredible CEO and founder, Seth Merrin.

I often refer to Liquidnet as "a Wall Street company with a Dot-com culture," where fun was one of the core values, no neck ties were allowed, there was unlimited food and drink, and an un-written "No Asshole" policy. And they set their people up for success by investing in professional development like no other company I had ever worked for, through their creation of the company's Learning & Development department known as LNU (Liquidnet University), headed by my boss, Jeff Schwartzman. One of the primary goals of LNU was to help the company develop people to be "the best in the world" at what they did, while making the company a place that no one would ever want to leave.

As head of the Liquidnet Leadership Institute, my first and biggest project was to create, from scratch, a six-session (three hours each) leadership program that we would put all our people managers through, globally. With seventy-five people managers in the New York City office, we would divide them into three groups of twenty-five, and I would deliver the program three times a week (on Tuesday, Wednesday, and Thursday afternoons) for six weeks to get everyone graduated.

Needless to say, it was extremely intense. But one of the things I loved about it was that, true to Liquidnet's lack of hierarchy, everyone in the company—including those in C-suite-level positions—went through the training together. Unlike other companies that might divide the managers by level, we didn't…which allowed the most junior to the most senior managers to mix and mingle and learn from one another. It sent the message: No one here—even if you have an MBA (which a few did)—is an expert in management and leadership…so we are all going to go through this experience and learn together.

Remember how I said that sometimes the "little things" end up being "big things"? Well, here's one of the extremely tiny, almost unnoticeable, things that Seth did that continues to impact me all these years later.

During one of the leadership sessions, I was introducing a table group discussion exercise when Seth blurted out, "I need a snack."

Still new to Liquidnet, from my experience working in the TV industry if one of the executives ever declared, "I need a snack," and the most junior employee in the room didn't leap up and run out of the room to get them one, that employee would have been unceremoniously berated, humiliated, and fired right in front of everyone. I am not kidding; I'd seen it happen…multiple times.

But not only did Seth get up on his own to run to the company kitchen, but he returned moments later with an entire basket of snacks—chips, cookies, nuts—and went table-to-table, person-to-person, around the training room offering them to everyone! Again, this may seem like nothing, but from the world where I had come from, this was unheard of for someone in a CEO position to do. To me it was an act of kindness and ego-free leadership that was few and far between in my previous career. While I don't love the term (for a variety of reasons), Seth's action was a great example of what is often referred to as "Servant Leadership." It was a real-life demonstration of a company CEO modeling the organization's core values.

Story Two: "Welcome to the Batcave"

Having run out of office space, my LNU colleague Brian Tally and I, along with our two interns, were all squeezed into a small, doorless alcove area that we lovingly referred to as "the Batcave." One day, I happened to be working alone in the Batcave when I glanced up and saw Seth quickly walking by, storming down the hall after a meeting, in a huff and with a scowl on his face.

We briefly made eye contact as he sped by, but as I put my head back down to continue working, I was shocked to find that Seth had turned back, entered the Batcave (!), plopped down in one of the empty chairs, and said to me, "My day's been shit. I need to hear something good that'll cheer me up. How's yours going? What are *you* working on?" Again, as mentioned previously, where I came from, the CEO of your company did not, typically, stop by your office for a chat and ask how your day was!

But I was working on creating a new executive coaching program for the company's managers at the time, so I told him all about it. He asked me a few great questions about it—demonstrating his interest, his caring, and his appreciation—and then, after our five-minute chat, he got up and said, "This all sounds great, thanks for filling me in—keep up the great work!"…and then, like Batman himself, he disappeared down the hall and into the night.

There's a management practice from the 1970s known as "MBWA"— which stands for "Management by Walking Around." This was more like "LBWA," or "Leading by Walking Around" as, in this situation, Seth was not managing but exhibiting leadership—simply by connecting, listening, and expressing genuine and sincere appreciation for one of his people. Again, this was just a simple act of being human, and making a person-to-person connection; but, based on my many years of experience, it was a rare occurrence and one that I still remember as if it happened yesterday, when it was more than ten years ago.

As Maya Angelou famously said, "I've learned that people will forget what you said, people will forget what you did, but people will never forget how you made them feel." And on that one ordinary, un-special day, I was made to feel extremely special by a simple act of leadership.

By the way, for more leadership lessons from Seth Merrin, I highly recommend his recently-published book, *The Power of Positive Destruction: How to Turn a Business Idea Into a Revolution.*

Story Three: "Step into My Office"

While they were renovating our floor at the Liquidnet corporate head-quarters for a few months, our four-person Liquidnet University (LNU) team—my boss, Jeff Schwartzman; Angelo Valenti, a senior-level external consultant; my colleague, Brian Tally; and me—was temporarily relocated to an office building across town a few blocks away. The problem was that there were four of us...but only two offices and two tiny cubicles. Of course, I assumed that Jeff and Angelo, being the most senior, would take the nice big offices with cushy, leather executive chairs, big wooden desks, tons of cabinet space, and an incredibly beautiful view of the Empire State Building.

But when we arrived, Jeff surprised us by giving me and Brian the big offices, while he and Angelo took the little cubicles. Wow. Again, based on all my prior career experiences, I never would have expected such a kind act of selfless, ego-free generosity. Having come from a world that was all about power, status, ego, control, and hierarchy, it would not have even crossed my mind that a manager would make such a kind gesture. In fact, at some of my previous companies, not only would an action such as this never been considered, but it would not even have been allowed! But this was representative not only of Liquidnet's culture, but of Jeff as a manager, as a leader...and as a person.

Before accepting the job offer from Liquidnet in 2007, I almost didn't...partially because of Jeff. We had first met back in 2002 when we were both new trainers for a nationally-known training company. We had very different styles and personalities (mainly, I'm an extreme introvert, while Jeff is an extreme extrovert). After discovering that we both played on multiple softball teams, were huge Yankees fans, and grew up five minutes away from each other in Commack, Long Island, however, we soon became good friends and occasional training partners. Four years later, Jeff was hired to head up Liquidnet University. A year later, when he was ready to create the Liquidnet Leadership Institute (LLI), he reached out to me to join him.

While I was honored and intrigued by this offer, working for a fintech (financial services and technology) company was not high on my list of industries; in fact, it was near the bottom. But even more, while I had enjoyed working *with* Jeff, I had huge concerns about working *for* him. Not only would I be working for a friend, and someone with a very different style, but one who was a few years younger than me. Could my ego handle that...and would our friendship be able to survive this new working relationship?

As it turned out, deciding to join Liquidnet was one of the best career and life decisions I've ever made. For, not only did we become even closer friends by working together, but Jeff turned out to be the best boss I've ever worked for; and it ended up being the best job I ever had. And a big part of the reason was Jeff's complete lack of ego (mentioned previously), along with his always-positive attitude and energy, not to mention numerous other important qualities and skills one would want in a manager.

Jeff always says that the top responsibility of any manager/leader is to set their people up for success, and he most definitely did that for me… every single day that we worked together. In *Good to Great*, Jim Collins advises, "Don't discipline people. Hire self-disciplined people, and turn them loose within the framework of a highly-developed system." This quote is all about empowerment, and creating a climate wherein people can bring their best, authentic selves to work, spread their wings, and fly. That's why I was *at* my best when working for a boss who *was* the best. Accepting me and all my many quirks (ok, neuroses), and supporting, empowering, and inspiring me to be the best I could be turned out to be a winning formula.

Unfortunately, my time at Liquidnet ended three years after it started, when Jeff had to break the bad news to me that I was being laid off (along with a number of others) as a result of the economic crisis. But, as always, he handled this difficult situation with professionalism, grace, empathy, and kindness, helping me to process and navigate what could, potentially under other circumstances, have been a really uncomfortable, awkward, and relationship-damaging situation.

But, referring back to my "Hierarchy of Followership" model mentioned earlier (Chapter 14), the "Liking, Admiration, Respect, and Trust" that we had built up over the years helped our relationship not only to survive, but to thrive. For, were it not for that layoff, I would not have founded my own company. And here we are seventeen years later, continuing to partner together on Liquidnet's leadership programs. Additionally, soon after I left Liquidnet, Jeff and I were invited to join the faculty of NYU as adjunct professors in their School of Professional Studies/ Division of Programs in Business, where we have been co-teaching our top-rated graduate course, "Leadership and Team Building," for their Human Capital Management master's program for the past nine years and counting. So, as we have evolved over the years through Bruce Tuckman's classic four stages of team development model—Forming, Storming (almost none of that!), Norming, and Performing—I look forward to enjoying our collaborative partnership long into the future.

A Few other Leadership Lessons from Jeff

I've learned and grown so much from working with, for, and again with Jeff over the past seventeen years that I could write an entire book just on that. But with our limited space, here are just a few of his greatest hits:

- "Don't be a victim of your environment": The very first time he had to deliver a workshop all on his own for a corporate client, he arrived at the location only to find that the training room was under construction; and so, he ended up having to deliver the entire workshop on the floor in a hallway. Being not quite as flexible and easy-going as Jeff, when facing an adverse situation I often ask myself, "WWJD?" ("What Would Jeff Do?")

- "Let it Go": Similarly, while I am one who tends to hold on to things and let them fester, Jeff often has to remind me of this mantra that we picked up from Marshall Goldsmith when we attended one of his workshops a number of years ago. Marshall, that day, also advised us in our two-on-one conversation with him after the workshop: "Don't coach people who don't want to be coached," which is a valuable and important reminder.

- "What am I going to learn about you ninety days from now that I may not like?": This is an excellent and insightful interviewing question that Jeff devised to ask potential job candidates. It's a powerful and revelatory way to gauge a candidate's self-awareness, integrity, and honesty. Having posed this always-challenging question to Brian when interviewing him for the first time, Brian realized afterwards that he regretted the superficial response that he had given to Jeff. So he called Jeff the next day to ask if he could change his answer. Partially because of that action, Jeff hired him… demonstrating Jeff's character…as well as Brian's.

- "The Three Expectations Questions": These questions are put to new hires. What do you expect from me as your manager? What do you expect from your colleagues/teammates? And what can we expect from you?

- "Inch by inch, life's a cinch; yard by yard, life is hard": Though he didn't originate this proverb, it serves as a reminder to take things one day at a time, as well as to break big things down into bite-sized pieces.

In Review

The Big Lesson: So many! When he produced the classic song and music video, "We Are the World," way back in 1985 performed by a choir of music superstars of that era, Quincy Jones famously hung a sign outside the room that said, "Leave your ego at the door." To me, being able to do that is one of the most valuable traits of an effective leader.

The Big Question: Who are the Seths and Jeffs that you've met and/or worked for? What are some examples of "little things" that have made a big difference in your life? What are the "great leader" stories that *you* like to tell based on *your* own personal experiences?

Your Big Insight:

Your Big Action:

CHAPTER 39

Generous Leadership: My Grant Tinker Story

When I was twenty-four years old, after getting my master's degree in communications from the State University of New York at Albany and then working for a year in the media buying department of Ogilvy & Mather advertising, I made the life-altering decision to move from New York to Los Angeles to pursue my dream of working in the entertainment industry.

I'd been an intern for NBC at Rockefeller Center while in college during the summer of 1984, and my vision, since I was a kid, had always been to work for NBC—the network of *Cheers*, *Family Ties*, *L.A. Law*, and so many other hit shows. *How exciting it will be*, I would say to myself, *to someday see that iconic, multicolored NBC peacock printed on my paycheck*.

Unfortunately, however, despite applying for one job after another, I just kept receiving one rejection letter after another, not only from NBC but from every other TV network and production company in New York City. I soon realized that if I was really serious about pursuing a career in television, I would have to head out west. In the most difficult and scariest decision I had made in my life, I shocked my parents, myself, and even my dog by giving my two weeks' notice and heading for Hollywood.

With two suitcases in hand, a couple of hundred dollars to my name, no job, no leads, and no contacts out there, my parents dropped me off at JFK airport. After a tearful farewell, I headed for my American Airlines flight to LAX, unsure now of whether I was making the right decision. With reality starting to sink in, I approached the gate with my hands shaking, my heart pounding, and my head spinning with self-doubt and second thoughts. But realizing that there was no turning back now, I boarded the plane.

I started to make my way down the aisle through first class, toward my coach seat way in the back. A white-haired businessman was blocking my path. As I stood there impatiently, waiting to get by, he finally turned around to take his cushy, luxurious aisle seat, at which point I froze in place: It was Grant Tinker…the chairman and CEO of, yes, NBC!

Fast-forward to two hours, then three hours into the five-hour flight. I'm still debating with myself: *Should I go up and talk to him, or should I not? Will I be bothering him if I do; or will I kick myself in regret for all eternity if I don't? Should I casually stroll by his seat, pretending that I am just stretching my legs and then "accidentally" drop one of my résumés onto his lap? Will he then be so impressed with my background that he offers me a job on the spot; or will he forever ban me from NBC for having the audacity to be such a clueless idiot?* Three times I go up and peek through the first class curtain, only to chicken out and scurry back to my seat.

Then, finally, with less than an hour to go before we land, it's now or never, do or die. So, somehow, despite my being the most introverted of introverts, I summon up the courage and the audacity, and, almost without even thinking, I just do it: I march down the coach cabin aisle, through the first class curtain, stop at his row, turn towards him and, in one long, rambling, run-on sentence, just start spouting out the words that I had been rehearsing and revising in my head for the past four hours:

"Excuse me, Mr. Tinker…I hate to bother you. I was an intern at NBC in New York last summer, and the reason I'm even on this flight is

because I'm moving out to L.A. to try to get a job in the TV industry— hopefully at NBC—though I'm open to any opportunities… Again, I'm sorry to bother you, but I was wondering if you might have a minute to give me some advice or anything that would help point me in the right direction."

After what seems like a painful, awkward, five-minute pause (though it was probably only a couple of seconds), he smiles, gets up from his big, cushiony aisle seat, moves over to the window seat, reaches out to shake my hand, and says, "Sure, sit down for a minute. What's your name?"

Wow.

So, there I was: twenty-four years old, unemployed, and possessing nothing but a dream, sitting there in first class, chatting about work and life with the head of NBC.

Without going into all of the details of what he had to say, the bottom line was that the CEO of the number one television network (and, by the way, the former husband of the amazing Mary Tyler Moore) generously took five minutes of his valuable time and attention to share the wisdom of his experience, and a few invaluable words of advice—as well as his business card—with a young, aspiring, relatively clueless and obviously overreaching job seeker.

As it turned out, despite my best efforts I never did end up working for NBC, but I left that brief, unforgettable conversation on an emotional high, beaming with hope and optimism…along with the confidence and self-assurance that I had, indeed, made the right career and life decision.

And though I am 99.9 percent certain that Mr. Tinker (who passed away just a few years ago) most likely would not have recalled that brief interaction, the leadership lessons that he left me with—through both his powerful words and his incredibly kind and generous actions—still resonate with me all these years later. And, for that, I am forever grateful.

In Review

The Big Lesson: So many life and leadership lessons packed into this one small story! Mr. Tinker's small act of ego-free humility and generosity of spirit reminds me that you are never too big to remember where you came from and help those who aspire to follow in your footsteps—even when you are the head of a TV network and flying in first class. And, from my younger self, finding the courage to push beyond one's comfort zone and into "the Zone of the Unknown" can have huge payoffs. After all...what do you have to lose?

The Big Question: What lessons in leadership and in life do *you* take from this story—from either my actions, or from Grant Tinker's— and what might you do differently in the future as a result?

Your Big Insight:

Your Big Action:

CHAPTER 40

Here Comes the Ice Cream Man

"The only emperor is the emperor of ice-cream."
—WALLACE STEVENS

After getting laid off from the theme park company where I managed
that robotic animals project in China, I was hired as a project manager
for Showscan Entertainment, an L.A.-based company that produced
motion simulator films and rides for theme parks around the world. My
new job was to oversee the construction and launch of the CineMania
motion simulation theater at Universal CityWalk, and it ended up being
both a challenging and amazing career experience.

After that project ended, I was made the manager of Customer
Support Services for all of the company's motion simulator theaters
around the world. Showscan manufactured and sold state-of-the-art,
super-high-definition projection systems to themed entertainment
venues around the world, and then licensed our three-to-five-minute

simulator ride films—for example, space adventures and roller coasters—to these venues. These shorts were fun, exciting, beautifully produced, and comparable in film quality to IMAX.

Unfortunately, my new Customer Support role was not nearly as glamorous or thrilling as these motion simulator rides were. This job was pretty much all about fielding complaints and fulfilling spare parts orders for our customers' theaters around the world. Although the projectors and the motion seats are incredible pieces of technology, the popularity of these attractions meant that all of this equipment was constantly breaking down. And that meant a constant need to identify, source, inventory, and ship these various spare parts to our clients' theaters in twenty countries around the globe.

This job was so frustrating, mundane, and unfulfilling that I am boring myself just thinking and writing about it. But hang in there with me for a minute, as there is a point! And it involves ice cream. Huge quantities of ice cream. I promise.

My biggest frustration in trying to do this job was the inefficiency and ineffectiveness of our warehousing operation, which was responsible for ordering and stocking all these spare parts and then shipping them out as quickly as possible to our customers. Because the warehousing system was such a mess, and because there wasn't a formal process in place, things took ten times longer than they should have, which often prevented us from getting the spare parts out to our customers in a timely fashion. And without these parts, neither the projectors nor the motion seats could operate. And nonfunctioning equipment meant no rides, and no rides meant no ticket sales. Which was a huge deal—and a huge problem—both for our clients' businesses and for the reputation and revenues of our company.

So, what was I to do? Caught in the middle between our upset and angry clients and our frustrated, overworked, and underappreciated warehouse people, all I could do was to keep walking into my company's senior management to complain about those nameless, faceless "people down in the warehouse who were not doing their jobs."

Well, guess what happened.

The CFO, whom I reported to, came to me one day and said, "You're the one who has the problem and is always complaining about it; so, fix it."

With that, I got both a promotion and a demotion at the same time: My title was expanded from "Manager of Customer Support Services" to "Manager of Customer Support Services, Warehousing, Inventory, and Shipping Operations."

Wow…thanks a lot.

And, along with that, with neither pomp nor ceremony, I was physically moved (basically, kicking and screaming), from my cushy, carpeted "Upstairs" office on the management floor, to a tiny broom-closet-sized office all the way "Downstairs" in the cold, dingy, dusty, warehouse. And did I mention that my tiny new office had a support beam—a pole, actually—right in the middle of it, wedging me between my desk and the wall? Well, it did. Needless to say, I was not at all happy. And I was now, officially, "one of those people down in the warehouse" that all the people "upstairs" barely knew but were always complaining about.

Long story short…fast-forward to four weeks later: Working with the warehouse foreman, we completely revamped the entire operation, creating an inventory system, automating certain processes, and getting the place organized. While things quickly started to visibly improve, we were still failing in one key area, the most important task: getting the parts shipped out the door to our customers by the Friday 4 p.m. deadline. Missing that FedEx and UPS pick-up time meant that our customers would not get their parts by the next morning, in time for them to get up and running for the weekend—their key revenue-generating days. And, not only that, but missing that shipping deadline meant that the company was paying a fortune—literally, thousands of dollars a year extra—in overtime pay and in rush shipping costs. If I could just figure out a way to have all our work completed by 4 p.m. Friday it would save the day…and I would be a hero. But how?

Well, after giving it much thought, I came up with a possible solution that could best be summed up in two words. My favorite pair of words in the English language: ice cream.

I announced to the warehouse staff that if we could find a way to speed things up and have all spare parts packages ready to ship by 4 p.m., I would bring in ice cream to celebrate, *and* I would authorize everyone to head home at 4:30 p.m., while being paid for the full day 'til 5 p.m., enabling them to hit the road and start their weekend. And if you know anything about fighting L.A. traffic during rush hour on a Friday night, getting to leave early is worth its weight in gold!

Well, that first Friday, we came close, missing the pick-up deadline by a half hour. But we were making huge progress. So, as a show of appreciation for the team's effort, I ran out and brought back fifty dollars' worth of chocolate, vanilla, and strawberry ice cream. Though we ended up working late and missed our goal, that symbolic gesture of recognition was appreciated.

The next week, however, we actually did it! All the spare parts shipments were packed and ready for pick-up, we had our ice cream celebration— along with a huge feeling of camaraderie and accomplishment—and everyone was out the door and on the road by 4:30 p.m. It worked!

After the weekend, first thing that Monday morning, I went upstairs to the executive offices to see my boss, the CFO, so excited to tell him the full story: How, in less than a month since I was sent "Downstairs," we not only streamlined the entire operation, but we also made our Friday evening shipping deadline for the first time ever, thereby saving the company hundreds of dollars in rush shipping costs and employee overtime. I also brought with me an expense reimbursement form for him to sign to cover the $100 in cash I had laid out from my own pocket for the two Fridays' worth of ice cream.

But, was I in for a big surprise: I wasn't expecting a gold medal and a ticker tape parade, but not only did he not congratulate me, he berated me for letting the warehouse people leave early on Friday when they were still "on the clock." *And* he took my $100 ice cream reimbursement form, ceremoniously crumbled it up into a ball, and slam-dunked it into his trash can, saying, "This whole ice cream idea is ridiculous—these are grown men being paid to do their jobs! It's a warehouse…not a little kid's birthday party!"

I was so demoralized. But I would not be defeated. I made a promise, and my plan was working. This was no time to backslide. So, that Friday, not only did I bring in ice cream, but (partially to spite my CFO) cones and sprinkles as well! And, for the second week in a row, with the help of our new system—and increased morale—we once again met our Friday deadline…as we did the week after, and the week after that.

As a junior-level manager who was not really making a ton of money, picking up the tab for all this ice cream every single Friday was starting to add up. On the one hand, I couldn't really afford to do it anymore, and yet, on the other hand, I had made this commitment to my team. We were starting to function as a well-oiled machine, and I didn't want to do anything to rock the boat. But I seriously didn't know how long I was going to be able to afford to keep doing this.

And then, about two months in, something happened that changed everything:

That particular Friday, one of the "Upstairs" people came downstairs to the warehouse to get some kind of paperwork signed around 4 p.m., just as I was setting up the ice cream bar. Even though he was "one of *them*" (that is, one of the "Upstairs" people), I invited him to make himself an ice cream cone.

The next thing I knew, he was yelling to everyone upstairs, "*Hey*! There's free ice cream down in the warehouse!!!"

Yeah…free.

Anyway, about ten people came down to grab some ice cream. And the following Friday, twenty more. Knowing that we were having "guests" from upstairs coming down to visit the warehouse motivated everyone to pitch in to make things as presentable and pleasing as possible. Before we knew it, "Fridays at Four" became the hottest party in town! OK, not really. But what it did do was give the warehouse people a feeling of pride and a sense of recognition that they never had before, as having the office people from upstairs coming down to visit leveled the playing field and created a common ground. People suddenly got to know one another for the first time.

And, if all that wasn't enough, how's this for an extra-happy ending to this story: A couple of weeks later, guess who came down from his ivory tower and stopped by the warehouse for an ice cream cone? Yup… the CFO—my boss who had originally slammed me for this "ridiculous" idea. And here's what he said:

"So *this* is where all the action is that I've been hearing about! I know when you came to me a couple of months ago I told you this was a dumb idea. But, apparently, it wasn't. Good job. Whatever you've laid out for all the ice cream, just put in a reimbursement form along with all the receipts and I'll sign it."

"You promise you won't crumple it up again?" I asked.

To which he just smiled, licked his ice cream cone, and headed back upstairs.

In Review

The Big Lesson: There are so many things I learned from this early-career episode! I had previously managed projects, and I had an assistant who I supervised, but this was my very first position in which I had a team of people directly reporting to me. And—with no prior management training of any kind—I had no other option but to figure things out as I went along.

It was not until years later that I learned Peter Drucker's famous quote, "Management is about doing things right; leadership is about doing the right thing." In this situation, I tried to do both by "managing the process" and "leading the people" in the only way I knew how.

And, the biggest lesson of all: Never underestimate the power of ice cream.

The Big Question: What would you have done in my situation? Have you ever been in a similar position? What lessons do you take from this story? And what did you learn that you might be able to apply in the future?

Your Insight:

Your Action:

CHAPTER 41

How Being a Quitter Can Make You a Winner

One of my NYU students was facing a dilemma: A few chapters into a highly recommended, award-winning, bestselling business book, she realized that she found it to be an uninteresting waste of her limited and valuable time. Meanwhile, she had a pile of other much more engaging and tempting titles sitting right there on her nightstand calling her name. She was excited about diving into one of them, only to find that when she put the boring book aside to embark on a new reading adventure, she suddenly and inexplicably found herself feeling extremely guilty.

Why?

As she put it, "The culture where I come from is really uptight about winning. People who quit are looked upon as 'failures.' And, so, quitting this book translated into a failure on my part. And this feeling of guilt comes on whenever I don't finish something."

"Always finish what you start."
"Don't be a quitter."

"No pain, no gain."
"Never, ever give up."
"Winners never quit, and quitters never win."
"Quitters are losers."

How many of these aphorisms sound familiar from parents, teachers, coaches, motivational speakers, and/or other authority figures, drilling these mantras into our heads? Or maybe you've come across some of these quotes:

"Many of life's failures are people who did not realize how close they were to success when they gave up." —THOMAS EDISON

"I hated every minute of training, but I said, 'Don't quit. Suffer now and live the rest of your life as a champion.'" —MUHAMMAD ALI

"If you quit once it becomes a habit. Never quit!" —MICHAEL JORDAN

No wonder we feel guilty when we decide not to continue with something!

But when is it OK to quit? How do we know when it's better to cut our losses and move on? What about "sunk costs" that cause us to dig ourselves into an even deeper hole? How do we decide when to drop something…and when to persevere? How do we determine whether to give something (or someone) a second or third or tenth chance vs. when to say, "That's it…enough is enough"?

And, is there a difference between "quitting" and "being a quitter"?

Confession: I Am a Quitter

I've quit jobs that weren't working out, and I've ended relationships that were dysfunctional. I've left many books unfinished, and I've walked out of many a bad play or movie. I quit piano lessons when I realized that I wasn't really very good. And I (with much hesitation and withdrawal) quit eating foods loaded with sugar and carbs, and replaced them with nuts, fruits, and vegetables. And I quit reading the *New York Times* while laying on my couch, and instead now read it every day while walking for thirty minutes on the treadmill.

So you can see where I'm going with this: When it comes to "quitting," it's all about context. In short, how you define it will determine how you feel about it. Simply replacing the word "quit" with the word "stop" can completely reframe quitting in a positive way. And, from a leadership perspective, Peter Drucker once said, "We spend a lot of time teaching our leaders what to do. We don't spend enough time teaching them what to stop."

In his classic leadership book *What Got You Here Won't Get You There*, legendary management guru Marshall Goldsmith explores the "20 Workplace Habits You Need to Break." In other words: there are unproductive and counterproductive behaviors that successful people need to stop (that is, "quit") doing in order to enable them to become even more successful. Many times, people are not necessarily successful *because of* how they are, but *in spite of* how they are. And so to get from "here" to "there" they may need to "quit" doing the behaviors that are, actually, working against them. For example, as Goldsmith mentions, it's great to be smart, but if you're always trying to prove that you're the smartest person in the room, there's a good chance that this approach could backfire on you one of these days.

So, while it is admirable to keep on keepin' on, there is no shame in movin' on if what you're doing just isn't working for you anymore. If you are disengaged, if you are unhappy, if you are frustrated, if you have given it your all and see little or no possibility of sunnier skies, then, perhaps, the best choice might just be to make a change.

As you get older (and, hopefully, wiser), you come to realize that life is short: too short to waste on books, or movies, or TV series, or projects, or jobs, or relationships that you no longer find valuable. The key, and the challenge, is that—although you can seek out others' input, advice, and opinions—when it comes to your life, *you* are the only one who can make the determination on whether to pass or to play.

It often helps to think about the fact that ending something negative—though leaving a void—creates the time and space for the start of something new. It's hard to start something new while our cup is full or when we're tenuously hanging onto the past.

To be clear…I'm not talking about quitting on a person who is relying on you, walking out on someone, leaving a project halfway done, or storming out of the office in a huff. I'm talking about those situations in which you reach a point wherein, after much thoughtful consideration of the respective pros and cons, you've made the well-thought-out decision that it's time to move on.

Why Didn't You Just Quit?

As mentioned throughout this book, I've worked for numerous awful bosses over the course of my long career. When people hear the unfathomable stories about them—after cringing and laughing in both disbelief and horror—they typically ask, "Why didn't you just quit?" This question can best be answered by this old vaudeville joke:

> *This guy works at the circus and his only job is to clean up after the elephants. All day long, day after day, his job is, literally, nothing but shoveling shit. And then, after work every night, he would meet up with his friends at the bar and bend their ears for hours complaining about it. Finally, fed up with the endless complaints and unable to hear about it anymore, one of the friends exclaims, "If you hate it so much, then why don't you just quit???" To which he replies, "What… and leave show business!?"*

Playing Quit and Seek: A Few Questions to Consider

- When should you quit your job…and seek a new opportunity?
- When should you quit that bad relationship…and seek a better one?
- When should you quit a bad habit…and replace it with something healthier and more productive?
- When should you quit complaining about problems…and start coming up with solutions?
- When should you quit venting…and start in-venting?
- How do you know if you should quit while you're ahead?
- How should you quit (if or when the time comes, what's the right way or the best way to do it)?

- Why are you quitting (is it the right decision, and are you quitting for the right reasons)?
- Who can you rely on and trust for counsel, advice, and support?
- Have you weighed the pros and cons of quitting vs. persevering?
- Have you explored all your alternatives?
- Are you giving up too soon?
- Or have you already stayed too long?
- Have you given it your best shot?
- Is it, simply, that time?

The best distinction I've heard between "quitting" and "being a quitter"

Quitting is never easy. It is often an emotionally wrenching and potentially confusing decision, and there are unlimited ways to approach it. And though making the decision to quit something is a tough one, the decision to *not* make a decision can be equally tough. In fact, as the saying goes, *not* making a decision is a decision. I've found that being stuck in limbo is one of the worst feelings there is. As the psychologist William James wrote, "There is no more miserable human being than one in whom nothing is habitual but indecision."

Perhaps this inspirational quote by author Osayi Emokpae Lasisi will serve to reframe what "quitting" is all about, and help you to decide what road to take, or what move—if any—to make:

Quitting is not giving up, it's choosing to focus your attention on something more important. Quitting is not losing confidence, it's realizing that there are more valuable ways you can spend your time. Quitting is not making excuses, it's learning to be more productive, efficient, and effective instead. Quitting is letting go of things (or people) that are sucking the life out of you, so you can do more things that will bring you strength.

To sum it all up: perhaps by ridding ourselves of the mind-set that "quitting is for losers," we will realize that, sometimes, quitting is exactly what you need to do in order to win.

In Review

The Big Lesson: Simply reframing what it means to "quit," and looking at quitting in a different and more positive light, will free you up and empower you to explore new possibilities.

The Big Question: What is something in your life that, if you made the decision to "quit," could potentially lead to bigger and better things?

Your Insight:

Your Action:

CHAPTER 42

How My Cardiologist Almost Gave Me a Heart Attack (Or, the Right and Wrong Ways to Communicate Numbers)

After going through a series of routine heart exams recently (an EKG, an echocardiogram, a cholesterol check, etc.), the cardiologist comes in and says:

"Based on all your lab results, and calculating all your risk factors, you have about a 5 percent chance of having a heart attack within the next ten years."

Getting weak in the knees, heart pounding through my chest, and feeling like I am about to pass out from the shock of this death sentence, I pause long enough to say:

"Wait. Doesn't that mean that there's more than a 95 percent chance that I *won't* have a heart attack within the next ten years?!"

To which he replies: "Yes...I guess that's another way of looking at it."

Um...yeah.

In fact, he goes on to say that my test results are excellent and that my heart is in perfect shape. As it turns out, statistically, 5 percent is the odds *of any* fifty-plus-year-old male having a heart attack within the next ten years! So, despite the temporary panic he caused, it turns out that I am completely normal…heart-wise, anyway.

So what can we learn from this near-fatal incident in terms of communicating numbers?

Everything!

Businesspeople communicate in numbers almost every single day. Regardless of what function you work in, numbers are typically how we gauge—and explain to others—how we're doing. And it is how most managers manage. As Peter Drucker famously put it, "If you can't measure it, you can't manage it."

But there is a crucially important point to keep in mind, whether you are delivering a presentation or writing a report for your boss, employees, customers, or patients: it's not the *numbers* themselves that matter, it's **the story the numbers tell**…and **the message** you intend to deliver.

Numbers without context are absolutely meaningless and confusing…and, in the worst cases, potentially damaging and (as in my example above) terrifying.

A few examples:

- If I tell you that I have "a 250 average" is that good or bad? The answer—as is the answer to most questions—is: "It depends"! If that "250" number is my baseball or softball batting average, it's not too great. If 250 is my bowling average, then you should sign me up right now for the Pro Bowlers Tour!

- When the iPod first came out way back in 2001, if Steve Jobs had announced with great fanfare that it had a 5GB hard drive, how many non-techies would have been so impressed that they raced out to buy one? Not too many, probably. But by saying that this tiny little gadget could fit "one thousand songs in your pocket," well, that visually exciting message changed the music industry…and the world.

- Let's say we're discussing high school graduation rates and I show you a complicated, dense graph that indicates that, nationwide, 30 percent of high school students will not graduate. Is that impactful? Maybe…once you've deciphered it. But what if, instead of saying "30 percent," I show you a photo of ten bright-faced high school students while stating: "See this group of ten kids? Three of them will not graduate from high school. Now that we know this…what are we going to do about it?" Which of those two presentation methods do you think will have the greater impact?

So, again, it's not the *numbers* that matter, but the story, and the meaning, and the humanity, and the emotion behind those numbers. That's what moves people and spurs them to action.

And when communicating numbers, whether spoken or written, keep in mind that it's not just *what* we say (the facts and figures), but *how* we say it (tone of voice, writing style, body language, facial expression, framing).

So, going forward, I urge you to consider your listeners or readers by putting yourself in their shoes. Use emotional intelligence, empathy, and compassion to visualize and anticipate how your message may ultimately be received.

Otherwise, a failure to do so can, literally, give someone a heart attack.

In Review

The Big Lesson: Data and numbers without context are meaningless. Ultimately, what's important is the story the numbers tell. So, think about how you can use data visualization methods, metaphors, and stories to help you to more effectively and persuasively get your message across.

The Big Question: How can you make your next number-based presentation more vivid and compelling?

Your Insight:

Your Action:

CHAPTER 43

How to Honk Your Way Out of a Job

When you go to Disneyland, your theme park experience does not start when you hop aboard your first ride. It starts as soon as you drive through those magical gates and set eyes upon the sign that welcomes you to "The Happiest Place on Earth."

Similarly, when you have a meeting or job interview, it's good to keep in mind that the process does not start when they come out to the lobby and call your name, but long before that. To explain why I say that, let me call this story, "Why It's Never a Good Idea to Be an A-hole to Anyone: A Cautionary Tale in Two Acts."

Act I

When I first moved out to Los Angeles at age twenty-four, to pursue my dream of working in the entertainment industry, I found myself struggling to even get an interview, let alone a job. But after months of working different part-time and temp jobs, I finally got called in to interview for a full-time, entry-level research job at a major film studio.

As I was in the midst of a week-long temp assignment at the time, my only option was to schedule the interview during lunchtime. Which meant that I had exactly one hour to drive to the studio, park my car, be interviewed, and race back to my job. If it sounds like *Mission: Impossible*—especially when you take into consideration the unpredictability of L.A. traffic—it was. But if all went according to plan, it was realistically doable since the studio was just about a fifteen-minute drive away under normal circumstances; plus, I had no other option.

So, I left my office and was relieved to find that the traffic was light that day, which enabled me to get to the studio right on schedule, with two minutes to spare. Only, as luck would have it, once I drove through the studio gates and into the parking lot, I got stuck behind an older, gray-haired gentlemen who was crawling along really, really, really slowly, looking for a parking space.

Getting more and more stressed by the second as he sat there motionless, despite the fact that there were no other cars in front of him, I waited patiently for about two minutes before the crazy, frustrated New York Driver in me kicked in: "*Come on, man…let's #$@&*#$ go!!!*" I started screaming, while pressing down obnoxiously on my horn.

Luckily, my windows were closed, and so were his, so he couldn't hear what I was saying. (Bear in mind, by the way, that—not that this excuses it—I was in my twenties at the time; I'm much more mature and mellow now.☺) Anyway, he finally pulled into a parking space, at which point I screeched past him, sped to the next aisle, careened into the first available space, and raced into the office building.

Completely stressed and frazzled at this point, I hurriedly checked in with the receptionist, who told me that the guy who was going to be interviewing me was running a few minutes late getting back from lunch, that I should have a seat, and that she'd call my name when he arrived.

As I sat there waiting, trying to compose myself for the interview, the elevator doors opened and—guess who steps out—yes, of course, it was the gray-haired gentleman from the parking lot. Picking up my résumé to cover my face, while slinking down in my chair, I'm thinking, "I hope he doesn't see me." At which point, the receptionist calls out to me, "Todd, Mr. Johnson"—not his real name—"is here and ready for you."

You can imagine how incredibly relieved I was when he greeted me, walked me back to his office, and spent ten minutes interviewing me for the job without having recognized me. Whew! I had dodged a bullet.

Shaking his hand, I thanked him for his time, and he said they'd "be in touch." I started heading for the door, free and clear…only to hear him say, "Oh, and by the way…when you drive, you really need to be a little more patient."

Act II

Cut to: Last year. I was sitting in the reception area at a Wall Street firm, a potential new client, waiting to meet with their head of training to discuss a possible leadership program, when this guy walks in. Let's just call him "Mr. Slick." With product-greased hair, an Armani suit, and a yellow power tie, this guy is straight out of central casting.

"I'm here to see April, the head of HR," he says to the receptionist, somewhat bluntly and arrogantly.

"And your name?" she asks.

"Rick," he replies. "Where's the men's room?"

"And your last name, Rick?"

"She knows. Is the bathroom this way?" he says, walking away in search of it.

Returning about five minutes later, he approaches the receptionist again: "Is she ready for me?"

To which the receptionist responds, "Not yet. It should only be a few more minutes. You can have a seat over there."

"That's OK, I'll stand—I don't wanna wrinkle my suit. And I hope it's soon, 'cause I'm kind of in a rush. You think you can grab me a water?"

The receptionist hands him a warm bottle of Poland Spring from a carton.

"I guess you guys don't have a refrigerator?" he asks, sarcastically. "Whatever, whatever, it's fine."

Not believing what I'm witnessing up until this point, but kind of enjoying the show, a young woman comes rushing in:

"Sorry, I'm late, April," she says to the woman who's been handling the reception duties this entire time. "Thanks so much for sitting in for me while I grabbed some lunch."

"Not a problem," April replies, with a genuine smile and a head shake indicating disbelief, "it's been interesting."

And then, with a complete change of demeanor, and a voice tough as nails, she turns to Mr. Slick: "OK, Rick, I guess I'm ready for you. I'm April, the head of HR. Nice to 'officially' meet you. You can follow me right this way."

I don't know whatever happened with Slick Rick, but if I had to venture a guess, I would say that his odds of being hired were about the same as mine were after my honking incident twenty years earlier.

In Review

The Big Lesson: Be nice, kind, and respectful to everyone you meet. One, because you just never know who it is that you're talking to. And two, because it's simply the right thing to do.

The Big Question: Have you ever had an embarrassing work incident which perhaps you didn't handle so well and it came back to bite you? What can you do going forward to make sure that nothing like this ever happens to you again?

Your Big Insight:

Your Big Action:

CHAPTER 44

How to Regain Your Confidence and Recapture Your Mojo After a Setback

Photo credit: My Mother

I really loved my job. And then one day, my boss walked in and informed me that I was being laid off. That was way back in January 2010… although it's as fresh in my mind as if it happened yesterday. There's a lot more to the story than that, but I want to talk about what happened immediately *after* I received that awful news.

I felt confused, disoriented, shocked, lost. It was around 10 a.m. on a Wednesday morning, and after going to the same office every single day for the past three years, I didn't know what I was supposed to do with the rest of my day. Or my week. Or my life. I guess I was just supposed to go home. But the reality hadn't really sunk in yet, and I wasn't quite ready to face my wife with this crushing and dispiriting news.

So, I left the office at 37th Street and Seventh Avenue and meandered mindlessly up Broadway with no specific destination in mind. As I was walking, millions of thoughts went zooming in and out of my head, including this dialogue from *Alice in Wonderland*:

Alice: *"Would you tell me, please, which way I ought to go from here?"*

The Cheshire Cat: *"That depends a good deal on where you want to get to."*

Alice: *"I don't much care where."*

The Cheshire Cat: *"Then it doesn't much matter which way you go."*

That pretty much sums up my state of mind at the time: At that point in my day, or in my life, it didn't really matter which way I went.

But before I realized it, maybe an hour or two—and around fifty blocks—later, I somehow ended up at 81st Street and Central Park West, right in front of the American Museum of Natural History. With nowhere else I had to be, I decided to just go in and wander around Africa and Asia for a while, and then the planetarium, before settling down under the big blue whale to rest and ponder my future and my fate.

About an hour later, still in a complete daze, I decided it was time to head home and break the news to my wife. But as I was leaving, I took one last look back. My gaze was drawn upward, toward the big dinosaur standing in the doorway. And as I did, something strange happened: a feeling of peace and calm came over me.

Somehow, my meditative walk around the museum and planetarium, followed by my encounter with this gargantuan dinosaur, mentally transported me through time and space. It gave me a newfound sense of perspective that made the layoff seem as though it was, perhaps, not the worst thing in the world. And while my beloved job was now "extinct," I myself was not. And so, it was now time for the next phase of my career and my life to begin.

Bounding down the museum steps, past the Teddy Roosevelt statue, I felt recharged and rejuvenated, with a clear head, a fresh perspective, and a burst of confidence. As I continued my walk home, I thought of the origin of the word "confidence," from the Latin "with trust or faith"—as if, though I had no real reason to believe it, I somehow had trust and faith that everything would turn out alright.

Our lives are constantly transformed by changes—both of our own making, and from outside forces. And, as the saying goes, we may not be able to control everything that happens to us, but—as difficult as it may be—we *can* control how we choose to react and respond.

Even if you are an inherently confident person, when you suffer rejections or setbacks, it's natural to lose that confidence, even temporarily. You can still feel this way in the case of a layoff, which isn't "personal" (as opposed to being *fired*, which *is* personal…and I've experienced that first-hand, too). And when you are let go, you lose that comfortable support network of colleagues and the guidance of a boss; it's common to have feelings of self-doubt, vulnerability, loneliness, isolation, and fear.

But confidence is so important to our well-being and to our future successes that, after a setback, it's crucial to do whatever it takes to regain it as quickly as possible…as it's extremely difficult to bounce back without it.

Confidence is often the key differentiator between those who succeed and those who don't. Earlier in my career, I learned the hard way that even though I possessed the requisite knowledge, intelligence, and experience, I lost out on a number of promotion opportunities simply because I lacked confidence…and it showed.

How to Get Your Groove Back

There are a lot of different ways to define confidence. I like this simple one from Harvard professor Rosabeth Moss Kanter, who sums it up as "the expectation of a positive outcome."

So what can you do to regain or maintain your confidence and increase your odds of a "positive outcome?" Here are five quick tips that might help:

1. **Build on your past successes and "keep your eyes on the prize."**
   Regardless of how confident you feel right now, stay focused on
   your ultimate goal. Keep in mind that you've succeeded in the
   past, and you will again. It's just a matter of time and persever-
   ance. It's not "if" you will bounce back, but "when." So, remaining
   positive and resilient are key to your future success.

2. **Leverage your strengths.** Don't dwell on your weaknesses or
   limitations. Be self-aware about—and make others aware of—
   what you have to offer. In fact, if you are "in between jobs," this
   is the perfect opportunity to take the time to learn new skills and
   work on taking your existing ones to the next level.

3. **Make everything a learning opportunity.** Einstein said: "Anyone
   who has never made a mistake has never tried anything new."
   Be ready and willing to fail, learn, and move forward. Reflect
   on what you learned from trying something new and know that
   this is just one more life experience that will help you grow both
   personally and professionally.

4. **Seek feedback and create a support network.** Build your own
   personal Board of Advisors. Appreciate that feedback is a gift. A
   lot of times, when we're feeling down, the tendency is to crawl
   under the covers until things improve. But you need to do the
   exact opposite! Get back out there and stay active. Work on
   your "3 Vs": Visibility, Voice, and Value. Be seen, be heard, and
   continue to make a contribution.

5. **"Act as if."** Behave as you believe, and your belief will eventually
   become reality. It sounds hokey, but it's true. I use this technique
   all the time: If you step up to the plate in softball "acting as if"
   you are a great hitter, you will, most likely, achieve better results
   than if you don't. Or, if you get up on a stage to deliver a presentation—assuming that you did all your preparation—then "acting
   as if" you are a powerful presenter will dramatically increase your
   odds of being one.

The Three Types of Confidence

Lastly, "self-confidence" is just one of what I call "The Three Types of Confidence":

1. **Self-Confidence**: Your belief in yourself.
2. **Other-Confidence:** Your ability to make others feel confident in you (that is, in your ability and in your potential to succeed).
3. **Leader-Confidence**: Your ability to make others feel confident in themselves (and in their ability and potential to succeed). That is, you lead by making others feel as if *they* are leaders.

The most successful leaders possess and exhibit all three types. But it all starts with Self-Confidence. It's very difficult to instill confidence in others when we don't feel confident in ourselves. It's kind of like the airplane instructions where they tell you that in case of emergency you need to put *your* oxygen mask on first, before you can help others.

And keep it in mind that confidence is not something that you either have or you don't. Even the most confident people in the world experience nervousness, anxiety, and self-doubt at various times. Especially when pushing themselves beyond their comfort zone…and into the Zone of the Unknown.

For example, even though I am now an experienced public speaker who feels comfortable presenting in front of large audiences, when I did my TEDx Talk last year, it was more challenging (and nerve-racking!) than a typical presentation. Why? Because it was a very special type of presentation experience—standing on that red circular rug in front of that big red TEDx sign!—with higher-than-usual stakes that pushed me beyond my comfort zone. But I spent months, with my wife's help, refining my script, and practicing my talk over and over and over again until I felt self-assured enough to eventually take that TEDx stage. And now that I've done it once, and proven to myself that I *can* do it, that classic red round rug is now part of my new and expanded comfort and confidence zone.

When you lose your confidence, the key to success is not to pretend that it hasn't happened, but to acknowledge that it's normal and natural for everyone, know that you will get past it, and push yourself to move forward regardless.

If you don't believe me, I suggest that you pay a brief visit to the American Museum of Natural History. And if you do, please do me a favor and stop by the big brontosaurus and tell him that I said to say "Hi"…and, "Thanks."

In Review

The Big Lesson: We will all face serious setbacks at one time or another. The key to bouncing back is finding a resilience in positivity and seeking to gain a fresh perspective.

The Big Question: When was a time that something happened that impacted your confidence…and what did you do to get it back? What advice would you offer to others going through a similar situation?

Your Insight:

Your Action:

CHAPTER 45

Ice, Rice, or Mice:
Has This Ever Happened to You?

Photo credit: Mark Fowler

My Diet Coke had gotten warm, so I asked the waiter for "some more ice." A few minutes later, instead of the ice, he brought me another bowl of rice.

I said "more *ice*"; he heard "more *rice*."

So the question is: Whose fault was it?

I guess you could blame it on my New York accent. And, good thing I didn't say "*some* ice"…or I might have ended up with…you know… some *mice*!

It happens all the time: we say something that is crystal clear in our own mind, and yet the person on the receiving end hears something completely different. The ice vs. rice mix-up was a relatively low-cost, low-stakes mistake (and, I actually wanted some more rice anyway), but what if the stakes were higher? What are the potential costs when a work-related message is lost in translation?

As mentioned in the introduction, earlier in my career I worked for a (now-defunct) themed entertainment design and production company in L.A. that produced audio-animatronic robotic figures for theme parks around the world. That was the project I managed in Shenzhen, China, in which I used visual thinking and visual communication—more specifically, drawing and gesturing, aka Pictionary and Charades—to communicate. But that was only one part of the story. I haven't yet discussed the serious and incredibly embarrassing (and costly!) miscommunication that occurred before we even arrived there.

To set the scene: A brand-new client, a theme park in Shenzhen, China, ordered a menagerie of life-sized robotic animals to be placed at various locations within their new theme park: three elephants, three sheep, and two cows. And my job, as the project manager, was to make sure they got designed and built, shipped from L.A. to China, and then installed to be fully operational in time for the grand opening which I would be flying all the way to China to attend.

It was my first-ever time as a project manager, as well as my first-ever trip outside of the United States, and I was so proud that everything was going according to plan. When finally installed, the giant elephants trumpeted and sprayed water from their trunks; the wooly sheep moved their heads, wagged their tails, and *baaaa*-ed; and the friendly cows chewed and *mooo*-ed. They all looked so real that the tourists initially believed that they were actually live animals.

So, "What went wrong?" you may be thinking.

Well, as it turned out, the client was completely confused by, and upset with, what they received, because what they wanted was not two "cows," but two "water buffaloes"!

Talk about lost in translation! When the client had ordered the two "cows" (by phone and fax—this was in the old days, pre-email and pre-internet), our expert design team did some research and determined that a Chinese yellow cow was what the client wanted.

And as a young, newbie, first-time project manager, who was *I* to question the judgment of our experienced and highly-skilled senior design team?

But despite all the design sketches, engineering drawings, and mock-up models that were created in order to produce the life-sized finished product, no one—including me—ever once thought to check in with the client to ask: "Is *this* what you want?" In hindsight, it's insane that we didn't do that. But of course (as the classic, visually-oriented metaphor goes), hindsight is 20/20.

So, what the client ended up with was two out-of-place mechanical yellow cows standing in a simulated rice paddy field where two water buffaloes should have been. To put this into perspective, this would be like placing a kangaroo on an American dairy farm. So out of place and incongruous as to be ridiculous. And all it would have taken to avoid this happening was to have simply stopped—at any earlier phase in the process—and asked the client: "Is this what you mean?"

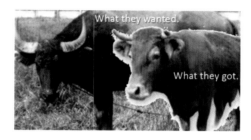

Six Simple Tips to Keep in Mind to Help Avoid Similar Miscommunication

When it comes to communication, you can't control the other party; you can only control yourself and what you say, ask, respond, and do. Here are six simple-yet-powerful tips to help you avoid potential misunderstandings in any personal or work situation:

1. **People are not mind readers:** One time, a manager asked me, "Did that package come in yet?" When I asked, "Which package?" her sarcastic response was: "The one I've been waiting for—which one do you think!" OK…that was helpful, thanks for clarifying.

   When communicating, use empathy to put yourself in the shoes of your listener (or reader, in the case of written communication), try to see things through their eyes, and ask yourself if your message is self-explanatory from *their* perspective…not from yours. And if not, then simplify and clarify. When on the receiving end of an ambiguous communication, it's always best to ask for clarification rather than to get the message wrong and potentially head down the wrong path based on false interpretations or assumptions.

2. **Validate understanding:** A boss once casually said to me, as we were strolling down the hall to a meeting, "That's a good point. We should look into that." A week later he asked me why I hadn't gotten back to him with an answer. I asked, "An answer to what?" To which he responded, "I thought I asked you to look into that issue and get back to me!" Apparently, that "we" (of "we should look into that") meant "me."

   So, keep in mind Stephen Covey's Habit #5 (from *The 7 Habits of Highly Effective People*): "Seek first to understand, then to be understood." Clarify that you're on the same page, especially if there is any potential for misinterpretation.

   One of my mantras, and one of my strongest recommendations, is to always think in terms of "Who's doing What by When." If you do not clearly establish responsibility and accountability, define exactly what needs to be done (that is, the deliverable), and agree on a delivery date, there's a very good chance that expectations will not be met. And it's one thing to confirm this verbally, but when you put it in writing—even in a simple text or email, although a more formalized progress report may be necessary—you will dramatically increase the odds of the right things getting done the right way.

3. **Read between the lines:** Peter Drucker said that the most important part of communication is to hear what *isn't* being said. In a classic joke from one of the old *Pink Panther* movies, a guy asks the hotel clerk, "Does your dog bite?" After getting bitten while trying to pet the dog, the guy exclaims, "I thought you said your dog doesn't bite!" The clerk's reply? "That is not my dog."

Keep an eye out for cues and clues as you seek to answer "the question behind the question" (also the title of an excellent book by John G. Miller, by the way). In other words, what is the other person really asking or looking for? This is especially important when meeting with a boss, client, or an interviewer. For example, if an interviewer were to ask you, "Have you ever done this type of work before?" don't take the question literally and simply answer with a "yes" or a "no." What they are really asking is, "Are you capable of doing this type of work here, in the future?" So that's the question you need to answer.

4. **It's not just your words—but your tone of voice and body language:** Let's say your manager questions you regarding the actions of one of your direct reports and you respond with the following simple, seven-word sentence. Notice how the meaning changes based solely on the word being emphasized:

   I never asked him to do that! (that is, someone else must have asked him to);

   I *never* asked him to do that! (emphatic denial that you ever made that request);

   I never asked *him* to do that! (that is, you asked someone else to do it);

   I never asked him to *do* that! (emphatic denial of the action taken);

   I never asked him to do *that!* (that is, you asked him to do something else).

   Be aware of how you say what you say (especially in emails or texts, where tone of voice is inferred by the message recipient!). A misinterpretation can completely distort your message and your intentions, as well as negatively impact the relationship. Be very aware of how your message could be misconstrued, because if there's any possibility it could happen, it most likely will. Just as in my "ice vs. rice" example, the burden of responsibility is on the communicator.

5. **Use visuals, nonverbal cues, analogies, and metaphors to get your ideas across:** Words don't always speak for themselves. Again, that's why a picture is worth a thousand of them. So, whenever possible, point, gesture, or use illustrations, diagrams, examples, metaphors, analogies, etc., to clarify your meaning and increase your odds of being understood.

   Remember that when it comes to metaphors, analogies, and examples, be sure to use ones that your audience/listener/reader will understand and be able to relate to. A baseball analogy (something, you can probably tell, I tend to use often) may not resonate with someone who doesn't know anything about baseball, but something different could—like soccer, or theater, or nature. Seeing a situation from your audience's point of view and speaking their language will go a long way.

6. **Be careful with jargon and acronyms:** They make for a great communicational shorthand with people who are "in the know," but end up having the opposite effect on people who are not. For example, I used to work at Liquidnet in their corporate university known, internally, as "LNU." When a senior manager told one of his new employees to get some information from LNU, she wasted hours searching the company for a nonexistent employee named "Ellen Yu."

   At a networking event, I once mentioned that I used to work for the "AMA." The guy thought I was talking about the American Medical Association, and the woman thought I meant the American Marketing Association, when I was actually talking about the American Management Association. Exact same initials; entirely different organizations; complete confusion.

   Every industry, company, department, and function has its own language. So, it's always best to define acronyms and/or jargon the first time they're being used…just to be sure. And if you're unsure on the receiving end, it's always best to just ask rather than operating under potentially mistaken assumptions.

Since effective communication is the key to any relationship and the primary unit of interaction and exchange in most of our work, it's more important than ever to make sure that we are heard and understood correctly—and that others correctly hear and understand us. And, if you are the communicator, the ball is in your court to get it right.

Take it from me…so that you don't end up with a bowl of rice the next time you want a glass of ice.

Or, even worse, a cow…when what you really needed was a water buffalo.

In Review

The Big Lesson: In brief, the burden of communication is on the communicator, so it is crucial to be self-aware and conscientious… and seek to view the conversation from your listener's or reader's point of view.

The Big Question: What are some of the biggest communication snafus you've ever experienced firsthand, what did you learn from them, and what can, or will, you do differently in the future as a result?

Your Big Insight:

Your Big Action:

CHAPTER 46

Listen Up!

Quick! Who's the best manager you've ever worked for? Picture him or her in your mind. Now ask yourself: What made you pick this person?

OK, now: Who was the *worst* manager you've ever had? Do the same thing: visualize working for this person while thinking about what made them so horrible.

I can't guarantee it, but if I had to guess, based on my own experience, one of the key differences between these two people was that the good manager actually *listened* to you, while the bad one didn't.

Am I right?

When you interacted with the good manager, how did he or she make you feel? Valued? Validated? Respected? Trusted? Confident? Engaged? Empowered? Effective? Smart? Successful?

And how did the bad manager make you feel most of the time? Most likely the exact opposite.

So if you are a manager—or even if you're not—look yourself in the mirror and answer this question honestly: **Are you a good listener?**

More importantly, if you were to ask other people that same question, what do you think they would (honestly) say?

If you're interested in becoming a better manager—and a more effective leader—you might find it valuable to reflect on how, how often, and how well you listen.

When we do 360-degree feedback evaluations, "Listening" is very often one of the categories that most managers rate themselves the highest in...while others around them rate them the lowest. In other words, we tend to find the biggest gap...between the ears.

For example, there was a manager who insisted that he was a tremendous listener and, as such, he was completely shocked to receive feedback to the contrary. Upon digging deeper, it turned out that he was, in fact, an exceptional listener—when he actually listened...which...as it turned out, was very rarely. In other words, if you were somehow able to capture and hold his attention, he hung on your every word, listened with empathy, remembered everything you said, and really made you feel understood. The problem was, he only did that with certain people, and not very often. Most of the time it was all about him.

Good Leaders Learn How to Listen

Early in my career, I temped in the PR department of one of the major Hollywood studios. Let's call them...um..."Disney"...since it was. Despite the excitement of working on a studio lot, the job itself was mind-numbingly boring, consisting mostly of answering phones, taking messages, and making copies. If you've ever temped, you know what it's like to sit there all day long, watching the minutes drag by, while your brain slowly turns to mush. Especially if you aspire to do something a little more creative and stimulating with your life.

One afternoon, one of the department managers came running out of her office, frantically looking for a PR rep to proofread and edit an urgent press release that needed to go out.

Finding the entire office empty, she barked at me: "Where the hell is everybody?" I told her that they were all out to lunch, but that I'd be more than happy to take a crack at proofing the press release. Without even looking at me, she snarled: "What are you talking about? You can't do this—you're just a temp!"

Even after I told her that I had a bachelor's degree in English, a master's degree in communication, and a year of experience working for a top New York ad agency, she didn't have any interest at all in anything I had to say. She just tossed the press release draft on my desk, told me to give it to the first PR rep I saw, and dashed out to a meeting.

While eating my lunch, I decided to read the draft and she was right: it was a mess. It contained all the necessary information, but it was badly written, poorly structured, and filled with numerous grammatical and spelling errors. So, with nothing else to do, and so as to alleviate my boredom, I took it upon myself to rewrite it…just as an exercise.

When one of the PR reps finally got back, I explained the urgent situation to him and gave him both the original copy and my revised version—without telling him I was the one who wrote it. His response regarding my revision: "This looks fine—what's the problem? Just send it out!" So they sent my version out to print…without making a single edit. And no one ever knew, or asked, who did it.

This department was always shorthanded, overworked, and in need of help. And I was right there in front of them, ready, willing, and able. I tried numerous times to bring this to their attention, but my offers to take on larger responsibilities went unheard, as no one was willing to listen to me. I was just "Todd the Temp."

But all's well that ends well, as two weeks later I was hired—full-time— by Disney to work as an assistant to a comedy writer/producer. On my first day on the job, I asked him what made him hire me over three other candidates who seemed to have stronger résumés. His response: "During the interview, you asked a lot of really good questions. And no one else did. It showed me you were thinking. I need the person who works for me to know how to listen."

So, it was asking and listening, not talking and telling, that got me the job.

And I soon discovered, working for him, that having a manager who was willing to listen to me made all the difference in the world.

The simple lesson: To be a better leader—as well as a better human being—be a better listener.

8 Quick Tips for Becoming a Better Listener: L-I-S-T-E-N-U-P!

Look at the person: Make eye contact. Pay attention to facial expressions, body language, and tone of voice. There's an old saying that we have two ears and one mouth, so we should spend twice as much time listening as talking. As Peter Drucker famously stated, "The most important thing in communication is to hear what *isn't* being said." And that can only happen if we make the time, and take the time, to truly stop, look, and listen.

Inquire: Ask questions. Ask follow-up questions. Delve deeper. Seek examples. Use paraphrasing and summary clarification to validate understanding. When someone asks you a question, don't just answer the question—care enough to answer the question behind the question. And when you listen to the response, actively listen to gain true understanding…rather than just selectively listening or listening to respond.

Show that you're interested: When someone is talking to you, it's important to physically demonstrate that you value the speaker—as well as what's being spoken. Put yourself in their shoes, try to see things from their point of view, and listen with empathy and compassion. Engage them in dialogue to make them feel like they're the most important person in the room. But it must be done genuinely and sincerely, or it doesn't count. People can see right through you when you're faking it.

Treat the person with respect: Even if you disagree with what they're saying, and you may not even like the person, show respect for their viewpoint and express appreciation for their candor and their contributions. If you disagree, use cushioning to disagree agreeably. Seek to connect with them on a human level, and on an equal level—person-to-person—regardless of title, status, or position, even if you are more senior, more knowledgeable, or more experienced. If you treat them with dignity and respect, you will earn their trust and respect in return. And that will open up the lines of communication even further.

Encourage the other person: Engage them in dialogue and empower them to speak their mind without hesitancy, self-censorship, or fear of retribution. Create an environment of dialogue, exchange, interaction, openness, honesty, self-disclosure, vulnerability, and trust. In other words, create a climate of what's now commonly known as "psychological safety" (thanks to Amy Edmondson of Harvard). Make a little extra effort when communicating with an introvert, as it may take a little more to get them to open up.

Never make someone regret that they opened up to you: Once you lose someone's trust and damage or destroy the relationship, it's almost impossible to get it back. Allow the other person to be vulnerable, and be willing to display your vulnerability as well. Maintain confidences and confidentiality. Don't gossip or talk behind anyone's back. And follow the "Vegas Rule": What's said here, stays here.

Understanding is your primary objective: It's not enough to simply hear the *words* being said; you must get at the *meaning* and the *intent* of those words. Listen not only with your ears, but with your eyes, your brain, your head, and your heart. When listening, it's not about *you*; it's about the other person. So, listen with empathy, compassion, and caring.

Put your smartphone down: This might be our biggest obstacle to meaningful listening in this day and age. We're so busy with our devices that we often ignore the person (or people) right in front of us. Ask yourself: Is the person on the other end of your device more important than the person (or people) right there in the room with you? If not, put the phone down. Seriously, put it down. Face down. Or in a pocket or drawer or briefcase. Be present. Be focused. Be here now. And give the person speaking to you your undivided attention. And make eye contact. Isn't that what you would want? We know that it is.

In closing, many managers feel and act as if their job is to do all of the talking and to have all of the answers. But the best leaders know that they don't. They know that wisdom comes not from answering questions, but from questioning answers. And they recognize the value and power of leveraging the collective brainpower of the diverse talent around them—and this can only happen if and when we make the time, and take the time, to listen.

Steve Jobs said that we shouldn't hire smart people only to tell *them* what to do; we should hire smart people so that they can tell *us* what to do.

So, for a leader, listening requires self-awareness, time, effort, vulnerability, and courage.

As Winston Churchill so eloquently put it: "Courage is what it takes to stand up and speak; courage is also what it takes to sit down and listen."

In Review

The Big Lesson: The best leaders know how to be good listeners.

The Big Question: How good a listener are you…and why? How do you think *others* would answer that question about you…and why? And what can you do to become an even better listener?

Your Big Insight:

Your Big Action:

CHAPTER 47

No Shirt for You

Photo of me getting Jerry Seinfeld's autograph at a 1993 Los Angeles book signing. And yes, I know...I do appear to be wearing a puffy shirt.

Years ago, when I lived in L.A., I went to see a live taping of *Seinfeld*—which, as a huge fan of the show, was an amazing and unforgettable life experience. But what made it most unforgettable—and regrettable—all these years later was something that *didn't* happen that night.

During a break in the taping, the warm-up guy, whose job it was to keep the audience entertained in between scenes, said: "It's time for some *Seinfeld* trivia! If you can tell me the middle name of Elaine Benes, you will win this *Seinfeld* T-shirt!" Having watched and pretty much memorized every single episode (I had taped them all on my VCR; yes, of course, on VHS tapes), I knew for 100 percent certain that the answer was *Marie*.

However, while other audience members randomly and stupidly shouted out one wrong guess after another, I sat there in anxious silence… not saying a word. Despite busting inside to shout out "Elaine *Marie* Benes!" and claim my prize, I suddenly started doubting myself. And, as an extreme introvert who was too shy and terrified to speak in public, I was afraid of the possibility of being wrong and embarrassing myself in front of this group of strangers who didn't know me, wouldn't have cared, and whom I would never see again. My introversion, lack of confidence, and self-doubt kept me from taking a chance. Within two minutes, time was up, no one won the prize, and that window of opportunity slammed shut forever. As the Soup Nazi might have put it, there would be "No shirt for you!"

So…what kept me from winning that *Seinfeld* souvenir that I wanted so badly? Absolutely nothing…except for a lack of trust in myself, the fear of being wrong, and my self-imposed inability to speak in public. That night, I wish that I had remembered the words of President Franklin Delano Roosevelt: "The only thing we have to fear…is fear itself." For, it was fear, and fear alone, that kept me from seizing an opportunity that was all mine to take.

I had briefly mentioned this incident earlier (when discussing the CAP: "Confidence, Assertiveness, and Presence" model in Chapter 7), but it bears repeating with just a little more detail, as this was such an impactful episode in my life, with such a transformative, and universal, lesson.

A number of years after the *Seinfeld* incident, I was working in New York as part of a six-person consulting team for a London-based leadership development training company. For each program we delivered to our client—let's just call them "Vandelay Industries"—they would appoint someone to serve as the Team Lead. Only, even after working for them for two years, and feeling that my skills were as good as, if not better than, some of the others', I was never—not once—named to be the Team Lead. And every single time that I wasn't, I grew more and more annoyed, frustrated, and resentful. "I can't believe they passed me over *again*!" I would say to myself and complain to my wife.

And then, one day, after being overlooked once more, feeling demoralized and depressed, I finally worked up the courage and the confidence to approach our supervisor—let's call her "Sally," which is not her real name. I tried not to come across as pissed-off, but I desperately needed an answer, as this constant rejection was starting to take its toll on my self-esteem. Our conversation went like this:

Todd: "Sally, can I speak with you for a minute. I've been doing this job for two years, and yet in all this time I have never once been named the Team Lead. So, I was just wondering why."

Sally: "Would you *like* to be a Team Lead?"

Todd: "Yes, of course!"

Sally: "Done! You can be the Team Lead on our next program that starts in two weeks."

Todd: "That's it? How come you never made me a Team Lead before?"

Sally: "Because you never asked."

Because you never asked. That was it. That was the entire reason. And it speaks to an incredibly valuable lesson, one that has stayed with me ever since.

The bottom line is that, very often, if we don't ask, we may not get. Yes, of course it is always nicer to be invited *without* having to ask, and sometimes we may feel, "Well, they should know; I shouldn't *have* to ask." But the reality is, everyone is in their own world and living in their own head—and not inside ours. People are not mind readers. This is such an important point that I'll say it again: People-Are-Not-Mind-Readers. If we want something, or need something, whether it is a *Seinfeld* T-shirt or a job assignment, or if you are a manager who just magically expects people to do things a certain way, or if you expect that your partner should just, automatically, "know" what you're thinking—if we don't speak up and speak out, and express what we want and need, we often have no one to blame but ourselves. It is entirely up to us to get others to "see what we're saying."

And I think you'll find that doing so—speaking up and speaking out for yourself, risking rejection, and simply raising your hand—will open the door to all kinds of opportunities you never thought possible. As the saying goes, when it comes to making sales, every "no" you receive brings you one step closer to a "yes." And, as Eleanor Roosevelt wrote in her wonderful book, *You Learn By Living*:

> *Fear has always seemed to me to be the worst stumbling block which anyone has to face.... The encouraging thing is that every time you meet a situation, though you may think at the time it is an impossibility...once you have met it and lived through it, you find that forever after you are freer than you ever were before. If you can live through that, you can live through anything. You gain strength, courage and confidence by every experience in which you really stop to look fear in the face. You are able to say to yourself, 'I have lived through this...I can take the next thing that comes along.' You must do the thing you think you cannot do.*

So, while there would be "no shirt for me" that night of the Seinfeld taping, and while I wasted almost two years frustratingly waiting to be picked for a role that I wanted, when all I would have needed to do was ask, I learned the hard way that "if you want something, say something."

And, though I am a very different person today than I was way back then, I will never forget, and always regret, the shirt that got away.

In Review

The Big Lesson: It is entirely within our power to speak up, speak out, and "claim our prize." And yet, too many times, we let fear and self-doubt get in the way...causing us to miss out on valuable and potentially life-changing opportunities. Yet that can all change—not overnight, but over time—if you are willing to work on it. Take it from me: if I was able to do it, anyone can.

The Big Question: Reflect back on a time when you didn't speak up when you could have, and therefore missed out on an opportunity. Are there similar situations you could approach differently today? What will you do in the future to make sure that this doesn't happen to you, or to others you know, ever again?

Your Insight:

Your Action:

CHAPTER 48

PTBD (Post-Traumatic Boss Disorder)

"The worst is not, so long as we can say 'This is the worst.'"

—WILLIAM SHAKESPEARE; *King Lear*, Act 4, Scene 1

That manager who threw the box of pens at my head wasn't the only "BFH" ("Boss From Hell") I've ever worked for. Unfortunately, there were many others. Way too many others. Almost as bad as the pain they caused is the painful memories—and the awful feelings—that still linger years later.

I was attending a conference when I glanced across the room and saw, sitting directly across from me, Ms. "X": one of the three worst managers I've ever had, and one of the most vile human beings I've ever met in my life. Worse than being incompetent, passive-aggressive, and power-hungry, she was mean, vicious, scary, sadistic, and abusive, and she made my life (and many of my colleagues' lives) a living hell. And she seemed to enjoy every minute of it.

But here's the crazy thing: Even though it had been exactly twenty years since I worked for her and last saw her, the instant I recognized her, every single one of those terrifying feelings I used to suffer while working for this evil woman immediately came flooding back. My body jolted into "fight, flight, or freeze" mode. Within seconds, I grew sick to my stomach, as if I were going to throw up. I started sweating profusely, my heart pounded through my chest, and my hands started to shake uncontrollably. I was having a full-fledged anxiety attack. Unable to catch my breath, I got up from my seat, legs wobbling, and bolted out of the room to compose myself in the men's room.

It was incredible: here I was, a successful and confident fifty-something-year-old business professional and college professor, suddenly reduced—in an instant—to a quivering abuse victim suffering from a post-traumatic stress reaction. Even though she no longer held any power or control over me, my mind and my body reacted involuntarily as if she did.

Amazingly, here is a person who made my life so unbelievably miserable and torturous, and who I can never forget; and, yet, if I had to put money on it, I would bet that if she saw me, she would neither recognize me nor remember who I was.

So, if you are a manager, due to the position and power you hold, your words and deeds will be magnified a thousandfold. And, in *any* relationship, it's good to keep in mind the potential emotional consequences—both positive and negative—of anything and everything we say and do.

Dale Carnegie, author of the classic book *How to Win Friends and Influence People*, noted that what we say to someone, *we* may forget a few minutes later…but those words could remain with that other person for the rest of their lives. Similarly, the poet Maya Angelou famously said, "I've learned that people will forget what you said. People will forget what you did. But people will never forget how you made them feel."

And I never experienced a truer and more powerful example of that than what I experienced upon encountering my former boss that day.

Even twenty years later, as William Faulkner once wrote, "The past is never dead. It's not even past."

In Review

The Big Lesson: In all of your relationships, and in every interaction, be consciously aware of what you say, how you say it, what you do, and how you act; for the impact of your words and actions, and how you treat people—regardless of your intentions—can have meaning and consequences above and beyond, and long after, what *you* can even imagine.

The Big Question: In what situations and in what relationships may you want to be more cognizant of how your words and/or actions are coming across? Have you ever had an experience comparable to the one I described? What can you take from your memory as you revisit it?

Your Big Insight:

Your Big Action:

CHAPTER 49

Rules Are Rules...or Are They?

When it comes to "rules," which of the following statements do you most agree with?

- **a.** Rules are rules…period.
- **b.** Rules are meant to be broken.
- **c.** It depends.
- **d.** All of the above.
- **e.** None of the above.

While there is no one "right" answer to the above question, the way you respond says a lot about you. The way you think and feel about rules in general will influence the decisions you make and the actions you take in different situations…as well as how you manage and how you lead.

Let me tell you about two contentious, thought-provoking, and emotional real-life incidents that happened to me, both of which involved "following the rules," and let's see what you think:

Incident #1

While playing softball in Central Park one night, our manager noticed that one of the players on the other team was wearing baseball cleats with metal spikes which, according to league rules, are not allowed (as someone could potentially get hurt). The player claimed that he didn't know about this rule, immediately apologized, and went back to the bench to change into his sneakers.

But not so fast! In the opinion of my team's manager, this opposing player's blatant and flagrant violation of league rules was too egregious to overlook or forgive. Ignorance of the law is no excuse. And what if he had spiked somebody and they got hurt? As far as our manager was concerned, there was no option but to go strictly by the book and demand that the umpire immediately throw this player out of the game.

The fact that it was a minor and inadvertent oversight, that the player apologized for his mistake, that no one got hurt, that a number of the guys on our own team pleaded, "Forget about it, just let him change his shoes and play," and that we were already losing 10–2 in the fourth inning, all didn't seem to matter. From our manager's perspective, "Rules are rules." No discussion. No debate. No warning. No second chances. One strike and you're out.

Following the letter of the law, the umpire (hesitantly, sympathetically, and apologetically) proceeded to inform the violator that he was sorry but, based on our manager's demand and the letter of the law, he had no choice but to ban him from the rest of the game.

Oh. And in case you were wondering, we went on to lose 20–2 as the angry opposing team, in the spirit of retribution, retaliation, and revenge, proceeded to pour it on and make us pay dearly.

Incident #2

Someone posted the following question on a LinkedIn HR discussion group: "One of my employees is an excellent worker, but he often does not report to the office on time. When I talk to him, he promises to be on time from now on, but that does not last more than two or three days. Any suggestions?"

The responses came pouring in: "Write him up!"; "Dock his pay"; "Demote him!"; "Put it on his permanent record!"; "Give him a final warning!"; "Show him who's boss!"; "Don't give him any more chances— I would fire him immediately!"; "This kind of insubordinate behavior simply cannot be tolerated! He's got to be made an example of and taught to obey the rules!"

Yup, rules are rules. Or are they?

Let me start by saying that, yes, rules are important. Whether we call them policies, operating procedures, guiding principles, or ground rules, every organization needs to have processes and structures in place or else there would be chaos. Rules enable organizations to be…well…organized. And they let the people within an organization (or a community or a society) know what is allowed, and what is expected.

However, when reflecting on the two incidents described above, my question is this: Might there be times when "the Rules" should be overruled?

Now, just for clarification, and before instigating any kind of legal backlash, I'm talking about "rules," not "laws," which are a more specific (though related) issue.

And I'm not talking about safety violations, integrity issues, or ethical lapses. I'm talking about situations in which mindlessly and unquestioningly following certain edicts and strictly following "the book" may not necessarily be the best or the right decision to make.

For example, in the softball incident, did the player on the other team "break the rules?" Yes, officially, he definitely did. But two key questions that should probably be asked are: (1) Was the rule violation intentional or accidental—and does that matter?; and (2) How serious of a rule violation was it; that is, was any advantage received or any damage done as a result?

Keeping things in perspective, we're not talking about a major league player caught taking steroids, corking his bat, or throwing a spitball; we're talking about a guy playing a fun, casual league game in the park who was discovered to be wearing the wrong kind of shoes. It was clear and obvious to everyone—including my manager, and the umpire—that this transgression was an accidental oversight. There was no intent to deceive, to defraud, or to reap any competitive advantage, and no harm of any kind was done. So, if that was the case, did the punishment, banishment from the game, fit the crime of wearing unsanctioned footwear? Or might this player's removal from the game have been a tad excessive under the circumstances? Was my manager "wrong?" No…he was not. But was he "*right*"? I'll let you play umpire and make that call.

In the second case of the online HR mob and the tardy employee, there are again two questions that come to mind: (1) What is the context?; and (2) What are the specific details?

What jumped out at me, and really pushed me over the edge, was that almost everyone—again, the respondents were all HR professionals—was calling for this guy's head with very limited information and pretty much no backstory!

Has this employee broken the rule that "everyone needs to get to work 'on time'"? Apparently so. But do we know anything else? No, absolutely nothing!

What type of job are we talking about? Is he a salaried or hourly worker? What exactly does "on time" mean anyway? How "late" is he… and how often? Is he expected to get there at 9 a.m. and is showing up at 9:05 a.m…or 10:05 a.m.? Is he "late" once a week or every single day? How long has this been going on? Two weeks, two months, two years? And what is the reason for, and the impact of, his lateness?

Most importantly, before reporting him to HR and putting him on a disciplinary plan (remember, he has been described as an "excellent worker"), has the employee's manager actually sat down and spoken to him one-on-one and heart-to-heart to find out what is going on with him—asking and listening, discussing expectations, making him aware of the business impact of the lateness (that is, on customers, team members, the organization, and on the manager himself), and exploring or offering possible solutions?

Years ago when I worked for CBS out in L.A., I was a high performer who had always gotten to work on time—until I hit a week of major car problems that resulted in my being about thirty to forty-five minutes late three days in a row. How did my tyrannical boss address this issue? By saying (and I quote): "I don't know what the hell is going on with you lately, but I'm sick of your marching in here late. If you can't start getting here on time, you better start looking for another job." Wow. So, you can see why I may be a little sensitive and overly empathetic when it comes to this particular situation.

But the bottom line is that I was really amazed, and incredibly disappointed, to see how many of the LinkedIn discussion responses were about "policy, policy, policy." Sad to say, but that's one of the problems with the HR mentality in many companies, and it's also why so many people, per the title of the classic *Fast Company* article, "hate HR."

As an honorary HR person who works in the learning and development field, I have seen too many human resources professionals who have lost sight of the fact that what we do is supposed to be all about engaging *people* and helping them maximize their performance, productivity, and potential. It's not simply about setting and enforcing *the rules*, or a written set of policies and procedures. The first initial of "HR" stands for "Human," and my belief is that we need to strive to treat our people more humanely.

The root of the word "policy" is the same as that of "police"—via Oxford, both words stem from the Old French word *policie*, or "civil administration." If HR representatives want to be viewed as something more than just the company police, perhaps companies need to rethink how we view, deal with, and find a gentle balance between the Rules and our People. Sometimes we need to go by the book; other times we need to go by "common sense." But, unfortunately, as the saying goes, common sense is not always common practice.

And from a leadership perspective, this classic saying from the legendary Peter Drucker comes to mind once again: "Management is about doing things right; leadership is about doing the right thing." As such, perhaps "by the book" is not always "the right thing" to do.

So, the question to ask yourself is, as you look to balance "the spirit of the rule" with "the letter of the law": Do "the Rules" rule, or do *you*?

In Review

The Big Lesson: Rules, policies, guidelines, and principles are important. Without them, there'd be chaos. However, as the saying goes, sometimes "rules are meant to be broken." And a part of leadership is often to challenge "the rules" and disrupt the status quo.

The Big Question: What is your perspective on "rules"? Personality-wise, do you consider yourself more of a "rule follower," "a rule breaker," or a "change maker"? What are some memorable times when you and "the rules" came head-to-head, and what was the outcome? And might considering these questions impact your decisions and actions in the future?

Your Insight:

Your Action:

CHAPTER 50

Slow Down Your Thinking to Speed Up Your Progress

You have an important job interview scheduled, or a big meeting coming up with the boss or with an important client. You've done your homework and you're prepared, primed, and pumped up.

But have you thought about your thinking speed?

We all know that interviews and high-stakes meetings can be very stressful, and when nerves flare up our tendency is to think and talk too fast, leading to our potentially blowing that meeting that we prepared so long and so hard for.

In his best-selling, award-winning book *Thinking, Fast and Slow*, Daniel Kahneman takes a deep dive into how we think, and shows us how we can be more effective…simply by slowing down. According to Kahneman, one of the biggest problems is that we tend to think too fast—especially when under stress.

When your brain reacts automatically and instinctively, almost thinking *without* really thinking, that's what Kahneman calls "thinking *fast.*" This is how we think most of the time. On the other hand, "thinking *slow*" is when your brain hits the pause button and takes a brief moment to consciously reason, consider, question, analyze, and decide—and *then* responds.

Of course, "thinking fast" is a good thing. We couldn't possibly—and wouldn't want to—have to overanalyze every single thought before responding. But, on the flip side, how often do we make mistakes motivated by knee-jerk reactions, or sudden jumps to conclusions, when we might have benefited from one momentary pause to devise a more well-considered response?

With that said, how can you leverage the power of "thinking slow" when on the spot in your next meeting, job interview, or high-pressure situation?

One simple and powerful way to do so is by harnessing the storytelling framework called "PARLA" (Problem, Action, Result, Learning, and Application) that I mentioned earlier.

Let's say a job interviewer asks you, "Can you tell me about a time when you faced a similar situation?" Or you're in a sales meeting and the potential client asks, "Have you ever worked with a company like ours before?" In either scenario, you might use the PARLA method to structure your five-part response as follows:

P—Problem: Let me tell you about the time I faced a similar situation…

A—Action: Here's the action I took…

R—Result: Here's the outcome of that action…

L—Learning: Here's what I learned…

A—Application: And—this is the most important and relevant part to the listener—here's how I would apply this Learning in the future…

· Very often, when an interviewer or a potential client asks us a question, we excitedly blurt out, in our excitement to win them over, something like, "Because I have a degree in x, and ten years' experience, and I'm a hard worker, and a team player, and blah blah blah." Not only are we thinking fast, we're talking fast, and often just rambling on and on. And that's exactly what so many people do.

Instead, why not try to differentiate yourself by taking a breath…and a brief, two-second pause…followed by a confident, PARLA-based *story* that will make you stand out from the crowd.

For example, one time a potential new client asked me "How much experience do you have working with millennials?"

My PARLA-structured response:

Problem: I've definitely spent a lot of time working with millennials! In fact, I teach a graduate course in 'Leadership & Team Building' in the HR master's program at NYU—and most of my students are millennials. And I've worked with a number of tech start-ups that have primarily millennial populations.

Action: One of the things I always ensure when training millennials is to keep things as fast-paced, varied, and highly-interactive and experiential as possible.

Result: I've found that when I do, as with any population, it dramatically increases the workshop attendees' attention, comprehension, and retention.

Learning: So, every one of my training programs is designed and delivered with our "3 E's"—Educate, Engage, and Excite—in mind.

Application: As such, I would definitely make sure that any leadership programs we create for your organization would be highly interactive and experiential as well.

It's that simple: PARLA.

By the way, in regard to the story you choose to tell to illustrate your experience and capability, the "P" for "Problem" that you describe simply refers to the *challenge, issue, situation,* or *opportunity* that you faced.

Also, even if things didn't go well in the Results phase of your example, what's most important is that you took an Action to address a Problem, and that you Learned something valuable from it that you can now Apply going forward. And, in truth, that's really what the interviewer or potential client is hoping to hear: based on your prior experience, whether you have the capability to do the job.

Lastly, PARLA is not just a storytelling technique to use when *being* interviewed; it is actually a classic technique that an interviewer may use to question *you*! So, if an interviewer ever begins a question with, "Tell me about a time when..." you will now immediately recognize that that is what they're doing...and what they are looking for in terms of a response. Not to give away any behind-the-scenes interviewing secrets, but now that you are aware of this popular methodology, you will be better prepared to take a breath and respond on the spot.

Ideally, when going into any meeting or interview, it's beneficial to have done your homework in advance and come prepared with a few relevant sample stories to share that will serve to bring your point to life and get people to "see what you're saying." But even if you feel unprepared or on-the-spot, if you can visualize the PARLA framework in your mind's eye, it will enable you to formulate a powerful and effective response in a moment's time.

Telling a well-structured personal story using the PARLA format will capture your listener's attention, bring your experience to life, show that you can think on your feet, and demonstrate with poise and confidence that you have what it takes to do the job...because you've been there before.

And that's the power of "thinking slow" in action.

In Review

The Big Lesson: Sometimes the fastest way to get your point across is to momentarily slow things down.

The Big Question: What is a situation in which the PARLA story-telling technique might come in handy for you? What are some stories you can formulate in advance to prepare yourself for the next time you need to show someone what you can do?

Your Big Insight:

Your Big Action:

CHAPTER 51

Spanning the Decades:
Career Advice for Every Age and Every Stage

"All the world's a stage,
And all the men and women merely players;
They have their exits and their entrances;
And one man in his time plays many parts.
His acts being seven ages."

—WILLIAM SHAKESPEARE, *As You Like It*, Act 2 Scene 7

Whenever anyone, including my students and my coaching clients, asks me for career advice, my answer is always the same: "It depends." And what does it depend on? A lot of different, individual factors. But among the most important considerations is: Where are they in terms of Shakespeare's "seven ages"—and at what stage are they at in their career?

While there is, of course, no "one-size-fits-all" answer, based on my personal and subjective experience here's my best career advice for every age and every stage:

Teens: The Age of Exploration

When you are in your teens, you don't know what you don't know. So, try to gain as much exposure to as many different types of experiences as possible. This way, you can get an idea of what you may be good at and what you're not, as well as what you may like to do and what you don't. Don't be afraid to try or to fail. That's what these years are for!

You should try to learn as much as you can about the realities of the workplace. Find internships, take temp or entry-level jobs, do volunteer work, and ask questions. Lots and lots of questions. Don't feel that any question is dumb, or that any job is beneath you. At this stage of your life, everything is new and, therefore, a learning experience. If you go into every situation with a positive attitude, you'll be amazed at how much you can learn and how fast you will grow.

20s: The Age of Experimentation

Now that you have a better sense of what's out there, take a more targeted approach toward finding your niche. You are still exploring and experimenting, but the stakes are a little higher now than when you were still in school. You want to do well, gain experience, build your network, and show that you are capable of producing real results.

Take chances, but be smart about it. And don't burn any bridges or do anything rash that could potentially come back to haunt you one day (including what you put out there on social media). You are now establishing your reputation, building your résumé, planting the seeds for your career, and—as Steve Jobs once put it—asking yourself how you are going to "put a ding in the universe."

30s: The Age of Self-Actualization

At this point in your life there is, hopefully, some connection between who you are and what you do, as well as having developed a strong sense of your "personal brand" and your "Eye-denity": the way you are seen by others.

One way to explore your personal brand is to think about how you want to define yourself: *What do you want to be known as, "the Guru of" or "the Go-to person" for?* Then, figure out what you need to do to make that vision a reality. Ideally, you want to be working in a field that you are good at (and/or aspire to be great at) and cultivating skills that you like or love. You want to be setting yourself up for success and becoming a subject matter expert in your field, while still creating opportunities to take risks and to grow.

You may have greater "adult responsibilities" now, so it may also be time to start thinking about and preparing for the future—financially and otherwise. The key is to be proactive in figuring out what you need to do to maximize your performance, your productivity, and your potential, both in your career and in your personal life.

40s: The Age of Expertise

Ideally, you'd like to now be settled into a career with a proven track record of success, a positive professional reputation, and a network of contacts. (And not just online "connections," but true, real-world relationships.) Building on the results you've produced, and with an eye toward the future, your thoughts will likely turn to further developing your leadership potential while continuing to hone your personal brand—both internally within your firm and externally within your industry.

But what do you do if you've had a setback and/or your career train has gone off the track? My feeling, from personal experience, is that it's never too late to reinvent oneself. As the saying about best-laid plans goes, they often go awry. Like getting knocked back to the starting square in a board game, you may occasionally need to return to the ages of Exploration and/or Experimentation again and start anew.

However: there's absolutely nothing wrong with that (!), as it happens to most of us at one point or another. The good news is that, this time around, you get to leverage the wisdom of your experience as you set out in search of new horizons and new possibilities.

50s: The Age of Mastery

Here's where and when you can up the ante of your reputation: based on years of experience, you can now market yourself as a credible subject-matter expert in your field. You've earned it. But it's equally important to keep learning!

Remember: "In an ever-changing world, if you're standing still, you're falling behind." Everything—technology, the marketplace, norms, and expectations—changes more quickly and more frequently than ever before. The shelf-life of knowledge is shorter than the expiration date on a container of milk. So it's a never-ending, twenty-four-hour-a-day race just to keep up. But you must try, as there is no other choice if you wish to stay relevant and valuable to others.

Your strength, at this stage, lies in combining your years of experience with your ability and willingness to proactively stay ahead of the curve. You may also be thinking about what you want your "leadership legacy" to be…and, if so, this is the time to start thinking about what you need to do between now and the future to make that vision a reality.

60s+: The Age of Wisdom

You've seen it all. Or have you?

As the world's changes seem to accelerate, we see something new every single day that we've never seen before. You want to make yourself marketable by branding yourself as a sage, and yet have the humility to look to those younger than you as your teachers. You want to *be* a mentor, and yet be open and willing to be mentored and coached yourself.

With that combination of attributes, you will have much to contribute and you will stay relevant and in demand. You want to experience the excitement and satisfaction of continuing on your own journey of development while, simultaneously, taking the time to pass the wisdom of your experience along to the next generation. It's also something you can take pride in, as you bear in mind my maxim that "Wisdom is where Knowledge and Experience meet."

A Few Thoughts to Keep in Mind as You Transition from One Stage to the Next

Bear in mind that this is all just one person's totally subjective broad advice, with which you are entirely free to agree or disagree. It is quite freeing, though, to remember that there are no "shoulds." For example, "At this point in my life, I 'should' be further along in my career."

The reality is that career paths take us where career paths take us. Just as in Robert Frost's "The Road Not Taken," our journeys are ultimately shaped by the choices we made...and the choices we didn't. Despite the common metaphor, most careers don't resemble a straight and linear "path" so much as a roller coaster ride of ups and downs, starts and stops, twists and turns, and victories and setbacks.

President John F. Kennedy wrote, "Leadership and learning are indispensable to each other." As such, with that realization in mind, a successful career journey seems inextricable from a life-long love of learning; a spirit of proactivity; a sense of resilience; a positive attitude of gratitude; and a growth mind-set that keeps you continuously looking—and moving—ever forward...at every age, and through every stage.

In Review

The Big Lesson: Considering where you are in your life and your career will help you to frame your situation with greater clarity and insight, as well as to make better career-related decisions.

The Big Question: In which stage of your career are you right now, and what can you learn from this framework that might guide you forward?

Your Big Insight:

Your Big Action:

CHAPTER 52

Taking the Leap

There's a classic riddle that I use in my leadership workshops that goes like this:

> There are five frogs on a log.
> One decides to jump into the pond.
> How many are left on the log?
> The answer: Still five.

Why?

Because he *decided* to jump in…but he didn't actually *do* it!

And it's the *doing* that counts.

When I was ten years old, my family went to a local pool club that had a high diving board. All the other kids were having so much fun scampering up that tall ladder and jumping into the water that, after much deliberation, I hesitantly decided to give it a try too, even though I had a debilitating fear of heights (which went along with my debilitating fear of all the other kids).

Gingerly climbing the ladder, I inched my way out to the edge of the diving board…only to look down and see that it was even more terrifying than I was expecting it to be!

So I quickly changed my mind and turned around with the intent of going back down the ladder. However, a line of about five other kids had already climbed up the ladder and were impatiently waiting their turn. "*Come on…let's go already*!!!" they were all screaming at me. So, completely embarrassed, and with, really, no other choice, I turned back around again, ran the length of the board, and dove in—headfirst!

What do you think I did the rest of that afternoon? Yup. I kept on climbing that ladder and diving back in, again and again, until the sun went down and it was time to go home.

This, again, reminds me of Seth Godin's simple-yet-powerful quote: "You don't need more time. You just need to decide." And after deciding, we need to act. Or, in Godin lingo, we need to "ship."

So often we are racked with indecision and/or paralyzed by fear that we put off making any decision—until the window of opportunity closes, and the decision is made for us.

In fact, if you think about it, *not* making a decision is a decision you've made.

Think about how many potentially positive, life-enhancing decisions might you have missed out on simply due to procrastination? We often come up with excuse after excuse about why something can't be done, but as futurist Joel Barker wrote in his amazing book, *Paradigms: The Business of Discovering the Future*—and as I experienced on that high diving board all those year ago—"Those who say 'it can't be done' need to get out of the way of those who are doing it."

The bottom line is that no one wants to *hear* excuses; they only want to *see* results.

So, unlike that hesitant frog on the log, I encourage you to take that leap. There's a good chance that if you do, you'll be very glad that you did.

In Review

The Big Lesson: When you reflect back on the times that you took a leap and landed successfully, it gives you the courage and confidence necessary to take on the next challenge.

The Big Question: What are some examples of times that you took a calculated risk, something that was a "big leap" for you, and what did you learn about yourself from that experience? And, what are some examples of times when you didn't take the leap, but looking back on it, you wish that you had? What held you back? With these examples in mind, what is the next big leap that you are going to take?

Your Big Insight:

Your Big Action:

CHAPTER 53

That's a Novel Idea!
How Reading Literature (and Other Nonbusiness Books) Can Benefit You at Work and in Life

Based on what I do for a living, most people assume that I have a degree in business.

But I don't. While I ended up getting a master's degree in communication, as an undergraduate I was an English literature major with a concentration in Shakespeare and poetry. (You might have sensed that from some of my examples and quotes. ☺)

And while I *love* reading business books (and have averaged one a week for the past twenty years), the truth is that today's businessperson cannot—and should not—live by business books alone!

With the word "novel" having the same Latin root—"*novus*" (meaning "new")—as the word "in-nov-ation," it follows that reading more nonbusiness writing may not only be an engaging and enjoyable escape, but also a catalyst for new ideas.

When people ask me, "What's the best way to become a better writer?" my response is always: "Becoming a better *writer* starts with becoming a better *reader.*"

When I am in need of business inspiration, I often find myself going not to a business book, but back to my English major roots to revisit the classics. As the French novelist Marcel Proust famously said, "The real voyage of discovery consists not in seeking new lands, but in seeing with new eyes." So every time I go to my bookshelf to grab some Shakespeare or poetry, or a play or a novel—even those (especially those) I have read before—I tend to find that these works not only hold up over time, but also take on new meaning, foster innovation, and provide fresh insights into the human condition. Surprisingly, these insights are often directly applicable to the world of work.

The Greek philosopher Heraclitus wrote that one "cannot set foot in the same river twice," for both the river and the person are, forever, in flux. So it is with reading and rereading the classics: Each time, a new adventure. Each time, a new voyage of discovery.

For example:

Shakespeare

The story of *Julius Caesar* is as current, meaningful, and impactful today as it was in 1599 when it was written…let alone in 44 BC, when the historical event actually happened. The play explores the world of individuals, organizations, and teams—as well as the themes of politics, public speaking, persuasion, and power. All one needs to do is open the newspaper, turn on the TV, or go online to draw parallels to what's going on in the world today.

And what about some of Shakespeare's other plays? How many times has your workplace turned into *A Comedy of Errors* in which you needed people to do things *As You Like It* so that *All's Well That Ends Well*…only to find yourself working for a boss who always makes *Much Ado About Nothing,* and is as indecisive as *Hamlet,* as weak as *Macbeth,* as emotionally hot-headed as *Othello,* and/or as mad as *King Lear.* There's nothing worse than having a boss who turns everything into a *Tempest*...as you yearn each day for the inspirational leadership of a *Henry V*.

Plays

Arthur Miller's classic dramas *Death of a Salesman* and *All My Sons* each explore timeless business-related themes, from core values and work/life balance to the exploration of relationships, communication, motivation, influence, and human nature.

In the devastating *All My Sons*, factory owner Joe Keller must make a choice between shipping a batch of cracked airplane parts (hoping nothing will happen) or admitting the truth and taking responsibility, thereby risking the loss of his government contract. You can probably guess which option he chooses and what the tragic outcome is (spoiler alert!). While this was a work of fiction, we see this type of tragedy play out in the news every single day.

Fiction

In this age of crowdsourcing and social media flaming, might there be a cautionary tale for us to heed hidden within Shirley Jackson's still-shocking, horrifying, and controversial 1948 short story of mob mentalities, "The Lottery"? And who hasn't wanted to say to his or her boss at one point or another, when asked to do something, "I would prefer not to," as the title character famously does in Herman Melville's classic 1853 short story "Bartleby, the Scrivener: A Story of Wall Street"?

Having recently reread five of my all-time favorite novels—*Catch-22*, *1984*, *Slaughterhouse-Five*, *One Flew Over the Cuckoo's Nest*, and *To Kill a Mockingbird*—the themes of great literature still prove timeless, and *timely*, several decades later. For instance, there is a powerful reason, from a leadership perspective, why the character of Atticus Finch (specifically in the original *To Kill a Mockingbird*, not his unsympathetic reappearance in 2015's *Go Set a Watchman*) is considered one of the greatest fictional heroes, role models, leaders, and real-life influences in the history of American literature (and film). His integrity, his morality, his empathy, his humility, and his intelligence, coupled with his ability to communicate and to impact, influence, and inspire others, are all timeless qualities of a great leader.

Poetry

Reading poetry by the likes of Keats, Shelley, Whitman, Dickinson, Frost, Cummings, Yeats, Eliot, and so many others reminds us of the importance of "poetic" language when seeking to effectively communicate. Poetry demonstrates the power of visual imagery, alliteration and allusion, rhyme and rhythm, meter and metaphor, and more. And the application of poetic elements in everyday speech lies at the foundation of visual thinking, visual communication, and visual leadership.

For example, a recent hot topic in the business world is "mindfulness." What better example of this idea is there than Wordsworth's 1804 poem, "I Wandered Lonely as a Cloud," aka "The Daffodils," in which he illustrates the concept of "emotion recollected in tranquility"! When it comes to decision-making, is there a more well-known, thought-provoking, and impactful metaphor than Frost's "The Road Not Taken" ("Two roads diverged in a yellow wood...")? And while we set off on the rat race each morning, striving to climb the corporate ladder (how's that for a mixed metaphor?), it's important to keep in mind our core values, maintain a sense of perspective, strive for work/life balance, and seek happiness, while taking heed of the fatal, cautionary tale of E.A. Robinson's "Richard Cory"...the rich businessman who seemed, on the outside, to have everything in the world, and yet his inner world was, apparently, a very different story.

Beyond entertainment, enjoyment, and escape, great literature transports us to another place and time, allowing us to experience—and view—the world through the eyes of others. It often brings us back to basics, while reminding us of the universality of the human condition. This makes us not only more informed and literate, but also more educated and enlightened, more aware and self-aware, more humane and more human. And, all together, this will (hopefully) make us both better business leaders and better people.

While the focus here is on the business value of reading fiction, the same can be said of reading nonbusiness, nonfiction books. It's all about opening yourself up to "seeing with new eyes": Whether you enjoy reading about the arts, sports, science, politics, history, biography, travel, self-help, etc., if you actively seek new perspectives and subjects, you are guaranteed to discover valuable business and life lessons hidden in plain sight.

So, if you are thinking about switching careers, looking for leadership lessons, or seeking fresh ideas and approaches, one of the best ways to stimulate innovation and open new possibilities is to look outside of, and beyond, your usual field of vision.

In addition to books, business and life lessons of all kinds can, of course, be gleaned every day, both online and offline, from such diverse media as newspapers, magazines, e-newsletters, blog posts, or even the back of a cereal box or a subway wall…if our eyes are open to noticing.

If "Wisdom is where Knowledge and Experience Meet"[1], then when we enhance our knowledge through reading, and combine that with our real-world, everyday experiences, we ultimately attain the wisdom that only time can teach.

And as the Fool put it to King Lear: "Thou shouldst not have been old before thou hadst been wise."

---

[1] Tip: visualize the Venn diagram.

In Review

The Big Lesson: When we think of "business reading," we often think only of business books. However, lessons in leadership and in life can be found hidden in plain sight in pretty much anything you read. Or watch. Or listen to. And if you are open to investigating the world around you through "a leadership lens," you will discover the world of possibilities that awaits.

The Big Question: What are some books you can read—that are not necessarily business books—from which you might pick up some valuable lessons for success, both in leadership and in life?

Your Insight:

Your Action:

CHAPTER 54

What Gets Recognized and Rewarded Is What Gets Done

Many years ago, early in his career, my brother Steve was working for a major entertainment conglomerate in their TV syndication department. Part of his job was to input data to a computer from various handwritten reports. One of five workers responsible for performing this tedious task day in and day out, for some reason, at the end of each day, everyone else had completed their allotted workload…except for Steve, as his paperwork continued to pile up on his desk.

On top of all of that, his supervisors would approach him and say, "You really need to speed things up. We don't know what's taking you so long, but everyone else always seems to be able to complete their workload by the end of the day, except for you."

Steve couldn't figure it out either. He was as competent and capable and diligent as any of them. So, why was he lagging so far behind?

Eventually, he discovered the answer. The issue had nothing to do with anything he was doing; it had to do with what he *wasn't* doing that everyone else was.

While Steve was diligent in making sure that he was accurately and completely inputting every single report assigned to him, it turned out that his coworkers were far less conscientious. In fact, it turned out that at the end of the day, they stuffed any and all unfinished paperwork into their backpacks, snuck it out of the office, and unceremoniously dumped it into the trash on their way home!

Upon learning this, Steve at least felt somewhat vindicated in knowing that he was not the problem. But now that he knew this…what to do about it? Join the club—sacrificing his integrity, but at least getting his boss off his back? Become a whistleblower, thereby proving to his bosses that he was not the problem? (Although he doubted that his bosses would even care, anyway, as long as they didn't have to see the work piling up.) Or keep doing what he was doing, and continue to bear the wrath of his bosses for his underperformance?

It's an interesting and challenging dilemma, but in the end, being a person of integrity, Steve just kept doing what he was doing, until he eventually found himself another job.

This is one of those stories that sounds like the movie *Office Space*, featuring the infamous TPS reports. But things like this actually happen… and then we wonder why the majority of employees in the workplace are disengaged.

Steve's story always brings to mind three of Peter Drucker's most well-known quotes:

1. *"What gets recognized and rewarded is what gets done."*

Steve's supervisors were recognizing and rewarding speed, with no regard at all for accuracy. Or integrity. Or any sense of purpose relative to the work at hand. It was just a meaningless task. And seeing as the only thing the supervisors seemed to care about was whether the workers ended their shift with a clear desk, that's exactly what they got.

2. *"If you can't measure it, you can't manage it."*

Similarly, Steve's supervisors measured success not by the *quality* of the work that was being done, but simply by the *quantity* of the work completed. And, by "completed," that meant that there were no reports left over...regardless of why that was. As long as everyone was able to "check their boxes" and cover their behinds, that was all that mattered.

3. *"Management is about doing things right; leadership is about doing the right thing."*

Steve's colleagues were being managed (poorly) and, most definitely, not being led. Everyone—except for Steve—failed to "do things right"...or do what anyone with a moral compass would consider "the right thing."

When it comes to balancing "doing things right" and "doing the right thing," everyone wants everything done "better, faster, and cheaper," but you can't always have all three; you sometimes need to prioritize. You can have things done *"right"* or you can have them done *"right now,"* but you can't always have it both ways. Ultimately, it all comes down to priorities...and values. And, without either—and, especially, without clear leadership—companies are going to get what they deserve.

If, at the end of the day, all that these managers care about is their staff leaving the office with a clean desktop, they might as well just toss their work directly into the trash right now and save them (and yourself) the time and trouble. But if a manager wants things done right—*and* the right things done—then they need to recognize and reward both productivity and performance.

Jim Collins, the author of the classic management book *Good to Great*, put it this way: "Don't discipline people. Hire self-disciplined people and give them the freedom and responsibility to act, within the framework of a highly developed system.

Unfortunately, based on Steve's experience—and mine—it seems that companies don't always follow such advice.

In Review

The Big Lesson: Be both aware and intentional regarding how you define responsibilities, assign tasks, and determine incentives, because how you *do* will directly influence what you *get*.

The Big Question: What lessons can you take from Steve's story, and have you ever been in a similar situation? What did, or what would *you* have done? And in light of Drucker's idea that recognition and rewards can strongly influence what gets done, how can you apply these principles to your own workplace so as to get the right things done the right way?

Your Big Action:

Your Big Insight:

CHAPTER 55

Why It's More Important to Be Interested than Interesting

My wife and I were at a New Year's Eve party at a friend's apartment when we ended up standing next to this guy who, as it turns out, was a struggling actor.

Cornering us in the kitchen, all he could talk about was his extensive acting background, and how hard it is—despite his considerable talent, experience, and marketability—to get invited to audition, even though he is continuously submitted by his agent for all of these roles that he's supposedly perfect for.

In the course of his ten-minute monologue on "the Trials and Tribulations of a New York Actor," he mentioned a couple of times that he really wished that he could meet this one famous and powerful New York casting director (so as to protect his identity, let's call this casting director "Mr. X").

Neither during this actor dude's monologue, nor any time afterwards, did he once make any attempt to engage with my wife or me by asking us anything…like, for instance, who we were, or what brought us to the party, or what *we* did for a living.

Had he asked my wife any questions, say, for example, "So, Karin, what do *you* do?" he might have discovered that she is a *casting associate* (!) who specializes in hiring actors for independent films. Yup, that's what she does.

But did he ask her any questions, or make any attempt to connect with her personally, in any way? No, he did not. So then, did he ever learn that she might, potentially, have been in a position to help further his career? Again, no he did not.

Had he made any attempt to engage directly with *me*, he might have learned that the powerful casting director—you know, "Mr. X" whom he mentioned—well, he just happens to be my former college roommate and one of my best friends. In fact, coincidentally, my wife and I had dinner with him just an hour prior to arriving at the party.

But did he ever find that out? Again, nope, he did not. Why? Well, in a nutshell, because all he appeared to be interested in was himself.

This is just one recent and all-too-common real-life example of why and how "networking" opportunities are all around us, hiding in plain sight…if we are only open to seeing them.

So, when meeting new people, rather than talking about ourselves the entire time and trying to sell others on how interesting and great *we* are, it might be valuable, less egotistical, and in many ways more interesting, to invest some time and energy in getting to know others.

In fact, I recommend keeping in mind this simple mantra: "Be Genuine and Generous."

Genuine: Being genuine in your interactions means being curious, and open, and natural, and authentic, and caring. It means asking sincere questions because you are genuinely interested in others…*and* listening attentively to their responses. When this is the case, your interaction becomes not a means to an end, but an end in itself. And if something more comes out of it, that's great, but it shouldn't be the sole or primary purpose; it's a bonus.

As Dale Carnegie wrote in his classic book *How to Win Friends and Influence People,* if you "become genuinely interested in other people," people are more likely to become genuinely interested in you. And when they are genuinely interested in you, they are more likely and willing to help.

Generous: When engaging with others, seek to *give* rather than to *get.* When you are asking and listening, and empathizing and connecting, are you thinking "how can I use what I'm hearing and learning so as to benefit myself?"…or are you thinking "how can I use what I am hearing and learning so as to potentially benefit this other person?"

As organizational psychologist Adam Grant discusses in his excellent book *Give and Take,* when you are a giver, you'll often find that what goes around, comes around—but even if it doesn't, being generous is still a good, and nice, thing to do. And when you do, you become the type of person whom other generous people genuinely want to know and to help.

So, remember that in the eyes of others, being more interest*ed* does, indeed, make you more interest*ing*. If we spend less time trying to promote ourselves, and a little more time listening to, and getting to know, others, you never know where it might lead. That chance conversation with a stranger could, potentially, turn out to be the one that someday leads to you seeing your name up there in lights.

In Review

The Big Lesson: It's not all about you. Taking a genuine interest in others and being generous with your time and attention is more likely to benefit you—and others—in the long run.

The Big Question: What are some things you can start doing differently to become more interesting...by becoming more genuinely and generously interested?

Your Insight:

Your Action:

CHAPTER 56

Why My Wife Doesn't Trust Me Anymore*
(aka The Cockroach Story)

*When it Comes to Bugs

Let me explain…

Early one Saturday morning I was awoken by the blood-curdling sound of my wife screaming from the other room. Still half-asleep and half-dressed, I bolted out of bed in a panic, yelling, "What happened!? What happened!?"

"There's a giant roach in the bathroom!!! It's so disgusting! It's like six inches long—and it just ran behind the sink! You have to kill it!"

So, I raced back into the bedroom to get my glasses, grabbed a rolled-up *New Yorker* magazine (after quickly checking to make sure I was done reading it), opened the bathroom door, slammed it behind me, and prepared for battle.

After multiple attempts of swiping and missing (and, yes, I must admit, yelling and cursing), I finally crushed this hideous beast, which was the size of a two-pound lobster, and flushed its remains down the toilet. (Alright, in all honesty, it wasn't *that* big, but it was sizable. And it was really, really disgusting.)

With that Kafkaesque horror story now over, I crawled back into bed with the intention of picking up where I left off to get a couple more hours of sleep. But just as I was about to doze off, my wife came in and sat down on the bed next to me:

"I have to ask you: Did you *really* kill it…or are you just lying to me again?"

Not fully awake or coherent, and after the exhaustion of my traumatic bug battle—combined with this now second rude awakening—I blurted out, "What—what are you talking about???"

At which point I remembered, and burst out laughing from the recollection of, the one and only time I had lied to my wife in all our years of marriage:

It was back in 2007 and we had just moved into our new apartment. Having just sat down to dinner, we were both jolted out of our seats in horror by the sight of a gigantic, disgusting roach (is there any other kind in New York City?) that had come crawling out of a still-open hole in the floorboard where we just had some construction work done.

After haphazardly swatting at it with a rolled-up newspaper, I finally yelled, "Got him!" gathered up the dead roach in a paper towel, and made a huge show of crumpling it up and, with a great flourish, tossing it into the kitchen trash can.

My wife's elated response, "My hero!"

Only, the truth is: I didn't get him. After much chasing and swatting and swinging and missing, my tiny tormentor had darted and dashed and evaded me, eventually scurrying back into the hole in the wall from whence he came. And I was hungry and just wanted to eat my dinner, which was getting cold. So, I doused the floorboard area with Raid, sealed up the hole with paper towels and aluminum foil, and sat back down to eat. Done.

Except that it wasn't done: the nightmare was just beginning.

Five minutes later, after finally settling back in to finish our dinner, my wife shrieks, "Oh my God—there's another one!!!"

Uh oh. This was a literal "moment of truth." Do I confess that I had failed miserably in my Battle of the Roach, and that I had given up the chase because I just wanted to eat—and, in so doing, sacrifice my newly-acquired "hero" status to be forever labeled, from this day forth, both a liar and a coward? Or: do I continue my charade of having killed the previous roach…which would then lead to my wife thinking that we had a large-scale infestation problem on our hands…in which case we would have no other alternative but to pack our bags and move?

Do I tell the truth…or was I now in what Jerry Seinfeld might label a "must-lie situation"?

So, I made the decision: I would come clean and tell the truth, the whole truth, and nothing but the truth.

And I made the promise—to myself and to my wife—to never lie to her about anything ever again.

A Few Leadership Lessons from This "Bug's Life" Tale

So, what lessons can we take from this episode that we can apply not only to our personal relationships, but also to the world of business and leadership?

Years ago, at a former company, we had an administrative assistant in our department who, for lack of a better term, could be labeled a pathological liar: she would, literally, lie about anything and everything. She lied about completing tasks that she had not even started yet, she made promises and commitments that she had no intention of keeping, and she would say things about other people that were completely untrue. At one point we actually all thought that *we* were going crazy, but the truth was that she was gaslighting us (that is, intentionally messing with people's heads so that they begin to question their own sanity) the entire time. It reached the point where if she said that it was raining out, we wouldn't have believed her. Ultimately, her dysfunctional behavior caught up with her and she was let go.

And the lies don't need to be that blatant. Even small, white lies will undermine your credibility and destroy trust. One of my previous bosses would habitually ask me (force me) to lie about her whereabouts on her behalf. For example, she would say that she needed to attend an important client meeting outside of the office when, in actuality, she would go shopping or get her hair done. So not only was she lying to others, but she put me in the awkward and uncomfortable position of having to sacrifice my integrity by covering for her. Ultimately, she, too, was discovered for what and who she was, and fired.

As the above examples illustrate, when you lie—about anything—that's it: you are now, in the eyes of others, branded "a liar." That is now your reputation. Once you plant a seed of doubt in someone's mind, no matter how trivial, that seed never goes away. In fact, it will most likely grow. For, it makes people start wondering, "If they lied to me about that, what else are they lying to me about?"

Luckily for me, my wife now only distrusts me when it comes to bugs. But if you are found to lie or to bend the truth repeatedly, everything you say thereafter will be subject to questioning. Your lie will live on in the hearts and minds of those you weren't honest with, and this label will cast doubts upon your trustworthiness, both as a person and a leader, forevermore.

Sadly, in our current "post-truth" world of fake news, falsified data, and alternative facts, it is more important than ever to be viewed as a person of integrity. Once you lose people's trust, it is almost impossible to get it back. This is deadly for a leader, or for anyone who aspires to be one. I am reminded of the old adage, "The truth doesn't cost anything; but a lie could cost you everything."

So, what can we do to be seen as one of those rare people of integrity, honesty, credibility, reliability, and trust? Here are a few simple tips to keep in mind:

- It sounds obvious, but always tell the truth. *Always*. Without spin, manipulation, or devious intent.
- Separate verifiable "facts" from claims or opinions…and make it clear at any given time which it is that you are stating.

- Back up your claims with concrete evidence.
- Be authentic, transparent, accountable, genuine, and sincere.
- Say what you mean, and mean what you say.
- Keep promises and commitments. Follow up, and follow through.
- Remember the old saying that "actions speak louder than words." It's true.
- If you don't know something, admit that you don't know it; people will respect that. Don't just make stuff up, as people can see right through the bullshit.
- If you know something, but honestly can't disclose it (that is, for reasons of confidentiality, or for ethical or legal reasons), just say, "I *do* know, but, I'm sorry…I'm not at liberty to say." People will respect that as well.
- If you have inadvertently provided untrue, inaccurate, or mistaken information, acknowledge it, admit it, apologize for it, and correct it. Again, people will respect and appreciate it. And you will regain their trust as a result.
- The same advice applies if you change your position on something. Don't try to bull your way through it; you can just say something like, "In light of this new information…" or, "Having considered this issue more fully…" to introduce the ways that you now feel differently. As the economist John Maynard Keynes was often quoted as saying, when accused of being a flip-flopper: "When the facts change, I change my mind. What do you do, sir?"

Lastly, based on my cautionary tale, remember that lying about one little thing (even one as tiny as an insect) could potentially continue to haunt you—and "bug" the person you lied to—for the rest of your life.

In Review

The Big Lesson: Tell the truth. All the time. Even when it's not easy.

The Big Question: Do you have a memorable story about a time you may have lied to someone, or in which someone lied to you? What did you learn from this experience?

Your Big Action:

Your Big Insight:

PART FIVE

VisuaLeadership: What Now, What Next?

Where do we go from here? As we wrap up our exploration of visual thinking and visual communication as applied to the world of management and leadership, why—when considering "the future of work"—might the use of visuals be even more important than ever? That is, in this fast-paced age of information overload and ever-shortening attention spans, how can we leverage the power of visuals to cut through the clutter so as to capture people's attention, enhance their comprehension, and increase retention?

As we ponder our need to continuously "learn how to learn, unlearn, and relearn," sometimes referred to as "reskilling and upskilling," we'll take a look at how VisuaLeadership can strengthen the competencies and abilities that today's workforce needs to survive and to thrive into the future.

We'll then explore my "Ten Tough Questions Every Self-Aware Leader Needs to Be Able to Answer" to not only challenge you, but also to set you up for success as you lead yourself and others into the future.

We'll then begin to bring our "Leadership Journey" to a close as we approach the final mile and set ourselves up to make the most of these new skills down the road.

And, lastly, I'll leave you with some final thoughts on the importance of reflection, introspection, and connection as a visual leader.

CHAPTER 57

VisuaLeadership and the Future of Work

In an ever-changing world, if you're standing still,
you're falling behind.

One of the hottest business topics out there right now is "The Future of Work": which is to say, how work is changing due to increasingly rapid technological flux, globalization, the gig economy, and other forces. And if you think about it, isn't *every* business book ever written in some way about "the future of work"? They all follow a similar formula (this book included!): Stories and examples from the past, combined with pronouncements about the state of things today, followed by recommendations for how to survive and to succeed in the future.

The main difference between "the past and the present of work" and "the future of work" is that everything seems to be changing at a rate, and on a scale, never before seen. As we've evolved from an agricultural/agrarian economy to the industrial/machine age to the information age to the current digital age, it's become more and more necessary to remain flexible, adaptable, and proactive. You can't just choose to say, "I'm gonna sit this one out"…unless you want to quickly become a dinosaur. For, in this ever-changing world, if you're standing still, you're falling behind.

As they say, we're living in an increasingly "VUCA" (Volatile, Uncertain, Complex, and Ambiguous) world, where we are dealing with rapidly evolving external "PESTLE" (Political, Economic, Sociological, Technological, Legal, and Environmental) forces. It's true that change has always been "the only constant," but when living in a twenty-four-hour, always-on, social media-driven "global village" (as Marshall McLuhan described this interconnectivity in the 1960s), we need to continuously simplify things as much as possible. Visual thinking can help us wrap our heads around this ever-shifting reality, and it will help us succeed in a globalized workplace, as we need to be as clear as possible in our communications as we collaborate across time zones, generations, languages, and cultures.

In terms of technological advances, the train has left the station—at 250 miles per hour—and is only going to speed up. As offices are transformed by artificial intelligence (AI), algorithms, machine learning, data mining and refining, blockchain, automation, outsourcing, gigsourcing, and the like, we're playing in an unfamiliar sandbox where most of us don't speak the language…let alone understand the vocabulary. As such, being equipped, enabled, and empowered to leverage the power of visual thinking and visual communication just might prove to be a huge competitive advantage as you set out to navigate this brave new world.

When it comes to leadership, the old days of "command-and-control"-style managing, and of multilevel organizational hierarchies, are over. We *all* need to be leaders and team builders in order to get things done through and with other people. If you are a manager, your employees have to listen to you because they report to you, but you are only a "leader" if people choose to follow you. So why should people want to follow you? Leadership is not a title or a position. It is a way of being, thinking, and acting. And the door is open to anyone and everyone—at any level, or in any role—with the right mind-set, tool set, and skill set to step up to leadership.

Leaders of the future need to be able to think strategically, see the big picture, and be proactive in gaining the knowledge and skills necessary to create a collaborative climate. One way to do this is to flip that "VUCA" acronym on its head and foster an environment that is its opposite: what I call "CCSC," which stands for: Calm, Certain, Simple, and Clear. We may find that each aspect's opposite offers its antidote:

- In the face of Volatility, leaders need to create an environment of Calmness so that people feel a sense of urgency, rather than a state of panic. As the legendary basketball coach and leadership guru John Wooden put it, we need to "be quick, but don't hurry"...for when you rush, you make mistakes.

- When things are Uncertain, it is the job of the leader to create some degree of Certainty. Uncertainty creates instability, and it is the job of the leader to make people feel that they are standing on a foundation of solid ground.

- In a Complex world, leaders need to Simplify that complexity so that people gain understanding. That does not mean "dumbing things down" or eliminating subtlety and nuance but finding a way to create understanding. As Einstein said, "Make things as simple as possible, but no simpler."

- And, within the Ambiguity, leaders must help people gain a sense of Clarity...so that they can find their way forward. This is done by providing people with a "lens," a perspective, and a vision through which they can see the world more clearly.

And, as you will hopefully see by now, one of the most powerful ways to do all of the above is by utilizing visual thinking and visual communication tools, tips, and techniques—including visual models, visual metaphors, and visual storytelling.

And lastly, we all need to prepare for jobs that don't yet exist, while facing the unavoidable question that so many are asking: in a world in which job functions and entire industries are disappearing, literally, overnight, and one in which many live in fear that "the robots are taking over," what do we humans need to do—or do differently, and better—going forward?

As we discussed in Chapter 10's "Five Levels of Proactivity," we need to be proactive and super-proactive rather than reactive. We need to be as agile, flexible, and innovative as possible; we need to continuously learn, unlearn, and relearn; and we need to open our eyes to envisioning the invisible…so that we will be prepared to do in the future what, today, may seem impossible.

In Review

The Big Lesson: The world—and the workplace—are changing faster than ever. So we need to be more agile, adaptable, flexible, and resilient than ever if we want to not just keep up with the curve but stay ahead of it.

The Big Question: When thinking about the future of work, what do you need to think about, and to do differently and better, in order to survive and to thrive?

Your Insight:

Your Action:

CHAPTER 58

Ten Tough Questions Every Self-Aware Leader Needs to Be Able to Answer

One of the keys to being an effective leader is emotional intelligence. And, as the foundation of emotional intelligence is self-awareness, here are ten powerful, thought-provoking, and challenging questions for you to reflect on—and be ready, willing and able to answer—if you truly want to be a more effective, reflective, introspective, and emotionally intelligent leader:

Question 1: How do you personally define "leadership"?

There's a great little book by Mark Sanborn called *You Don't Need a Title to Be a Leader*. In a nutshell, as the title implies, true leadership is not about rank or position; it's about exhibiting leadership qualities, demonstrating leadership behaviors, and stepping up to leadership when leadership is needed. And it is always needed.

There are almost as many different definitions of leadership out there as there are actual leaders. Peter Drucker contended, "The only definition of a leader is someone who has followers." President John Quincy Adams wrote, "If your actions inspire others to dream more, learn more, do more, and become more, you are a leader." So if someone came up to you and asked for *your* personal definition of leadership, how would *you* respond?

Question 2: Who are some of the leaders ("public figures") that you admire—and why?

Who are the leaders throughout history, or current leaders out there today—from the world of business, politics, the arts, sports, etc.—whom you most admire, and why? What relevant characteristics, qualities, or traits do they possess? Conversely, think of other leaders who you do *not* find effective...and why? Oftentimes we can learn as much about leadership from people who have failed as from those who have succeeded. And while we're at it, regarding the classic question, "Are leaders born or made?" how would you answer that one?

Question 3: Who have been some of the influential people in your own life ("private figures") from whom you have learned something valuable about leadership?

While we often look to the famous and to the history books for examples of leadership, it is more than likely that the most impactful leaders in each of our own lives are the people we've known personally. So who are those who have shaped who you are, how you are, and what you believe in? Who are the people in your life who influenced your ethics, core values, and personal leadership style?

Parents and grandparents, friends and family members, neighbors, teachers, coaches, and bosses (both good and bad!) have all put their stamp on who you are and how you are as a person...and as a leader. Who are the *best* people you've worked for or with—and who are the *worst*? What did you learn from them, and how have they influenced who you are and how you lead today?

Question 4: What have been some of the "defining leadership moments" in your life?

As we go about our lives, most days can be described as "business as usual." But every once in a while something happens that transforms us in a profound and game-changing way. Think back on some of the stories and examples throughout this book: memorable leadership moments can happen over time, or in an instant; at work, at home, or out in the world; and can be as small and seemingly insignificant as a pair of black socks, a little yellow ball, or a tiny pink spoon…or as majestic and awe-inspiring as the Grand Canyon.

Sometimes we realize it right then and there; other times it does not become apparent until long down the road. But these incidents and interactions are the "defining moments" that impart the vivid leadership lessons that we carry with us throughout the years. These are the "home movies" that we play over and over again in our minds that remind us of who we are and how we got here. These are the stories that make up the fabric of your being and function as your guiding compass.

So what are some of those unforgettable leadership-related moments from your past that shape who you are today?

Question 5: What are you truly passionate about?

What gets you up and out of bed in the morning? And what keeps you up at night? What gives you a sense of purpose and energizes you? And what doesn't? If you do not demonstrate passion and purpose, how can you expect the people around you to do the same?

Passion is contagious. Negativity is, too. So, again, as mentioned earlier, ask yourself, "What is my 'Leadership Weather Report' today?" Are you being a ray of sunshine…or a cloud of doom and gloom? Are you trying to light a fire under people…or helping them to light a fire within themselves? Do you demonstrate passion and purpose…and instill that feeling in others? Or do you (knowingly or unknowingly) do the opposite?

Question 6: Why should anyone be led by you?

How would you answer this incredibly personal and challenging (and scary!) question posed by authors Goffee & Jones in their classic *Harvard Business Review* article and book of that name? If you're someone's manager, they have to be *managed* by you because you're their boss. But they don't have to be led by you…unless they choose to.

So why should someone voluntarily and willingly choose to follow you? What leadership characteristics do you believe you possess? And how do you gain others' respect and trust? If you left your current role, would your people leap at the chance to join you…or would they leap in the air in celebration of your exit?

I've had a few (very few!) bosses that I would have followed to the ends of the earth: the leaders who inspired me to "dream more, learn more, do more, and become more." And I've had other bosses who I wouldn't have followed across the street for a million dollars. (Alright, maybe a *million* dollars…but not a penny less!) So, now tell us: why should we hire you as our leader?

Question 7: What are some of the key leadership lessons you would want to pass along to others?

It is often said that one of the most important responsibilities—and privileges—of being a leader is developing the next generation of leaders. Think about the "Leadership Journey" metaphor where the windshield represents your vision of the future, the dashboard represents the metrics by which you gauge your progress and measure success, and the rearview mirror represents how you got to where you are today…as well as the crucial importance of taking time out for introspection and "reflection."

As you think about your personal leadership journey, what are some of the nuggets you have picked up along the way that you would like to share with others? What advice would you have given to your eighteen-year-old self? Or to a new college graduate today? And if you were to fast-forward to your retirement party, what would you want your "leadership legacy" to be? What do you want to be known for, and known as?

How would you like to be remembered? And, with that in mind, what do you need to do between now and then to turn that vision into reality?

Question 8: Who are the people in your life right now who make you a better person—and a better leader?

I previously asked who some of the people were from your past who shaped who you are today. Building on that, who are the people in your life right now who help to make you a better leader? Who can you count on to be open and honest and candid and truthful with you, with no other agenda other than wanting to help you be the best person and the best leader you can be?

President Eisenhower wrote in his memoir *At Ease*, "Always try to associate yourself with and learn as much as you can from those who know more than you do, who do better than you, and who see more clearly than you." We can't do it alone.

If "Wisdom is where Knowledge and Experience Meet," who are the people who help you to be wiser? The best leaders surround themselves on all sides with people whom they trust implicitly without question, doubt, or hesitation. So if you were going to create "a personal board of directors," who would you ask to be on it?

Question 9: What are you reading (and listening to, and watching)?

Harvard Business School professor John Kotter once said that "the most notable trait of great leaders is their continuous quest for learning." President John F. Kennedy wrote that "leadership and learning are indispensable to each other." And President Harry S. Truman declared, "Not all readers are leaders; but all leaders are readers."

Many people think and act as if, once you're done with school, you're done with learning. But the best leaders know that nothing could be further from the truth. Yes, we learn much of what we know from real-world experiences, as well as from formal training, coaching, and feedback. But it's also absolutely crucial for leaders to always be reading, and listening, and watching, as the next book, article, blog post, video, or TED Talk you expose yourself to could, potentially, forever change your life. And it's not just business content that I'm talking about: as mentioned throughout this book, lessons in leadership are hiding in plain sight everywhere…if we are just aware enough to open our eyes, ears, and hearts to seeing them.

As legendary basketball coach John Wooden said, "It's what you learn after you know it all that counts." So…have you read any good books lately?

Question 10: Are you a good follower?

Lastly, to be a good leader, it's also important, when the situation warrants, to be a good follower. Thomas Paine wrote that we need to either "lead, follow, or get out of the way." The key is to have the wisdom to know when to do which.

In Rob Reiner's movie *The American President*, Michael J. Fox's character says to (President) Michael Douglas, "People want leadership. And in the absence of genuine leadership, they will listen to anyone who steps up to the microphone." So, as a leader, sometimes you need to be the one who steps up to the microphone. But other times, the most appropriate and valiant act of leadership is to step aside—and let someone else take the lead. Winston Churchill stated that it takes courage to stand up and speak, but courage is also what it takes to sit down and listen.

So, as mentioned back in Question 1, you do not need a leadership title in order to be a leader; all it takes is the desire and the willingness to step up to leadership when leadership is needed. And leadership is needed all the time.

So as you travel along throughout your career, remember that leadership is not a destination, but a journey; it's also not a position, but a choice. And the best news of all is that the choice to lead is entirely up to you.

In Review

The Big Lesson: One of the best things about exploring the concept of leadership is that unlike many other domains, there is no "one right answer" to any of these questions. Your answers are going to continuously change as you change. And that's perfectly fine. In fact, it's more than fine: it's ideal, as it shows that you are learning, evolving, growing, transforming into the leader you were destined to be.

The Big Question: How would you answer each of these ten questions? Which ones came easily to you, and which were the most challenging...and why?

Your Big Insight:

Your Big Action:

CHAPTER 59

Your Leadership Journey: The Road Ahead

As we come to the end of our journey together, it's time to pull over, take a brief glance in the rearview mirror, and reflect on how far we've come. Just to refresh your memory regarding the three key components of the Leadership Journey metaphor, which we discussed briefly in the introduction:

- The **Rearview Mirror** represents the Past: where we came from… and how we got here. And, as a mirror, it literally reminds us to take the time, as we move along on our journey, to stop…and to "reflect."
- The **Dashboard**, with its dials and gauges, represents the Present, and allows us to examine how we're doing. As Peter Drucker famously put it, "If you can't measure it, you can't manage it."
- And, lastly, the **Windshield** represents the Future…and directs our attention to the road ahead. While it appears to be blue skies and smooth sailing as far as the eye can see, what's beyond the horizon is unknown, as our future is unwritten.

But what else? What other metaphors do we see…and not see? And what other questions might we need to answer along the way?

What does the steering wheel symbolize to you, and the tires, and the engine, and the glove compartment, and the trunk?

Should you continue to stay on this road, or take a different route on a road less traveled?

You're moving full speed ahead. But are you headed in the right direction? What is your map or your GPS telling you? And do you have enough fuel to get you to where you're going?

Are you prepared for what's beyond the horizon, should you hit a patch of stormy weather, bumps in the road, or a sudden, unforeseen traffic jam or detour?

Is the fact that there seems to be no other vehicles in sight a good thing or a bad thing? Are you so far ahead that you've left everyone else in the dust…or so far behind that you are out of the race?

As important a question as any: who will be accompanying you on your journey?

What about the culture and the climate? The outside conditions are beyond your control…but the climate inside the car is entirely up to you. Are the windows clear enough to see out of? What's the temperature like? What's the soundtrack of your journey going to be…and at what volume will you be playing it? From a diversity, inclusion, and belonging perspective…how do the people around you factor into the environment you've created?

And, lastly, where should *you* be, as the leader: when should you be in the driver's seat, when should you move over to the passenger's seat to navigate, and when might it be best to take a back seat? As mentioned, Thomas Paine declared that we need to either "lead, follow, or get out of the way"; so, how do you, as a leader, know and decide which to do?

With all of these important questions in mind, now might be as good a time as any to "pull over" and "reflect" on what you may need to do to realize your leadership vision and to reach your ultimate destination… whatever, or wherever, that may be.

In Review

The Big Lesson: The metaphor of "the leadership journey" is a universal and powerful one. While each and every one of us is on our own, individual, life-long journey, at the same time we are all on one big gigantic journey together.

The Big Question: As you reflect on your own journey—past, present, and future—how can you use this metaphor to help you to navigate your life...and to successfully reach your desired destination?

Your Big Insight:

Your Big Action:

CHAPTER 60

Final Thoughts:
Reflection, Introspection, and Connection

This book began with one of my all-time favorite *New Yorker* cartoons: the one with the two guys looking up at the giant billboard that reads, in gigantic letters, "STOP AND THINK," while the caption below reads: "It sort of makes you stop and think, doesn't it?"

As we race around each day from home to work and back—often with our heads buried in our phones—too many of us don't make the time and take the time to hit the pause button and just allow ourselves to stop…and to think. Mindfulness is a resonant trend these days because, as we hurtle through the constant flux of work and life, it's more important than ever to allow ourselves to be more present, focused, and aware of what's going on around us. Only then can we find a way to see the invisible…so that we can do the impossible.

One way to be more mindful is to keep in mind these three words: "Reflection, Introspection, and Connection." This mantra of mine simply calls for making and taking the time to look backward ("Reflection"), look inward ("Introspection"), and look outward towards others ("Connection").

As you continue on your leadership journey—and especially now, as a more visual leader, with this collection of models, metaphors, and stories now part of your VisuaLeadership tool kit—I encourage you to consciously seek to view things through this new lens…as well as to continue to Reflect, Introspect, and Connect with yourself and with others along the way.

And I have no doubt that, if you do—if you continue to leverage the power of visual thinking and visual communication to get your ideas out of your head and into the heads of others—you will not only change *their* world…but *the* world.

Appendix

Twelve Authors Who Had the Greatest Impact and Influence on My Thinking, My Work, and My Life[1]

Dale Carnegie: *How to Win Friends and Influence People; How to Stop Worrying and Start Living;* and many others

Daniel H. Pink: *Drive: The Surprising Truth About What Motivates Us; A Whole New Mind: Why Right-Brainers Will Rule the Future; Free Agent Nation: The Future of Working for Yourself*

Edward de Bono: *Six Thinking Hats*

Garr Reynolds: *Presentation Zen: Simple Ideas on Presentation Design and Delivery; The Naked Presenter: Delivering Powerful Presentations With or Without Slides*

Joel Arthur Barker: *Paradigms: The Business of Discovering the Future*

John Kotter: *What Leaders Really Do; Leading Change; Buy-in;* and others

---

[1] In alphabetical order by first name.

Marshall Goldsmith: *What Got You Here Won't Get You There: How Successful People Become Even More Successful;* and others

Nancy Duarte: *Slide:ology: The Art and Science of Creating Great Presentations; Resonate: Present Visual Stories that Transform Audiences; DataStory: Explain Data and Inspire Action Through Story*

Peter Drucker: *The Effective Executive: The Definitive Guide to Getting the Right Things Done; The Essential Drucker: The Best of Sixty Years of Peter Drucker's Essential Writings on Management; Managing Oneself;* and others

Seth Godin: *Linchpin: Are You Indispensable?;* (and pretty much every other amazing book and blog post he's ever written!)

Stephen R. Covey: *The 7 Habits of Highly Effective People: Powerful Lessons in Personal Change*

William Shakespeare: The Complete Works

Todd's Bookshelf: Forty-plus Favorite Authors/Book Recommendations to Help You Become a Better VisuaLeader[2]

Having read an average of more than one business book per week over the past twenty-plus years, I surpassed my one thousandth book sometime around last year. Of all those books related to management, leadership, innovation, communication, presentation, learning, and more, I came up with this list of forty of the top authors, and their books, that I tend to recommend to my clients, students, and friends…and that I would like to now share with you.

I'm not necessarily saying these are the top forty business books ever written (in case you are thinking of questioning my selections, or contacting me to say, "How could you have included *that* book on your list!" or, "How could you *not* have included this one!"). This is my own, totally biased and subjective, list of personal favorites that I tend to refer back to and/or recommend to others time and time again.

My criteria for inclusion are simply that these are some of the key books that opened my eyes to new ideas, new perspectives, and/or new tools, tips, or techniques. Additionally, rather than listing many of the bestsellers that everyone is already familiar with, I tried to include a number of selections that are less well-known, including a few hidden gems that were written by personal friends of mine. And, to make it onto this list, they had to be terrific and well worth reading.

With that, I hope you will enjoy and benefit from this collection of books as much as I did…and as much as I still do.

---

[2] In alphabetical order by first name.

Adam Bryant: *The Corner Office: Indispensable and Unexpected Lessons from CEOs on How to Live and Succeed*; and *Quick and Nimble: Lessons from Leading CEOs on How to Create a Culture of Innovation*

Adam Grant: *Give and Take: Why Helping Others Drives Our Success*

Annette Simmons: *The Story Factor: Inspiration, Influence, and Persuasion Through the Art of Storytelling*

Ayse Birsel: *Design the Life You Love: A Step-by-Step Guide to Building a Meaningful Future*

Barry Schwartz: *Why We Work*; and *The Paradox of Choice: Why More Is Less*

Benedict Carey: *How We Learn: The Surprising Truth About When, Where, and Why It Happens*

Brad Szollose: *Liquid Leadership: From Woodstock to Wikipedia*

Brene Brown: *Dare to Lead: Brave Work, Tough Conversations, Whole Hearts*

Bryan Mattimore: *Idea Stormers: How to Lead and Inspire Creative Breakthroughs*; and *21 Days to a Big Idea: Creating Breakthrough Business Concepts*

Charles Duhigg: *The Power of Habit: Why We Do What We Do in Life and Business*

Chris Anderson: *TED Talks: The Official TED Guide to Public Speaking*

Dan Roam: *The Back of the Napkin*; *Unfolding the Napkin*; and others

Daniel Kahneman: *Thinking, Fast and Slow*

Dave Gray, Sunni Brown, and James Macanufo: *Gamestorming: A Playbook for Innovators, Rulebreakers, and Changemakers*

David Rock: *Your Brain at Work: Strategies for Overcoming Distraction, Regaining Focus, and Working Smarter All Day Long*

David Sibbet: *Visual Meetings, Visual Teams, Visual Consulting, Visual Leaders*

Edgar H. Schein: *Humble Inquiry: The Gentle Art of Asking Instead of Telling*

James E. Zull: *The Art of Changing the Brain: Enriching the Practice of Teaching By Exploring the Biology of Learning*

Jason Fried and David Heinemeier Hansson: *Rework*

Jerry Colonna: *Reboot: Leadership and the Art of Growing Up*

John Medina: *Brain Rules: 12 Principles for Surviving and Thriving at Work, Home, and School*

Julie Dirksen: *Design for How People Learn*

Ken Robinson: *The Element: How Finding Your Passion Changes Everything*

Lee Lefever: *The Art of Explanation: Making Your Ideas, Products, and Services Easier to Understand*

Marc Emmer: *Momentum: How Companies Decide What to Do Next*

Mark Sanborn: *You Don't Need a Title to Be a Leader*

Mike Figliuolo: *One Piece of Paper: The Simple Approach to Powerful, Personal Leadership*

Peter Bregman: *18 Minutes: Find Your Focus, Master Distraction, and Get the Right Things Done*; *Leading With Emotional Courage: How to Have Hard Conversations, Create Accountability, And Inspire Action On Your Most Important Work*

Nancy Ancowitz: *Self-Promotion for Introverts: The Quiet Guide to Getting Ahead*

Rick Wormeli: *Metaphors & Analogies: Power Tools for Teaching Any Subject*

Rob Salafia: *Leading From Your Best Self: Develop Executive Poise, Presence, and Influence to Maximize Your Potential*

Robert I. Sutton: *The No Asshole Rule: Building a Civilized Workplace and Surviving One That Isn't*

Roger von Oech: *A Whack on the Side of the Head: How You Can Be More Creative*

Ron Ashkenas: *The Harvard Business Review Leader's Handbook: Make an Impact, Inspire Your Organization, and Get to the Next Level*

Rosamund Stone Zander and Benjamin Zander: *The Art of Possibility: Transforming Professional and Personal Life*

Seth Merrin: *The Power of Positive Destruction: How to Turn a Business Idea Into a Revolution*

Sunni Brown: *The Doodle Revolution: Unlock the Power to Think Differently*

Susan Cain: *Quiet: The Power of Introverts in a World That Can't Stop Talking*

Susan Weinschenk: *100 Things Every Presenter Needs to Know About People*; and *How to Get People to Do Stuff*

William L. Maw: *The Work-Life Equation: Six Key Values That Drive Happiness and Success*

Forty Classic Leadership Models or Concepts That Every Business Professional Should Know (or At Least Know About)

These are some of the classic leadership-related models, frameworks, and constructs—*not* created by me, and not focused on in this book—that I often either teach in my classes, introduce to my consulting, training, and/or coaching clients, or use myself to enhance my own performance.

Some are well-known, others are less known, but each one will be a valuable addition to your VisuaLeadership tool kit. I may not, necessarily, like or agree with every single one, but I believe that every concept on this list is worthy of, at the very least, being familiar with.

Easily searchable online, I encourage you to dive beneath the surface to explore each one. Just think: If you look up one or two per day, you can learn about all forty in less than a month.

And, of course, there are a *lot* more where these came from; but you've got to start somewhere!

The 7 Habits of Highly Effective People (Stephen R. Covey)

9-Box (Productivity and Potential) Talent Matrix

20 Workplace Habits You Need to Break (Marshall Goldsmith: *What Got You Here Won't Get You There*)

70-20-10 Learning and Development Model (Center for Creative Leadership)

AIDA: Awareness, Interest, Desire, Action

AMP: Autonomy, Mastery, Purpose (Dan Pink: *Drive*)

Belbin's 9 Team Roles

Cialdini's Six Influencing Strategies

Consciousness/Competence model

Dale Carnegie's 30 Principles

DISC: Dominance, Influence, Steadiness, Conscientiousness

Five Dysfunctions of a Team (Patrick Lencioni)

Fixed vs. Growth Mindset (Carol Dweck)

Gallup's 12 Employee Engagement Questions (Buckingham and Coffman: *First Break All the Rules*)

Golden Circle (Simon Sinek)

Good to Great models: Flywheel, Hedgehog, Level Five Leadership, etc. (Jim Collins)

GROW: Goal, Reality, Options, Will Do coaching model (Sir John Whitmore)

Herzberg's Two-Factor Motivation Theory

Johari Window

Kirkpatrick Model: The Four Levels of Learning Evaluation

Kotter's 8-Step Change Process (John Kotter: *Leading Change*)

Maslow's Hierarchy of Needs (Abraham Maslow)

McClelland's Needs Theory

Myers-Briggs Theory, aka MBTI

McKinsey 7S Framework

Pareto Principle, aka the 80/20 Rule

Progress Principle (Teresa Amabile and Steven Kramer)

Project Aristotle (Google's study of team effectiveness)

Project Oxygen (Google's study of manager effectiveness)

RACI: Responsible, Accountable, Consulted, Informed

Radical Candor feedback matrix (Kim Scott)

SCARF: Status, Certainty, Autonomy, Relatedness, Fairness (David Rock: *Your Brain at Work*)

Situational Leadership (Paul Hersey and Ken Blanchard)

Six Thinking Hats (Edward de Bono)

SMART Goals: Specific, Measurable, Achievable, Relevant, Time-bound

Social Styles

SWOT (Strengths, Weaknesses, Opportunities, Threats) Analysis

Theory X and Theory Y (Douglas McGregor)

Time Management Matrix, aka the Eisenhower Matrix

Tuckman's Four Stages of Team Development: Forming, Storming, Norming, Performing

Question: What are some of *your* top recommendations that *you* would add to this list? Please feel free to write them below and then email your suggestions to me!

Some of My All-Time Favorite VisuaLeadership-related Quotes

But first, a disclaimer:

I've learned from experience that "Wanting something to be true does not make it so." So, what does this quote (by me…as far as I know) have to do with famous quotations from famous people? Well, over the years I've been repeatedly disappointed to discover that many of the famous quotes that we all know and love were either not said exactly in the way that we know them…and/or were not originated by the person to whom they are usually attributed.

For example, I truly hate to burst any bubbles, but there seems to be no record anywhere of Gandhi ever having said, "Be the change you wish to see in the world." It's a powerful and inspirational quote. It sounds exactly like something Gandhi would have believed and said. And we probably all wish that he had said it in those very words. Unfortunately, however, after much research into the matter, there seems to be no evidence anywhere that he did. He did say many things similar to that, and in that spirit, but just not that particular quote, in those exact words.

But that shouldn't keep us from continuing to quote him as having said it, right? Or should it? I guess that's up to each of us to decide. As far as I'm concerned, if it's printed on a greeting card, a T-shirt, a bumper sticker, or a refrigerator magnet—or if it's a meme on the internet—then it's official. Or not. And you can quote me on that. Or not. Who knows. Even the all-time King of Quotes Yogi Berra once said: "I really didn't say everything I said. Then again, I might have said 'em, but you never know." And, as Abraham Lincoln warned: "Don't believe everything you read on the internet just because there's a picture with a quote next to it." And you can look that up. Seriously…look it up. I'll wait. [Pause.] OK, welcome back. See what I mean!

So, again, all I can say when it comes to quotes is that you could look them up for yourself to try to find out what's true and what's not. However, as Dr. Zaius says in the final scene of the original *Planet of the Apes* movie (and we have filmed proof that he said this, so I can confirm that this quote is, in fact, valid): "Don't look for it, Taylor. You may not like what you find."

That said, I am happy to share with you this collection of some of my favorite, go-to leadership-related quotations, quoted as accurately as possible and attributed to the appropriate person to the very best of my ability.

I hope you find the words, regardless of the source, to be as inspirational as I always do.

A few "Todd-isms"

- No one wants to *hear* excuses; they only want to *see* results.
- The true value of knowledge is not in its accumulation, but in its application.
- Wisdom is where Knowledge and Experience meet.
- Knowledge comes not from answering questions, but from questioning answers.
- In an ever-changing world, if you're standing still, you're falling behind.
- The difference between an explanation and an excuse is accountability.
- In the absence of feedback, our tendency is to fill that void of silence with negativity.
- When someone says, "I know what I'm trying to say, I just can't explain it," they usually don't. Otherwise they could.
- What did the inventors of the drawing board go back to when the first one didn't work out?
- Is it within walking distance? *Everything* is within walking distance…if you have the time and are willing to put in the effort.
- Managers try to get the *most* out of their people; leaders try to get the *best* out of them.

- Managers focus on the *position*; leaders focus on the person *in* the position.
- The impact of leadership can be seen not only in how people act in your presence, but how they act in your absence.
- Team-bonding needs to come before team-building. You need to connect to each other, if you want to work better *with* each other.
- After a major setback, failure, or loss, the reality is that you may never get over it, but you *will* get through it. And as difficult as it may be to move *on*, you must find a way to move *forward*.
- Change happens not overnight, but over time.
- With the trees outside our window fiercely swaying to and fro, my wife said, "Wow—look at that wind!" But we cannot see the wind; we can only see its impact. Similarly, the words we say and the actions we take cannot always be seen; and yet their impact on others can have the force of a hurricane.

A few of my father's favorite "Dad sayings"[3]

- I never made a mistake. I once thought I did, but I was wrong.
- People make mistakes; that's why pencils have erasers.
- Good, better, best. Never let it rest, 'til the good is better, and the better is best.

From my wife, Karin:

- Focus on the donut, not the hole.
- I can't hear you when you're yelling.
- Turn that frown upside down!

---

[3] Although not original, they were part of his repertoire, and relevant to work and to life.

Appendix

And some of my other favorites…in no particular order:

"It is only with the heart that one can see rightly; what is essential is invisible to the eye."

—ANTOINE DE SAINT EXUPÉRY

"What you *get* by achieving your goals is not as important as what you *become* by achieving your goals."

—HENRY DAVID THOREAU

"I found that if you have a goal, you might not reach it. But if you *don't* have one, then you are never disappointed. And I've gotta tell you, it feels phenomenal."

—VINCE VAUGHN in *Dodgeball*

"If they don't give you a seat at the table, bring a folding chair."

—SHIRLEY CHISHOLM

"I never lose. I either win or I learn."[4]

—NELSON MANDELA

"Many of life's failures are people who did not realize how close they were to success when they gave up."

—THOMAS EDISON

"Anyone who has never made a mistake has never tried anything new."

—ALBERT EINSTEIN

"Whatever you do, always give 100 percent. Unless you're donating blood."

—BILL MURRAY

"People don't care how much you know, until they know how much you care."

—UNKNOWN

---

[4] Although, if it were up to me, I would add that we "win and learn" as well, as we should seek to learn something from our wins as well as from our losses.

"Simplicity is the ultimate sophistication."

—LEONARDO DE VINCI

"To be prepared is half the victory."

—CERVANTES

"The fight is won or lost far away from witnesses—behind the lines, in the gym, and out there on the road, long before I dance under those lights."

—MUHAMMAD ALI

"Compassion is empathy in action."

—DR. LINDA LAUSELL BRYANT

"The greatest thing by far is to be a master of metaphor; it is the one thing that cannot be learned from others; and it is also a sign of genius, since a good metaphor implies an intuitive perception of the similarity of the dissimilar."

—ARISTOTLE

"A wonderful harmony arises when we join together the seemingly unconnected."

—HERACLITUS

"Every single thing that has ever happened to you in your life is preparing you for a moment that is yet to come."

—UNKNOWN

"Enjoy the little things, for one day you may look back and realize they were the big things."

—ROBERT BRAULT

"Every man is my superior in that I may learn from him."

—THOMAS CARLYLE

"Everyone you will ever meet knows something that you don't."

—BILL NYE THE SCIENCE GUY

Appendix

"In a minute there is time/For decisions and revisions which a minute will reverse."

—T.S. ELIOT ("The Love Song of J. Alfred Prufrock")

"When it comes to knowledge, the more you give it away, the less likely you are to ever lose it…*and* the more you get back."

—UNKNOWN

"Everyone smiles in the same language."

—UNKNOWN

"Know thyself."

— ANCIENT GREEK APHORISM

"All I know is that I know nothing."

—SOCRATES

"We spend a lot of time helping leaders learn what to do, but we don't spend enough time helping leaders learn what to stop."

—PETER DRUCKER

"Leadership is not about doing what's popular, it's about doing what's right."

—UNKNOWN

"If you don't know where you're going, you might not get there."

—YOGI BERRA

"The best way to predict the future is to create it."

—PETER DRUCKER

"The best way to predict the future is to invent it."

—ALAN KAY

"How sweet a thing it is to wear a crown."

—WILLIAM SHAKESPEARE, *Henry VI Part III*

"Uneasy lies the head that wears a crown."

—WILLIAM SHAKESPEARE, *Henry IV Part II*

"Those who cannot remember the past are condemned to repeat it."

—GEORGE SANTAYANA

"It infuriates me to be wrong when I know I'm right."

—MOLIERE

"Thou shouldst not have been old till thou hadst been wise."

—WILLIAM SHAKESPEARE, *King Lear*

"Success is peace of mind attained only through self-satisfaction in knowing you made the effort to do the best of which you are capable."

—JOHN WOODEN

"Education is not the filling of a pail, but the lighting of a fire."

—WILLIAM BUTLER YEATS

"To know even one life has breathed easier because you have lived—this is to have succeeded."

—RALPH WALDO EMERSON

The boss drives [people]; the leader coaches them.
The boss depends upon authority; the leader on goodwill.
The boss inspires fear; the leader inspires enthusiasm.
The boss says "I"; the leader, "We."
The boss knows how; the leader shows how.
The boss says "Go"; the leader says "Let's go!"

—HARRY GORDON SELFRIDGE

By cartoonist, Dan Reynolds

THE ~~END~~ BEGINNING

Acknowledgments

To those below (as well as to the so many others not mentioned by name), I thank you for your Impact, Influence, and Inspiration (the "3 I's"), as you all played a huge part in making this book happen:

My wife, Karin, Mom and Dad, my brother Steve, and my mother-in-law, Myra for all their love and support.

Jeff Schwartzman: from colleague, to boss, to client, to teaching partner, to one of my closest friends, it's always a pleasure working, and hanging, together. You introduced me to the mantra "if you love what you do, you'll never work a day in your life." Though that's not *entirely* true—as we both work pretty damn hard—I always do my best work, and have the most fun, when working together.

Joe Armentano: mentor, coach, and friend—you recognized my potential before I did and took a chance on me, changing the course of my career...and my life.

Seth Foster (who, after helping me to get a job at his company once advised me, "Never let them know that you have no idea what you're doing and you'll be fine,"—advice I've followed ever since)—and my college roommate and great friend Mark Saks: you both "knew me when," and have been along for the long, wild ride every step of the way.

Mr. Hugh Patterson, Mr. Robert Ballentine, and Professor Jeffrey Berman: the three teachers who took a special interest in me and not only taught me how to learn, but—without realizing it—how to teach.

My incredible agent Ken Lizotte and his wonderfully brilliant and amazing editors, Elena Petricone and Chloe Lizotte at emerson consulting group, who helped to make this dream a reality. Thank you, also, to

Bill Maw (author of *The Work-Life Equation*) for originally introducing me to Ken…*and* to Rob Salafia (author of *Leading From Your Best Self*) who, by coincidence, reintroduced me to Ken two years later, confirming that this relationship was meant to be.

The terrific people of Post Hill Press, especially president Michael L. Wilson, acquisitions editor Debra Englander, managing editor Heather King, and publicist Meredith Didier, as well as the folks at Simon & Schuster.

My excellent IP attorneys at FisherBroyles, Lisa Carroll and Richard (Rick) Lehrer, who (especially for lawyers) are always such a pleasure to work with.

NYU School of Professional Studies/Division of Programs in Business: Associate Dean Martin Ihrig, Dr. Negar Farakish, Dr. Anna Tavis, Mary-anne Spatola, all my wonderful faculty colleagues, the tremendous support staff—especially Daniel Amaranto, Amanda Charnley, Lisa Hoang, Nicole Howe—and my amazing students who inspire me to do what I do.

Columbia University: Dean Jason Wingard, Tatum Thomas, Joshua Mackey, Arabella Pollack, and all my fantastic students and colleagues, with special thanks to Michael J. Passaro.

Adam Bryant (author of *The Corner Office* and *Quick and Nimble*), whose hundreds of CEO interviews in the *New York Times* validated the fact that senior leaders are just regular people and provided me with so much valuable content for my NYU classes over the years: I've enjoyed our various collaborations and always appreciate your humble generosity.

All my friends and colleagues at Liquidnet—both past and present—especially CEO Seth Merrin and the Liquidnet University (LNU) all-star team of Jeff Schwartzman, Angelo Valenti, and Brian Tally.

The entire Leadership Forum community—too many amazing people to mention!—with a special shout-out to Steve Gardiner, who is always one of my biggest and most enthusiastic supporters.

The Ferguson Library Pro Speaker Group: Sandra Long (author of *LinkedIn for Personal Branding*), Mary Abbazia (co-author of *The Accidental Marketer*), fellow bookworm Helena Escalante, and the rest of our amazing group of speakers, as well as our sponsors, Alice Knapp, Susan LaPerla, Elizabeth Joseph, and Connie Hubbard.

All my amazing consulting, training, and coaching clients who provide me with the opportunity to put into practice what I preach.

And, lastly, to all of my other wonderful friends, family, colleagues and clients for all their advice, support, and encouragement over the years, especially…my grandparents, Mindy and Fred Nelson and family, my beloved Aunt Irma and Uncle Paul Cherches, the Schuman/Shapiro/Myers family, the Marcus/Somerfield clan, Nick Sibrava, Tala Robinson, Bill Keisler, Marc Levine, Sue Foster and Hannah Foster, Joanne and Brad Bartmess, Robin T. Jonah, Barbara J. Spence, Eileen Noon, Martin Van Treuren, Bill and Theresa Mollica, Chris and Caryn Berlingieri, Adam Varsano, Marc Emmer, Dario Palombi, Karyn Wulbrun, Beverly Helton, Derek Jones, Lourdes Olvera-Marshall, Dr. Linda Lausell Bryant, Andrea Nierenberg, Peter Phelan, Rob Polishook, Deborah Grayson Riegel, Nolan Haims, Kevin Lupowitz, Brett Kotch, Bryan Mattimore, Brad Szollose, JP Laqueur, Donna Scarola, Rich Kuepper, David Kruczlnicki, Elise Silverman, Ellen Anthony, Edward Fleischman, Glenn Bernstein, Margaret McLean Walsh, Mary Walsh, Allison Hemming, Nancy Ancowitz, Roseanna DeMaria, Karen Miner-Romanoff, Monica Glina, Angela Wright, Ajay Chitharanjan, Janet Lyden, Dina Friedel, Jessica Palacios, Cholda Techamani, Madeleine Weinberg, Melissa Brachfeld, Seth Godin, Adam Grant, Susan Cain, Dan Pink, Nancy Duarte, Marshall Goldsmith, Ayse Birsel, Peter Bregman, Sunni Brown, Jerry Colonna, Ron Ashkenas, Mike Figliuolo, Steven Heller, Jennifer Goldman-Wetzler, Fawn Germer, Enrique Rubio and the Hacking HR community, Mark Taylor and Vistage, Nicos Marcou and the TEDx ChelseaPark team, Alicia Pierro and Gail Morse of Big Apple Greeter, and one of the most incredible and inspirational individuals I've ever met, Phillip Butler, PhD—CDR, USN (Ret.), former POW, and author of *Three Lives of a Warrior*—who is living proof of his quote that "optimism and humor are the grease and glue of life." And, I would be remiss if I did not also thank Dr. Ronald Ruden (author of *The Craving Brain* and *When the Past is Always Present*), who has saved me more times than I can count.

About the Author

Photo credit: Jingtao (Vincent) Wen

Todd Cherches is the CEO and co-founder of BigBlueGumball LLC, an innovative New York City-based management and leadership consulting, training, and executive coaching firm. BigBlueGumball's patented VisuaLeadership® methodology leverages the power of visual thinking and visual communication to equip, enable, and empower business professionals of all levels—from individual contributors to senior-level executives—to maximize their performance, their productivity, and their potential.

Cherches is also a TEDx speaker ("The Power of Visual Thinking") and Vistage speaker, as well as a two-time award-winning Adjunct Professor at the NYU School of Professional Studies in their Division of Programs in Business, where he teaches the top-rated graduate course "Leadership & Team Building" for their Human Capital Management master's degree program. A specialist in experiential learning and faculty development, Cherches has received the prestigious NYU "Excellence in Teaching" award (2016), as well as an NYU Center for Academic Excellence and Support (CAES) "Impact Award" (2018).

He is also a Lecturer on leadership at Columbia University, where he has taught in their Executive M.S. in Strategic Communication graduate program, as well as guest lecturing on the subject of leadership in the Columbia MFA Theater program and Columbia University's Teachers College.

A popular blogger, keynote speaker, and panelist, Cherches is the creator of the highly-acclaimed BigBlueGumball PowerDial™ model, as well as the BigBlueGumball Passion/Skill Matrix™.

Cherches is a graduate of the State University of New York at Albany, from which he holds a Master of Arts degree in organizational and inter-personal communication from their School of Social and Behavioral Sciences, as well as a bachelor's degree in English Literature (magna cum laude) with a concentration in Shakespeare and poetry.